Heidegger's
Pragmatism

Kwang Dae Lee
September 3, 1999
Kent

Heidegger's Pragmatism

Understanding, Being, and the Critique of Metaphysics

MARK OKRENT

Cornell University Press

Ithaca and London

First published 1988 by Cornell University Press.

International Standard Book Number 0-8014-2094-6
Library of Congress Catalog Card Number 87-26014

Printed in the United States of America

Librarians: Library of Congress cataloging information appears on the last page of the book.

The paper in this book is acid-free and meets the guidelines for permanence and durability of the Committee on Production Guidelines for Book Longevity of the Council on Library Resources.

To Charlotte

Contents

Acknowledgments

Much of the work for this book was supported by a leave from Bates College and a year-long grant from the National Endowment for the Humanities. I spent that year in Berkeley, California, as a research associate at the University of California, and I thank the members of the Department of Philosophy at Berkeley for their hospitality. In California my work was helped substantially by the comments, criticisms, and conversation of Michael Philips, Theodore Schatzki, Charles Guignon, and, especially, Hubert Dreyfus. It is hard to imagine what this book would have looked like without my interactions, over several years, with Bert Dreyfus.

I owe a special debt of gratitude to Joseph Rouse of Wesleyan University. He was kind enough to read and comment on several drafts of this manuscript, and both his criticisms and his conversation have been invaluable. I also thank my many colleagues over the years in the Philosophy Department at Bates College. In particular I must acknowledge my long-time relationship with David Kolb, who has always been a tough critic, a stimulating associate, and, most important, a good friend.

My children, Nicholas and Valerie Okrent, provided me with essential emotional support. They cheerfully put up with a fair amount of inconvenience and, I suspect, more than a little obsessional behavior. For all this I thank them.

Finally, I must thank Charlotte Witt. She gave more to me while I was writing this book, both personally and professionally, than I knew it was possible for one person to give another. Charlotte read every word of every version of every chapter. Her support, her suggestions, her insightful criticisms, and the courage with which she communicated them to me made this book possible.

MARK OKRENT

Lewiston, Maine

Works of Heidegger Cited in the Notes

The abbreviations listed below are used to cite both the German and English editions. I have generally quoted from published English translations, although I have made occasional changes in the interest of consistent terminology. In particular, 'vorhanden' and its derivatives have been translated consistently by 'extant' and its derivatives, instead of Macquarrie and Robinson's 'present-at-hand'.

Note references give the page numbers in the translation first, followed by the page numbers in the German edition.

A.W.P. "Die Zeit des Weltbildes." 1950. In *Holzwege* (Frankfurt am Main: Klostermann, 1963), pp. 69–104.

"The Age of the World Picture." Translated by William Lovitt. In *The Question concerning Technology and Other Essays* (New York: Harper & Row, 1977), pp. 115–154.

B.P. *Die Grundprobleme der Phänomenologie.* 1927. Frankfurt am Main: Klostermann, 1975.

The Basic Problems of Phenomenology. Translated by Albert Hofstadter. Bloomington: Indiana University Press, 1982.

B.T. *Sein und Zeit.* 1927. Tübingen: Niemeyer, 1957.

Being and Time. Translated by John Macquarrie and Edward Robinson. New York: Harper & Row, 1962.

E.O.P. "Das Ende der Philosophie und die Aufgabe des Denkens." 1964. In *Zur Sache des Denkens* (Tübingen: Niemeyer, 1969), pp. 61–80.

"The End of Philosophy and the Task of Thinking." Translated by Joan Stambaugh. In *On Time and Being* (New York: Harper & Row, 1972), pp. 55–73.

H.C.T.   *Prolegomena zur Geschichte des Zeitbegriffs.* 1925. Frankfurt am Main: Klostermann, 1979.

History of the Concept of Time: Prolegomena. Translated by Theodore Kisiel. Bloomington: Indiana University Press, 1985.

I.D.   *Identität und Differenz.* 1957.

Identity and Difference. Translated by Joan Stambaugh. New York: Harper & Row, 1969. Dual-language text.

K.P.M.   *Kant und das Problem der Metaphysik.* 1929. Frankfurt am Main: Klostermann, 1973.

Kant and the Problem of Metaphysics. Translated by James Churchill. Bloomington: Indiana University Press, 1962.

L.H.   *Brief über den Humanismus.* 1946. In *Wegmarken* (Frankfurt am Main: Klostermann, 1976), pp. 313–362.

Letter on Humanism. Translated by Frank Capuzzi and J. Glenn Gray. In *Basic Writings* (New York: Harper & Row, 1977), pp. 193–242.

M.F.L.   *Metaphysische Anfangsgrunde der Logik im Ausgang von Leibniz.* 1928. Frankfurt am Main: Klostermann, 1978.

The Metaphysical Foundations of Logic. Translated by Michael Heim. Bloomington: Indiana University Press, 1984.

M.H.B.   "Die Metaphysik als Geschichte des Seins." In *Nietzsche II* (Pfullingen: Neske, 1961), pp. 399–457.

"Metaphysics as History of Being." Translated by Joan Stambaugh. In *The End of Philosophy* (New York: Harper & Row, 1973), pp. 1–54.

M.H.C.   *Martin Heidegger im Gesprach.* Freiburg: Karl Alber, 1970.

Martin Heidegger in Conversation. Translated by B. S. Murthy. New Delhi: Arnold Heinemann, 1977.

O.E.T.   *Von Wesen der Wahrheit.* 1930. In *Wegmarken* (Frankfurt am Main: Klostermann, 1976), pp. 13–44.

On the Essence of Truth. Translated by John Sallis. In *Basic Writings* (New York: Harper & Row, 1977), pp. 117–141.

O.G.C.   "Nur noch ein Gott kann uns retten." In *Der Spiegel,* May 1976, pp. 193–219.

"Only a God Can Save Us." Translated by William Richardson. In *Heidegger: The Man and His Thought* (Chicago: Precedent, 1981), pp. 45–72.

Q.C.T.   "Die Frage nach der Technik." 1954. In *Vorträge und Aufsätze* (Pfullingen: Neske, 1954), pp. 13–44.

"The Question concerning Technology." Translated by William Lovett. In *The Question concerning Technology and Other Essays* (New York: Harper & Row, 1977), pp. 3–35.

S.H.B.   "Entwürfe zur Geschichte des Seins als Metaphysik." In *Nietzsche II* (Pfullingen: Neske, 1961), pp. 458–480.

"Sketches for a History of Being as Metaphysics." Translated by Joan Stambaugh. In *The End of Philosophy* (New York: Harper & Row, 1973), pp. 55–74.

S.S.   "Protokoll zu einem Seminar über den Vortrag 'Zeit und Sein.'" 1969. In *Zur Sache des Denkens* (Tübingen: Niemeyer, 1969), pp. 27–60.

"Summary of a Seminar on the Lecture 'Time and Being.'" Translated by Joan Stambaugh. In *On Time and Being* (New York: Harper & Row, 1972), pp. 25–54.

T.B.   "Zeit und Sein." 1968. In *Zur Sache des Denkens* (Tübingen: Niemeyer, 1969), pp. 1–25.

"Time and Being." Translated by Joan Stambaugh. In *On Time and Being* (New York: Harper & Row, 1972), pp. 1–24.

Heidegger's
Pragmatism

Introduction

⌜A group of American philosophers led by Hubert Dreyfus, John Haugeland, Richard Rorty, and Robert Brandom have been suggesting that the work of Martin Heidegger has important implications for a range of crucial issues in contemporary philosophy of mind and metaphysics. This claim, by itself, is hardly surprising. After all, Heidegger was perhaps the most prominent German thinker working in these areas in the first two-thirds of the twentieth century and has always had devoted admirers among the 'continental' philosophers active in the United States. What is surprising is not *that* someone has been saying Heidegger is important but *who* has been saying it. All the philosophers listed above are primarily analytic philosophers, in the rather vague sense that they were trained in the tradition of Gottlob Frege, Rudolf Carnap, Ludwig Wittgenstein, W. V. O. Quine, and Wilfrid Sellars rather than in that of Edmund Husserl and Heidegger, and that the bulk of their work has been addressed to the problems raised by, for example, Donald Davidson, John Searle, and Jerry Fodor rather than those posed by, for example, Hans-Georg Gadamer and Jacques Derrida.

⌜Those analytic philosophers who have become interested in Heidegger have not always been able to agree on precisely what it is that Heidegger says or why it is important. Dreyfus, on the one hand, thinks that the important aspects of Heidegger's work lie in his early analysis of what it is to be 'Dasein' (or a being of the same ontological sort that we are), which, for Dreyfus, implies that certain types of method in the social sciences are unlikely to be successful and that a certain understanding of intelligence derived from computer models is unlikely to be correct.

3

Rorty, on the other hand, considers the early metaphysical work on the meaning of the being of Dasein to be part of Heidegger's 'juvenalia'; for him, what is important is the late anti-metaphysical stance, which Rorty takes to be derived from Heidegger's implicit pragmatism. For Dreyfus, in turn, such a pragmatic reading of late Heidegger misses the central importance of the 'truth of being' and '*Ereignis*' and commits Heidegger to just the sort of nihilism he abhorred.

Obviously, what is missing in such debates is a clear, acceptable statement of just what Heidegger did say concerning metaphysics, intentionality, and being a person, together with a statement of his reasons for saying it. Not that there is any lack of interpretive studies of Heidegger; on the contrary, there is a host of recent books, led by those of Joseph Kockelmans and Reiner Schürmann. But almost all these works presuppose an idiom, a type of argument, a style of rhetoric, and a philosophical context that are alien to the dominant strain of American philosophy; thus they often occasion as much confusion as enlightenment. What is needed is an interpretation comprehensible to all philosophers—including those trained in an analytic way—which shows in a straightforward though not uncontroversial manner the impact of Heidegger's work on central questions in contemporary analytic philosophy: 'Are meanings in the head?' 'Is it appropriate to think of mental states, such as beliefs and desires, as causes of behavior?' 'What is the status of metaphysical claims concerning being, identity, and essence?' 'What is the status of theories of truth?' 'Is there warrant for accepting a pragmatic view of mind and language, and, if so, what are the metaphysical, or antimetaphysical, implications of that view?' Such an interpretation would need to discuss clearly the evidence, and thus the arguments, that Heidegger advances in favor of his positions. The aim of this study is to address this need.

The book falls naturally into two parts. Part I, "Understanding," offers an interpretation of the early Heidegger which sees him as giving a transcendental argument concerning the necessary conditions for the possibility of intentionality. Roughly, Heidegger argues seven points. (1) No being can count as intending, having intentional states, or being an intentional being unless it specifically understands or possesses 'understanding'. (2) The primary type of understanding is practical and agent-oriented ('understanding how') rather than theoretical or mental ('understanding that'); and understanding that something is such and such, or believing that some proposition is true, is impossible without understanding how to perform various actions or how to use a variety of tools.

(3) To understand how to do something, one must be capable of acting in order to reach an end; conversely, to act in order to reach an end, one must understand how to do a range of things. (4) To act in order to reach an end is to act so as to reach some future possibility of oneself, and to act in this way *is* what it is to have self-understanding. Therefore, self-understanding, acting purposively in order to realize ends, and understanding how to perform actions always occur together. No being can have any one of these determinations without having all of them. (5) Understanding how is always holistic. To understand any one entity practically, or how to perform any given action for a purpose, one must have practical understanding of a wide variety of entities and understand how to perform a wide variety of purposive actions. (6) Among humans, objects have standardized functions, and there are proper ways of doing things among a group of beings who establish standard ends and communally shared ways of achieving those ends. To be Dasein, or a being such as we are, one must be a member of such a group. (7) Only a being who is Dasein in the sense just indicated can make assertions (which may be true or false), and only a being who can make assertions is capable of understanding (believing) that extant (*vorhanden* = present, at hand) entities—that is, substantial entities, substances—have natural, as opposed to functional, determinations. Assertions are tools for communicating interpretations, which are ways of taking a thing as something. Assertions can be true or false—that is, have semantic content—only insofar as they have roles within the purposive behavior of Dasein.

I contend that the structure of the argument that the early Heidegger uses to justify these claims is thoroughly verificationist, even though the verificationism involved is both holistic and pragmatic. That is, it is an essential premise of the transcendental argument that Heidegger constructs concerning the necessary conditions for intentionality that the meaning of any overt act, intention, or assertion is a function of the evidence that would count in favor of its truth or success. This formula clearly differs from the standard verificationist slogan ("the meaning of a sentence turns purely on what would count as evidence for its truth")[1] in two interrelated respects. First, for Heidegger, not only sentences or propositional contents but also overt actions have meanings. Second, the conditions under which it would be correct to conclude that an action has

---

1. W. V. O. Quine, "Epistemology Naturalized," in *Ontological Relativity and Other Essays* (New York: Columbia University Press, 1969), p. 80.

been successfully performed play an analogous role vis-à-vis the meaning of practical actions to the role that justification conditions play vis-à-vis the meaning of assertions. This pragmatic form of verificationism, which, as it turns out, is also holistic, is central to the transcendental argument leading to the claim that purposeful agency is a necessary condition for all intentionality. But, as we shall see, the pragmatic verificationist premise does not beg any important question concerning early Heidegger's pragmatic conclusions.

Part II of this book, "Being," discusses the metaphysical, or anti-metaphysical, implications of the early Heidegger's pragmatism in regard to intentionality. All transcendental arguments since Immanuel Kant have proceeded in two stages. First, one argues that some set of conditions is necessary for intentionality or some particular kind of intentional state (consciousness, experience, reference, language, or whatever). Second, one argues that these conditions also fix the necessary conditions that an object or entity must satisfy if it is to be capable of being intended (or thought of, or experienced, or referred to, or meant, or whatever). In the classical transcendental argument, then, the transcendental analysis of intentionality is taken as grounding metaphysical claims concerning the necessary conditions for being a being, or an entity capable of being intended. (As has often been pointed out—by Barry Stroud, for example—all such arguments, from Kant to Peter Strawson, are essentially verificationist.)[2] I argue in the second half of this book that the early Heidegger hoped to complete just such a metaphysical form of transcendental argument. He hoped to arrive at conclusions about what it means for an entity to be (that is, a statement of the necessary conditions for being an entity), as well as conclusions concerning the ontological sorts of entities there are and the appropriate way of understanding each different ontological sort of entity, on the basis of a transcendental analysis of intentionality and of intentions directed toward 'being' in particular.

The early Heidegger, however, thought of *his* transcendental argument as distinct in two ways. First, he thought that the thinkers prior to himself had skipped a critical step. They had gone directly from a transcendental discussion of intentionality to the attempt to ground a metaphysics—without pausing to consider what it meant to be an intender,

2. Barry Stroud, "Transcendental Arguments," *Journal of Philosophy* 65 (1968), 241–256.

without discussing the conditions under which an entity can be one who intends or (in Heidegger's own terminology) without asking the question of the meaning of the being of Dasein. Heidegger thought that because of this all his predecessors had fallen into the trap of thinking of the intentional agent as a substance that happened to have an odd range of properties: mental properties that involved thinking of things and itself, or being conscious and self-conscious. In contrast, Heidegger's own analysis of the meaning of the being of Dasein led him to assert that that meaning is temporality, that to be an intentional agent of the sort we are is to be temporal. As we shall see, this amounts to the claim that to be an intentional agent is to be a certain sort of organized activity itself, not to be a thinking thing that happens to have private mental states such as beliefs and desires, which cause that being to act for a purpose.

The early Heidegger further thought that the 'subjectivism' he found prevalent in modern metaphysics all the way back to René Descartes— the emphasis on the character of the intentional subject and its intentionality as the ground for all determinations in regard to what it is for any entity to be—was itself a function of this Cartesian error in regard to the ontology of the intender. In the completion of *Being and Time,* the early Heidegger hoped to show how the appropriate answer to the question of the meaning of Dasein's being (that is, the pragmatic, anti-mentalistic, agency-centered answer to the question 'what are the necessary conditions for being an intentional agent?') led to the appropriate, anti-subjectivistic answer to the question of the meaning of being (that is, to a non-subject-centered account of the conditions under which any entity can appropriately be said to be).[3]

But the early Heidegger was wrong about all this. What's more, he discovered that he was wrong relatively quickly. *Being and Time* was

---

3. 'The question of the meaning of being' is an ambiguous phrase in Heidegger; the early Heidegger often interprets the question of the meaning of being as the question of what the term 'being' means in general, or even the question of what it means to say of some entity that it is (see Chapter 6 and the first section of Chapter 7). In this sense, the question of the meaning of being is a question concerning what Thomas Sheehan (*Heidegger: The Man and His Thought* [Chicago: Precedent, 1981], p. ix) calls 'beingness', or whatever it is that is said when it is said that something is. (One must be careful here because Heidegger agrees with Kant that 'being' cannot be treated as a predicate.) It is in this sense that I use 'the meaning of being' here. Yet there is a legitimate sense in which the early Heidegger uses the phrase to mean 'the necessary conditions under which anything like "being" can be understood at all'. When the late Heidegger looks back at the early Heidegger, he always interprets 'the meaning of being' in this latter way.

never completed, although we do have what Heidegger called a new working-out of Division 1, Part 3. This volume, *The Basic Problems of Phenomenology*, represents Heidegger's best attempt to construct the antisubjectivistic metaphysics that he then thought must follow from his pragmatic analysis of intentionality—and it is a failure. In Chapter 6 I reconstruct the argument of *Basic Problems* and show that it leads to an *aporia*. As a first approximation, the problem consists in the fact that Heidegger had misidentified the source of metaphysical subjectivism. It doesn't always arise out of Cartesianism; in some cases it arises out of the transcendental mode of argument. All transcendental arguments, including the early Heidegger's own, are verificationist; and verificationism, even of a pragmatic sort, leads to subjectivism in metaphysics. But the early Heidegger has a prior and overwhelming bias against such a subjectivist metaphysics, a commitment that cannot be supported by the argument of *Being and Time*.

The rest of Part II develops the late Heidegger's response to the collapse of the metaphysical project of *Being and Time*. This response has two sides. First, Heidegger came to believe that metaphysics had reached its 'end' or 'completion' in the present age, a completion understood as taking place in 'the scientific attitude of socially active humanity'. That is, the questions of what it means for some entity to be or for any entity to be, and which ontological sorts of entities there are, are all questions that we now see can be answered only pragmatically, either directly through seeing what kinds of activities are successful or indirectly through the ontological commitments of a pragmatically understood science. The late Heidegger isn't always *happy* that metaphysics has been completed in this way, that philosophy has found its *telos* in science and technology, but he is consistent in his assertion that it has. As we shall see, these antimetaphysical, pragmatic assertions concerning ontology follow directly from the analysis of intentionality carried out in the published portion of *Being and Time*.

But there is a second side to Heidegger's response to the collapse of the anti-subjectivistic program of *Being and Time*. Late Heidegger thought that over and beyond metaphysics, over and beyond questions concerning what it means for something to be or which sorts of things there are—questions that he came to see as both definitive of philosophy and capable of being answered only pragmatically—there was another question that has a unique status and cannot be answered either scientifically or pragmatically. This is the question of 'the truth of being'—the *aletheia*, opening, or lighting of being. In Chapters 7 and 8 I argue that with appropriate modifications this question should be identified with Heidegger's initial question concerning the necessary conditions for the possibility of intentionality. I further argue that the late Heidegger thought this question was neither metaphysical nor scientific, because the answer was neither contingent and grounded in a scientific investigation of any entity or capacity of any entity, nor analytic and grounded in an a priori analysis of what it means for any entity to be. Positively, this amounts to the claim that the answer to the question of the truth of being (the question of the conditions under which 'being' can be understood or intended) is derived from a transcendental argument that (1) has no metaphysical implications whatsoever and (2) does not involve any *a priori* analysis of the being of any entity, including any transcendental subject, subject of consciousness, or Dasein.

The Heidegger who emerges from these pages is thus transcendental, anti-mentalistic, verificationist, pragmatic, and anti-metaphysical. In addition, instead of simply making assertions on the basis of more or less perspicacious phenomenological descriptions, he is rather good at constructing powerful arguments. In all these respects this Heidegger may be a bit unfamiliar, perhaps even disconcerting, to some of those who are already quite familiar with his works. To call late Heidegger transcendental and pragmatic, for example, goes against a variety of specific claims that he makes about himself. Similarly, it is clear that the *early* Heidegger considered himself both a metaphysician and a phenomenologist, and thus 'mentalistic' in at least some of the senses of that overloaded term. Finally, to say that Heidegger was a verificationist seems to bed him down with Carnap, and they are indeed strange bedfellows.

Potential surprise at these implications of my interpretation can be overcome, however, if one carefully examines Heidegger's uses of the terms in question, the structure of his arguments, and the sense in which I use these terms. There is no question, for example, that the late Heidegger considered himself anti-transcendental, but that belief is a function of what *he* meant by the word 'transcendental'. For him, a transcendental argument necessarily involved (a) metaphysical, a priori conclusions concerning the objects that can be intended and (b) a metaphysical analysis of the being who is intending. I see (a) and (b) as features that have historically characterized transcendental arguments but are inessential to them; rather, as I use the word, any discussion that asks after the necessary conditions for intentionality is thereby 'transcendental'. Understood in this way, the late Heidegger's argument structure *is* transcendental. Similarly, for late Heidegger, to be pragmatic is to adhere to the view that all questions are to be answered pragmatically, that there is only one kind of assertion. As I am using the term, however, any position asserting that all *metaphysical* questions can legitimately be answered only pragmatically is pragmatic. Under this criterion, late Heidegger is just as much a pragmatist as Rorty. To call Heidegger, early and late, 'antimentalistic' will surprise some but not those who, like Dreyfus and Haugeland, have insisted that for Heidegger the key to the existential analysis of both Dasein and intentionality is practical understanding as embodied in overt action.

What may surprise even them, however, is the emphasis I place on the importance of understanding Husserl for the proper interpretation of both the argument structure of the early Heidegger and his understanding of the word 'being'. Husserl, after all, is a mentalist; nevertheless, as soon as one realizes that, for Heidegger, intentionality is always practical rather than cognitive and that the primary form of intending is doing something for a purpose rather than being conscious of something, the structural analogies between the argument strategies of Husserl and Heidegger become apparent. This is the case regardless of the important differences in the content of what is said and what it is being said about— intentional action in the one case and consciousness in the other. It is in this light that we must understand Heidegger's verificationism. It is holistic and pragmatic, and what can count as evidence for it is very different from what can count as evidence for Husserl or Carnap, but it is verificationism nonetheless.

The final test of any interpretation is whether it makes sense of a body of texts, and the final test of an interpretation of a great philosopher is whether it clarifies what that philosopher thought, why he thought it, and why what he thought is worth attending to. And these ultimately must be the tests of this discussion of Heidegger. It is in this spirit that I submit this work to the philosophical community, both 'continental' and 'analytic'.

PART I
Understanding

Introduction

Traditionally, the word 'understanding' has been used to refer to a certain range of cognitive abilities and performances that result in knowledge. Prior to Kant (and even in Kant) it was common to contrast understanding, as a source of knowledge, with sensation, which was frequently taken to be an entirely separate origin of our knowledge of the world. Sensibility was thought of as the capacity to be affected by the external world through being caused to have sensations; understanding consisted in our ability to *think,* according to concepts, the things given to us in sensible intuition. The typical result of an exercise of sensibility was considered to be an intuition or a direct presentation, a having. The typical result of an exercise of understanding was a judgment that some thing, presented to us in intuition, had some definite characteristic or was similar to some other things in some particular respect.[1] To form judgments, one had to use concepts, general terms, representations, or characters (depending upon one's philosophical orientation). Such concepts contained and expressed various ways in which things might be and in which one thing could be similar to another. Every judgment was considered to involve the subsumption of one representation, intuition, or concept under another concept. To form a judgment, then, was thought to involve taking one thing or intuition as having a characteristic that it could share with others.

1. In David Hume, following Descartes and George Berkeley, the problem emerged of whether actions of our understanding resulted in judgments that referred to real things or in judgments that referred merely to our intuitions. Kant's work very largely concerned this issue.

The act of taking one thing as having a definite character, as falling under some concept, has been traditionally considered to be the act of understanding par excellence; our ability to take things as this or that has been called the faculty of understanding; and the judgments that result from taking this as that have been taken to be the fruit of understanding. With Kant, however, the long tradition of thinking of knowledge as consisting in direct intuitions, and of truth as the correct mirroring of the world in those intuitions, appeared finally to come to an end. Since Kant, knowledge has been thought to consist in judgments: what is known are true judgments, and only judgments can be true or false. Thus knowledge and truth are firmly associated with understanding understood as the ability to take something as having a definite character or determination, even though it is generally acknowledged that unless we can sense things, we can have nothing to exercise our understanding on.

In addition to these philosophical senses of 'understand', there are colloquial ways in which the word is used. We frequently say of people who are good with cars that they 'understand' them in the sense that they know how to deal with, fix, or handle them. We might say that I understand my son in the sense that I know and appreciate what motivates him, and that therefore I know how to cope with him so as to take those motivations into account. There is a sense in which someone who can say very little that is true about a movie can nevertheless understand it better than someone who knows a great many facts about it. And it is certainly possible that someone can understand nothing about making movies even though he or she is a film school graduate. In each of these uses it seems as if 'understanding' is associated with some practical ability or other. To understand in this way is to know how to do something, or how to cope with some thing, or how to deal with some range of situations. Given these uses, it is reasonable to ask whether and how theoretical understanding, or the subsumption under a concept which results in a judgment of the form that x is y, is related to the practical understanding involved in knowing how to accomplish a number of tasks and deal with the ordinary problems of life. And this relationship, under a variety of labels and in a number of different ways, has been a major theme in twentieth-century philosophy.[2]

When we turn to the early Heidegger and his prominent use of the

---

2. E.g., theory and praxis, meaning and speech act, theoretical judgment and practical judgment, knowing how and knowing that.

word 'understanding', we seem to be all at sea. There is very little in either of the traditional uses of 'understanding' to prepare us for the kinds of claims Heidegger makes, or even for their tone. What, for example, are we to make of these 'definitions'? "In the 'for the sake of which', existing being-in-the-world is disclosed as such, and this disclosedness we have called 'understanding'."[3] "Understanding is the being of such potentiality-for-being, which is never something still outstanding as not yet extant but which, as something which is essentially never extant, 'is' with the being of Dasein, in the sense of existence."[4]

Part I of this book is a systematic treatment of Heidegger's concept of understanding as it is developed in the period of *Being and Time*. The first three chapters offer an extensive interpretation of Heidegger's assertions and positions in regard to understanding. This interpretation aims to make these positions intelligible by showing how his use of 'understanding' is related to and is meant to have implications for both of the more traditional philosophical uses of 'understanding'. Chapters 4 and 5 construct an argument that supports many of Heidegger's important claims concerning understanding and the relations between Heideggerian understanding and theoretical understanding.

3. *B.T.*, p. 182/143.
4. *B.T.*, pp. 183–184/144. Translation modified.

1 Dasein's Understanding

Even if not much is initially clear in Heidegger's conception of understanding in *Being and Time,* three features of his approach stand out. First, Dasein is the one who understands, and only entities that are ontologically characterized as being Dasein can understand. Second, Dasein *always* understands. Understanding is not one determination among others which Dasein might have, or one intentional comportment among others which Dasein might occasionally engage in. Rather, to be Dasein is to understand, in the sense that understanding is essential to Dasein. There could be no Dasein without understanding. Third, *what* Dasein primarily understands is itself or, more properly, its own being. While it is true to say that Dasein understands many things, of a variety of sorts, there is some kind of priority granted by Heidegger to the self-understanding of Dasein. This chapter deals with each of these points in turn.

Understanding Belongs to Dasein

What is Heidegger talking about when he speaks about Dasein? If we take this question as asking which things the word 'Dasein' refers to, or as concerning the extension of the term 'Dasein', then the answer seems easy. We are Dasein. All of us who could read this book, or Heidegger's book, are Dasein. "We are ourselves the entities to be analyzed [Dasein]."[1] This simple answer, however, even as a response to the question

1. *B.T.,* p. 67/41.

in regard to extension, is inadequate because it is ambiguous. Is it the people who read German who count as Dasein, those who read at all, those who in virtue of their capacities could be eventually taught to read, those who can speak and understand any language, all those who are genetically and biologically human, all rational beings? What about infants, chimpanzees, aliens, and the feebleminded?

Heidegger spends very little time directly addressing the question of the extension of the term 'Dasein'. He is content with the general indication that roughly, we are talking about things that are significantly like us, and then turns to an attempt to determine what it is about us that is significant. It is in the determination of the character and characteristics of those things that are Dasein that the concept gets its determinacy. But Heidegger doesn't start with a fixed list of entities that are Dasein and can be compared to find their common traits. How then does he proceed?

In fact, Heidegger's definition of 'Dasein' seems very traditional in two different ways. 'Dasein' is defined by mentioning a trait which all things that count as Dasein must possess insofar as they are Dasein, and which no being that is not Dasein possesses. That is, 'Dasein' is defined intensionally. Further, the trait used to define 'Dasein' appears to be just the one that has traditionally been taken to be distinctive to human beings, at least *qua* thinkers and intenders, since Descartes: self-awareness, or self-consciousness. "These entities [Dasein], in their being, comport themselves towards their being. As entities with such being they are delivered over to their own being."[2] But self-comportment is *not* self-awareness.

This passage needs some elucidation. At this period Heidegger uses the word 'comportment' (*Verhaltung*) as a general term for any kind of intentional act directed toward any object whatsoever. Every time there is a comportment, there is an intention, because what makes a comportment a comportment is that it is intentionally directed toward . . . Thus willing, believing, wishing, hoping, fearing, imagining, and manipulating are all comportments in that they are intentional. "As structure of comportments, intentionality is itself a structure of the self-comporting subject. . . . It [intentionality] belongs to the essential nature of comportments, so that to speak of intentional comportments is already a pleonasm and is somewhat equivalent to my speaking of a spatial triangle."[3] So, to say, as Heidegger does here, that Dasein essentially comports itself toward its own being is just to say that it is a distinctive trait of Dasein that it intends itself or its 'own being'.

2. *B.T.*, p. 67/42.
3. *B.P.*, p. 61/85.

Two things about Heidegger's formulation of this traditional-sounding claim should alert us that everything isn't quite as traditional as it seems, however. Most obviously, there is no hint that he thinks it is anything like a mind that is the subject of self-intentions. Just as is true of many other twentieth-century thinkers, it is people who are self-intending for Heidegger, not nonbodily parts, aspects, or components of people. More important and distinctive, Heidegger's statement of the view that we are distinguished by self-intending makes two essential mentions of 'being'. Dasein, *in its* being, comports itself toward its *being*. That Dasein intends itself is taken to be an ontological differentiation, and what it intends is seen precisely as its being, so differentiated. We will deal with the first of these appeals to 'being' in this section and return to the second in the second section of this chapter.

Heidegger clearly conceives of the trait of being self-intending as different in kind from other traits, such as being white, being square, or being a house. In fact, for Heidegger, it is inappropriate to see self-intentionality as a 'trait' or 'property' at all, essential or inessential. Rather, Dasein's essence consists in its being and not in some necessary property that makes it distinctive. "The 'essence' of this entity lies in its 'to be' (*Zu-sein* = being toward). Its being-what-it-is (*Was-sein; essentia*) must, so far as we can speak of it at all, be conceived in terms of its being (*existentia*).[4] (We should note what is in any case obvious. Heidegger reserves the term 'existence' for the being of Dasein and uses other locutions for the traditional ontological concept of existence. How Heidegger understands existence in the traditional philosophical sense will concern us throughout this book.) The distinctive mark of Dasein is that it intends itself; what is distinctive about Dasein is that it has a distinctive kind of being; intending itself is what makes Dasein ontologically distinct, and Dasein's ontological distinctiveness consists in being self-comporting. Heidegger's name for the distinctive kind of being of Dasein is 'existence'. Dasein is distinguished from everything else not by its essential property but by its kind of being, existence; and existence consists in self-intending. "The 'essence' of Dasein lies in its existence."[5] What are we to make of all of this talk about 'being'?[6]

Since the Greeks introduced careful reflection on the notion of being

4. *B.T.*, p. 67/42.
5. *B.T.*, p. 67/42.
6. Part II examines Heidegger's thought concerning being; at this point we go into the question of being as Heidegger sees it only so far as is necessary to make sense of Heideggerian understanding.

and Aristotle introduced the concept of a category, it has been common (though not universal) to think of beings (entities, things that are) as divided among various categories. Although Aristotle has ten categories, the only categorical difference that concerns us here is the distinction he makes between substance and the other nine categories (quality, quantity, time, place, and so on). A being is in one of the nine categories only insofar as it is a modification or qualification of a being that is a substance, while a being that is a (primary) substance is neither 'in' nor 'said of' anything else. That is, it is some thing that is white, not some white that is thingy. Although the way in which being a substance is different from being a modification is much contested in the tradition, it at least seems to be the case that substances are individuals that can be subjects of modification, while the other categories of being are different types of modifications that can pertain to substances. The most obvious way, then, to interpret Heidegger's suggestion that Dasein has a kind of being distinct from substances and all other kinds of being is to think of Heidegger's 'existence' as a distinctive way in which substances can be modified. Thus, it might be thought that just as all sensible substances can be qualified in having a temporal location, and all physical substances are modifiable by spatial position and extension, those substances that happen to be Dasein are characterizable by intentional properties, such as believing that or seeing that. This, in fact, is precisely the analysis of thinking being that Heidegger ascribes to Descartes and, to a lesser degree, to Kant. It is definitely *not* Heidegger's account of the ontological distinctiveness of Dasein.

Existing beings, Dasein, are both individuals and primary subjects of predication. Dasein isn't a substance with a distinctive kind of essential property; for Heidegger, it is a subject of predication which is not a substance at all. This means that for Heidegger it is always wrong to think of existence or of being self-intending as a property of some ordinary substance. Rather, the difference between beings that exist and ordinary substances is thought of as a difference in the way they are subjects that can be modified, and a difference in what it is for each of these kinds of being *to be* modified. What ontologically differentiates Dasein from substance is not that the one can be an individual subject and the other cannot but that what it is to have properties (to be an individual subject) is different for substances than it is for existing beings. "Those characteristics which can be exhibited in this entity [Dasein] are not extant properties of some entity which looks so and so and is itself extant [*vorhanden,* Heidegger's word for the ontological character of ordinary physical substances as objects of theoretical understanding]; they are in each case possible ways for it to be, and no more than that."[7] "Because Dasein's characters of being are defined in terms of existentiality, we call them 'existentialia'. These are to be sharply distinguished from what we call 'categories'—characteristics of being for entities whose character is not that of Dasein."[8] To be Dasein, to exist, is to be an individual that has a way of having characteristics and, (associated with this) a type of characteristic essentially different from the way of having characteristics and the types of characteristics appropriate to substances.

So, to say, as Heidegger does, that the distinctive trait of Dasein is intentionality directed toward self but that this trait should be conceived as a difference in being instead of a difference in property is to say that (1) to be self-intentional is not a property of a substance in the way that being a house is a property of a substance; (2) being self-intentional is a determination of what sort of modification can count as being a property or characteristic of the being that is self-intending, just as, for Heidegger, being a substance is a determination of what can count as a modification of the entity that is a substance; and (3) existentiality (the way of being of existing beings, Dasein) determines a manner of having properties, just as, for Heidegger, substantiality determines a distinctive way in which substances can be modified. But what is distinctive about Dasein's being is that it intends itself. To say of some thing that it is a Dasein, then, or that it exists, is to say that it is capable of being characterized by various means, ways, or procedures through which it intends itself. Such ways of intending are the existentialia mentioned above, and the specific concrete realizations of the different possible ways of intending itself are the different distinctive properties of any given Dasein.

But what are the multiple ways in which Dasein can intend itself? What are the 'existential' divisions that correspond with the various categories in which substances can be modified? These existentialia amount to ways in which a self-intention can be determined, modified, or characterized— much as, for Aristotle, substances can be determined in quantity or quality. In *Being and Time* there are several such kinds of existential being, but in *The Basic Problems of Phenomenology, The Essence of Reasons, The Metaphysical Foundations of Logic,* and the rest of the works from this

7. *B.T.,* p. 67/42. Translation modified.
8. *B.T.,* p. 70/44.

period, they all shrink to insignificance in the face of the primary way in which self-intending beings can intend themselves. Dasein, insofar as it exists, is capable of understanding and is capable of having some particular understanding or other. Understanding is primarily, then, one of the ways in which self-intending entities are self-comporting. "If we interpret understanding as a fundamental existentiale, this indicates that this phenomenon is conceived as a basic mode of Dasein's being."[9]

Dasein Always Understands Itself in Its Being

As we have developed the notion to this point, Heidegger's conception of understanding involves seeing understanding as one of the ways in which intentions directed toward self occur. There are clearly several oddities about this conception, two of which demand immediate attention. First, while it is certainly appropriate to say in ordinary or philosophical contexts that one understands oneself, this is not the most typical use of the term. More frequently, what is understood is something other than the one who understands. Indeed, Heidegger himself often speaks of understanding things other than Dasein. Nevertheless, in tying understanding to Dasein's ontological constitution and associating that constitution with self-comportment, Heidegger does seem to grant some sort of priority to self-understanding. Second, understanding, whether taken in the cognitive or practical sense, is most frequently thought of as one among several sorts of intentional relations that human beings can have to objects. As such, understanding seems to be something a human might do occasionally, in the same way that she might see occasionally, or hope occasionally, or manipulate occasionally. But if, as Heidegger claims, it is appropriate to think of understanding as analogous to categorial determinations of substance, then it should follow that insofar as there is an existing being, it is always possible to characterize that being as having some understanding or other. That is, just as every substance always has some quality, whatever it might be, every Dasein should always have some understanding, whatever it might be. This is, indeed, precisely what Heidegger suggests. "To exist is essentially, even if not only, to understand."[10] For Heidegger, one can't exist at all or at any time without understanding.

9. *B.T.*, p. 182/143.
10. *B.P.*, p. 276/391.

What might it mean to assert, as Heidegger does, that in order to exist, a being must understand? Existence, as Dasein's kind of being, itself is initially characterized in terms of a certain sort of comportment, self-comportment; that is, to exist means to be such as to intend oneself in some manner. To say, then, that there is no existence without understanding is just to say that understanding, whatever it might be, is a necessary feature of all self-directed intentions. In fact, Heidegger goes even further. He maintains that understanding is a necessary condition not only for self-directed intentions but for all intentions, insofar as he holds that only beings that exist are capable of intentions at all. "If understanding is a basic determination of existence, it is as such the condition of possibility for all of the Dasein's particular possible manners of comportment. It is the condition of possibility for all kinds of comportment, not only practical but also cognitive."[11] From what standpoint, and in terms of which conception of understanding, is it plausible to maintain that there can be no self-directed intentions without understanding?

In the traditional cognitive sense, understanding amounts to taking something as something or having a belief in regard to it. When such understanding is contrasted with and distinguished from other kinds of intentional comportment (as one among several kinds), such as sensing, it is being suggested that it is possible to be aware of 'something' without having any beliefs in regard to it or being aware of it as something with a definite character. I can see the house, it is claimed, without taking what I see as anything definite at all. If there are such 'things' as sense data, they are the sorts of things that can be intended without any understanding. To claim, then, that there can be no intentions without understanding in this traditional cognitive sense would amount to the assertion that there can be no intentions that do not intend their objects as determined in some way. This would not imply that there was no difference between sensing and believing; it would merely state that it is impossible to sense unless what one senses is qualified in the sensing as belonging to some type. Interestingly, at several points Heidegger appears to make just this claim. "What we 'first' hear is never noises or complexes of sound, but the creaking wagon, the motorcycle. We hear the column on the march, the north wind, the woodpecker tapping, the fire crackling . . . it [Dasein] certainly does not dwell proximally alongside sensations; nor would it

11. *B.P.*, p. 276/392.

first have to give shape to the swirl of sensations to provide the spring-board from which the subject leaps off and finally arrives at a 'world'."[12] To extend this point and suggest that there can be no existence—that is, no self-directed intentions—without understanding would merely be to assert that all self-awareness necessarily involves the awareness of oneself as something, that we can't be aware of ourselves unless we are aware of ourselves as having some definite characteristics.

But if we interpret Heidegger's claim concerning the ubiquitousness of understanding for existence as a claim that one could not intend oneself without practical understanding, then we get what appears to be a very different assertion. One understands something practically if one knows how to deal with it and how to cope with it. I understand cars practically when I know how to drive them or how to fix them, depending on the context. So, if one said that one couldn't intend cars without understand-ing them in this practical sense, it would mean that one couldn't intend a car without knowing how to use or fix it as a car. This, of course, is wildly implausible. But Heidegger doesn't claim that there can be no intentions directed toward a thing unless we understand *it*. Rather, he asserts that one can't intend oneself unless one understands oneself, and that one can't intend anything else unless one intends oneself. Because, as we have already emphasized, understanding is primarily self-understanding, to assert that there are no self-directed intentions without understanding is to say only that we couldn't intend ourselves without understanding ourselves. The further point quoted above, to the effect that there are no intentions at all without understanding, would then be the assertion that there are no intentions without practical self-understanding—not, as it first seemed, without practical understanding of the thing intended.

It is certainly the case that when Heidegger talks about understanding he is always using the word in a way that is meant to be somehow akin to the ordinary practical use of the word. "In German we say that someone can *vorstehen* something—literally stand in front of or ahead of it, that is, stand at its head, administer, manage, preside over it. This is equivalent to saying that he *versteht sich darauf*, understands in the sense of being skilled or expert at it, has the know how of it. The meaning of the term 'understanding' . . . is intended to go back to this usage in ordinary language."[13] What distinguishes Heidegger's use of 'understanding'

12. *B.T.*, p. 207/163–164.
13. *B.P.*, p. 276/392.

from the ordinary practical use is that what is primarily understood for Heidegger is always Dasein itself, insofar as it exists, that is, in its being as self-intending. "When we are talking ontically we sometimes use the expression 'understanding something' with the signification of 'being able to manage something'; 'being a match for it'; 'being competent to do something'. In understanding, as an existentiale, that which we have such competence over is not a 'what', but being as existing."[14]

To recapitulate, Heidegger holds that it is impossible to exist without understanding: that is, that all self-directed intentionality demands understanding. He thinks of understanding primarily in terms of understanding oneself rather than understanding other things, so his claim is that all self-intending involves self-understanding. This could be interpreted in two ways, depending upon whether Heidegger's use of 'understand' is derived from the cognitive or the practical use of that word. If it is derived from the former, then Heidegger's assertion would amount to the claim that, perhaps as a function of the role of beliefs in all intentions, one cannot intend any thing without having some beliefs in regard to that thing, and that one cannot intend oneself without having some beliefs in regard to oneself.[15] If we are to take 'understanding' in some practical sense, then to say that all existence involves self-understanding is to say that we couldn't intend ourselves unless we had a certain competence over ourselves and our 'being as existing'. The further proposition that there can be no intentional comportment directed toward anything without understanding would then be the claim that we couldn't intend anything at all unless we had competence over 'being as existing'. The textual evidence is overwhelming that Heidegger uses the word 'understanding' in the sense of practical coping (and indeed that he sees cognitive understanding as derivative from practical understanding), so the claim that Dasein, as existing, always understands must be interpreted as the assertion that nothing can intend itself unless it has 'competence over being as existing'.

This conclusion as it stands is hardly an aid to interpretation, however. We have managed to explain the obscure with the more obscure. What can it possibly mean to talk about 'competence over being as existing'? What are we to make of Heidegger's insistence that we primarily under-

14. *B.T.*, p. 183/143.
15. We will see later on that if we appropriately define 'belief', Heidegger does hold this position. It is not, however, the proper interpretation of his claim that all existence demands understanding, a claim that occupies a central position in his thought.

stand ourselves rather than other things; that to understand ourselves is to understand our 'being', and to understand our being is to have competence over our being?

According to Heidegger, existing beings are those entities that intend themselves and, in intending themselves, constantly understand themselves. As we have already seen, however, for Heidegger, existing beings do not merely understand themselves; they always have an understanding of their own *being*. The preliminary description of the being of existing entities, given above, suggested that we should think of the difference in ontology between Dasein and substances as a difference in the way in which they are respectively subjects of predication and in what it means for them to have properties or characteristics. At this point we must further clarify what could be meant by the claim that existing beings not only constantly intend themselves but that they do so in such a way as to constantly understand their own being.

Similar to Heidegger's claim in regard to the priority and necessity of Dasein's understanding of its own being is Kant's assertion in Section 25 of the Transcendental Deduction in the B edition of *The Critique of Pure Reason:* "In the transcendental synthesis of the manifold of representations in general, and therefore in the synthetic original unity of apperception, I am conscious of myself, not as I appear to myself, nor as I am in myself, but only that I am."[16] Kant's point is multifaceted. First, as the "transcendental synthesis of the manifold of representations" is a necessary condition for the possibility of experiencing any object whatsoever, the consciousness of myself that consists in "the synthetic original unity of apperception" must constantly accompany, be capable of accompanying, or be presupposed in any intentional giving of any object at all. I am implicitly aware of myself in every experience insofar as that experience is organized with others into a coherent and ordered pattern, and I am the subject of that organized experience in that it is *my* experience. My consciousness of myself is my consciousness of the ability to combine various intuitions into a unitary consciousness: "I exist as an intelligence which is conscious solely of its power of combination."[17] As Heidegger himself puts it in his gloss on this passage: "The ego is 'I think', which in

---

16. Immanuel Kant, *The Critique of Pure Reason,* trans. Norman Kemp Smith (New York: St. Martin's Press, 1965), p. 168, B157 (henceforth cited as Kant, *C.P.R.*).
17. Ibid., p. 169, B158.

every thinking is thought along with it as the conditioning ground of the unifying 'I-combine'."[18]

So, for Kant as for Heidegger, there is no possibility of intending things other than ourselves unless we are capable of intending ourselves. But what is it to be aware of myself and of what sort of thing am I aware when I am aware of myself? For Kant, the categories, the various kinds of determination of a substance in general, arise out of the various ways in which thinking can perform its task of combining. But as the sentence cited makes clear, the categories are inapplicable to ourselves insofar as we are the subject of experience. There are two reasons for this. First, the 'I think' is thought of as the ground for the combination of representations in understanding that is accomplished in and through the categories, and there is something incongruous about applying the results of an activity to the source of the activity.[19] More important, the categories, as modes of combination, are applicable only where there is something to be combined: that is, for Kant, when we have been given some intuitions to work with. But I have no intuition of myself as the determining ground of combination; I intuit myself only in the temporally successive manifold of my particular experience, a manifold in which, as Kant puts it, my existence is *determinable* (by the categories) but not *determining* (as it is when I think of myself as the 'I think'). So, whatever mode of being the pure self (of which I am conscious in the synthetic unity of apperception) has, it does not have that kind of being which substances have, the kind of being that is determined in and through the categories. In fact, it is a mistake to think of this subject as a substance at all.

Kant draws from this argument the conclusion that because we have no knowledge or understanding of the 'I think' according to the categories—that is, as a substance—we have no knowledge or understanding of it at all. We have only a consciousness of ourselves as a spontaneous, active power of combination which is in no way determined further. Early Heidegger rejects this inference. "It does not follow from the inadequacy of the categories of nature that every ontological interpretation whatever of the ego is impossible."[20]

18. *B.P.*, p. 144/204.
19. Heidegger emphasizes this point (cf. *B.P.*, pp. 144/204–205, and *K.P.M.*), even though Kant does not. There is in fact serious question whether this observation could be turned into anything like a valid argument.
20. *B.P.*, p. 145/207.

Heidegger follows Kant in seeing the subject as the source of the unity among our various intentions of objects—a unity that is necessary if we are to intend objects at all—and in conceiving the self-intention of this subject in terms of the comportment toward this organized structure. He diverges from Kant, however, in thinking of the primary unity of experience as a practical (that is, action-oriented) unity rather than as a theoretical unity. Things can be understood only in relation to one another, but for Heidegger, those relations are principally instrumental rather than causal (as they are for Kant), and the properties these things are understood as having are functional. It follows that Dasein, the subject of this structured intentionality, must be thought of as that in terms of which entities can be understood or thought of as instruments, or the *end* or *purpose* for the realization of which things can be made to function. Dasein exists, or intends itself, insofar as the understanding of things as having functions also always involves an implicit understanding of the end these things can serve.

This reorientation of the Kantian notion of apperception from a theoretical to a practical context stands behind Heidegger's contention that it is possible to understand the subject of experience, even though it is impossible to understand it as a substance. Heidegger holds that even though it is inappropriate to understand Dasein as a substance, this does not mean that it is impossible to understand Dasein as existing. In fact, as we have seen, Heidegger thinks that such understanding is not only possible but is in some sense necessary if there is to be self-intending at all. But in what manner does Dasein understand itself as existing? Once again, Heidegger takes his cue in regard to the ontological character of this self, and of the understanding that grasps it, from his interpretation of Kant—in this case of Kant's ethics. "What is the ontological meaning of the person thus made manifest in respect? Kant says: 'Now I maintain that man and every rational being in general exists as an end in himself, not merely as a means to be used arbitrarily by this or that will; instead in all his actions, whether they are addressed to himself or to other rational beings, he must always be considered at the same time as an end.' . . . The moral person exists as its own end; it is itself an end."[21] The notion of the person as developed in Kant's moral philosophy suggests to Heidegger that there is "a sharp ontological distinction between person and thing as *two* basic kinds of being."[22]

21. *B.P.,* p. 138/195.
22. *B.P.,* p. 139/197.

To be a person, as opposed to being a substance, is to be an end or purpose. The being of Dasein as existing is to be thought of as being an end. For Dasein to understand that being is for Dasein to intend *itself* as being an end. There are, of course, many possible ends or kinds of purposes: I can intend that my car run properly, or that I be a good philosopher, or, more prosaically, that I be at class on time. Heidegger is primarily concerned with the intending that intends some possibility of myself as an end, for it is this sort of intention that counts as an understanding of myself as an end and anchors my experience of entities other than myself as instrumentally related to one another. In the period of *Being and Time,* Heidegger calls an existing being's intending of itself as end the 'for-the-sake-of' (*das Umwillen*). The 'for-the-sake-of' always consists of some possibility of the Dasein itself. Hence, to be an existing being necessarily involves understanding that being as an end, and to understand that being as an end is to intend *oneself* as an end to be accomplished, or as a 'for-the-sake-of'. "To be for its own sake is an essential determination of the being of that being we call Dasein. This constitution, which we will now, for brevity, call the for-the-sake-of, provides the intrinsic possibility for this being to be itself, i.e. for self-hood to belong to its being. To be in the mode of a self means to be fundamentally towards oneself. Being towards oneself constitutes the being of Dasein and is not something like an additional capacity to observe oneself over and above just existing. Existing is precisely this being towards oneself, only the latter must be understood in its full metaphysical scope and must not be restricted to some activity or capability or to any mode of apprehension such as knowledge or appercep-tion."[23] Finally, 'understanding' is just our having of ourselves as end insofar as we are directed toward some 'for-the-sake-of', a having that *is* our understanding of ourselves as being an end, or as existing. "In the 'for-the-sake-of-which' existing Being-in-the-world is disclosed as such, and this disclosedness we have called 'understanding'."[24]

We are now in position to recapitulate and to translate these results out of Heidegger's peculiar idiom. The central prerequisite for comprehending the early Heidegger is to see that, as he understands it, to be a person is precisely to be an end or a purpose. As his comments on Kant and his rejection of the conception of the person as substance make clear, this should not be interpreted to mean that he regards people as things that

23. *M.F.L.,* pp. 189/243–244.
24. *B.T.,* p. 182/143.

happen to have the intentional property of willing or desiring. Rather, the being of Dasein itself is thought of as *purposiveness*, or being toward an end, and a particular Dasein's determinate characteristics are all definite ways in which that entity is purposive. To exist, in Heidegger's sense, is simply to intend some possibility of oneself as a purpose. According to Heidegger it is necessary for intending ends that one understand oneself as intending *some* end. But what is it to intend oneself as intending some end, or to have an understanding of one's own being as existing? Heidegger suggests that we understand ourselves indirectly as the purpose in terms of which various things in the world can appear to us as serviceable or detrimental. He calls this overriding purpose, in light of which things have significance as useful, the 'for-the-sake-of'; he sees the for-the-sake-of as some possible manner in which we might come to be and claims that the for-the-sake-of is the principle vehicle of our self-understanding.

To say, as Heidegger does, that Dasein, or existing beings, understand is to say that only beings who are purposive can understand either themselves or anything else. To say, as Heidegger does, that existing beings essentially understand, or necessarily understand, is to say that one can intend oneself (in the sense of intentional comportment toward oneself) only if one intends (in the sense of intentionally striving or attempting) to realize some possibility for oneself. To say, as Heidegger does, that Dasein primarily understands *itself* and does so by understanding its own being, is to say that understanding *consists* in projecting an end or purpose for oneself in terms of which those things other than Dasein have a significance, and that one's understanding of oneself is as an end to be accomplished. I understand myself, in particular, as what I am trying to be; I understand myself in general as something that can attempt to achieve such a result; and unless I understand myself in those ways, I cannot, according to Heidegger, understand anything else.

We still have not seen, however, why this should be so or, in detail, what it means to claim that self-understanding as purposiveness is necessary for understanding anything at all. And so, by a roundabout route, we are led back to one of the questions we raised above. What, specifically, does Heidegger take to be the relations among our self-understanding as ends, our cognitive understanding of things as substances with properties, and our practical understanding of how to cope with and deal with things in a variety of situations? Further, we still need to interpret Heidegger's odd suggestion that to understand our being (now seen as 'purposing') is to have 'competence over our being'. These issues lead us into an analysis of the notions of 'projection' and 'world'.

Practical Understanding and Projection

Given Heidegger's belief that intending oneself involves the intention to accomplish some end or realize some possibility of Dasein, it is hardly surprising that he considers practical understanding to be the primary form of our understanding of entities other than ourselves. We will be able to interpret how Heidegger handles cognitive subsumption only after we have become clear on the status of 'understanding how'.

What is involved in understanding how to use a tool? We say that we understand how to *use* a tool (hammer, computer, car), but we also say that we understand how to perform the activity appropriate to that tool (to hammer, to compute, to drive). We will tend to use these locutions interchangeably, but the reader should realize that even though Heidegger frequently speaks simply of understanding tools, his analysis demands a strict priority for the verbal rather than the nominal form. That is, to understand *x* (for example, a hammer) is primarily to understand how to do *y* with *x* (to hammer) or how to use *x* (to use *x* as a hammer).

First, then, understanding how to use a tool consists strictly in an ability. To understand how to use a hammer, one must be able to use it at the appropriate time, in the appropriate circumstances, and in the appropriate way. What one is capable of when one has an understanding of how to hammer is a certain kind of overt performance or activity.[25] The exercise of the ability to hammer, in which the practical understanding of hammers is realized, is no kind of private mental act. Rather, what we are capable of when we understand how to use a hammer or how to hammer, or have a practical understanding of hammers, is just the overt activity of hammering. The practical understanding of one kind of tool consists in the capacity to use tools of that kind correctly, and nothing else. "Equipment can genuinely show itself only in dealings cut to its own measure (hammering with a hammer, for example); but in such dealings an entity of this kind is not grasped thematically as an occurring thing. . . . The hammering does not simply have knowledge about the hammer's charac-

---

25. Notice, we certainly ascribe an understanding of hammers—in the sense of understanding that some thing is a hammer, or in the sense of understanding what hammers are for and what it is to be a hammer—to persons such as quadraplegics who are incapable, for physical reasons, of hammering. It seems a bit odder to say of such people that they understand how to hammer. When we do so, I suggest that we are ascribing to them an assertoric 'understanding-that' in regard to tools (cf. Chapters 2 and 3) and that their ability to *x* is treated as a certain sort of counterfactual ability: they would be able to *x* (in the usual sense) if they did not have the disability they do have.

ter as equipment, but it has appropriated this equipment in a way which could not possibly be more suitable."[26]

Heidegger says that things understood in this practical way—that is, by being tools that we are capable of using in a certain manner—have a different kind of *being* from ordinary substances, which are the objects of cognitive understanding. "The hammering itself uncovers the specific 'manipulability' of the hammer. The kind of being which equipment possesses—in which it manifests itself in its own right—we call 'readiness to hand' [*Zuhandenheit*]"[27] This demands clarification. What Heidegger is suggesting here is that to be a tool, such as a hammer, is to be nothing other than to be capable of use or service. I practically understand something as a hammer insofar as I understand how to hammer with it: that is, insofar as I am able to use this thing as hammers are used. But not everything that I can attempt to hammer with, even if I am hammering correctly, is capable of performing the function of a hammer. I can practically understand something to be a hammer by using it in hammering without its being a hammer. It could, for example, be made of brittle glass, so that when I hammer with it, it shatters. What must the thing be to be actually a hammer? It must be such as to be actually capable of being used in hammering. As Heidegger says, "the hammering itself uncovers the manipulability of the hammer"; that is the test of a hammer is in the hammering. To be a tool of a certain kind, then, is to be useful in a certain kind of practical activity. The class of hammers is composed of all things, and only those things, that could be useful in hammering, and whether or not something is a hammer can be determined only by hammering with it. To be a tool as such, to be 'ready to hand', in Heidegger's expression, is to be such that *what* the thing is is determined as its specific utility, which in turn is determinable only in and through its being used.

Practical understanding consists in an ability to use things appropriately, and such understanding understands the objects used as useful in such operations. The two sides go together. We don't understand how to hammer if we habitually choose the wrong instrument to hammer with. But what, in general, characterizes the operations we must be capable of if we are to count as practically understanding how to do something? I said above that to understand how to hammer, one must understand how to use hammers at the appropriate time, in the appropriate circum-

26. *B.T.*, p. 98/69.
27. *B.T.*, p. 98/69.

stances, and in the appropriate way. But what is it to use hammers appropriately? What is it for an activity to be 'appropriately' timed or performed in the 'appropriate' way? We would say of someone that he understands how to hammer if, in a situation that 'calls for' hammering, he successfully completes the operation of hammering and tends to be able to do so habitually. This formula has two sides (in addition to the capacity clause): the ability to respond differentially to a situation that 'calls for' the operation, and the successful completion of the operation. To count as understanding how to hammer, one must fulfill both these conditions. One must know when to hammer, and one must know how to do it so as to get the job done. The 'situation that calls for hammering' is some state of things in relation to some job to be accomplished.

If one wants to build a house, one needs to build a frame. To do this one must have boards from which to make the frame, nails to hold the boards together, and a hammer to drive the nails into the boards so as to hold them fast. It is appropriate to engage in the activity of hammering in the situation just defined, and that situation in turn is defined in terms of (1) an end to be realized (the completion of the house), (2) a set of functionally defined tools (the frame, the boards, nails, hammer), and (3) the present state of relations among those tools (the frame hasn't yet been built from the boards and nails). Similarly, what counts as the successful completion of a task or operation is fixed as a certain functionally defined resolution in light of the ultimate end to be accomplished. One has hammered successfully in this situation if the result of the action is two boards bound together tightly enough to support the weight to be placed upon them in the house and thus to contribute to the stability of the house that is being built.

In other words, both the 'situation' that fixes the time when it is appropriate to hammer and the end result that the hammering must bring about if it is to be successful are functions of the ultimate end to be realized through the series of actions of which hammering is a part and through the relations among a variety of functionally defined tools. But one can't understand how to hammer unless one understands when to hammer and how to complete the task of hammering successfully. And to understand when to hammer is to understand the role hammering is to play within a longer-range project: that is, to be able to distinguish those 'situations' that call for hammering from those that don't and to be able to respond differentially to them. (To understand when to hammer is to understand how to cope with a situation.) Since the situation itself is a function of the end to be realized and the current state of the tools to be used in relation to that end, understanding how to hammer implies understanding what is to be done with hammering, the instrumental relations that define the other tools used along with hammers, and how to use those tools themselves. Understanding when to hammer is necessary to understanding how to hammer, and understanding what the hammering is for and how other tools are to be used is necessary for an understanding of when to hammer. Practical understanding presupposes an ability to orient one's activity toward a future end to be accomplished; it is necessarily holistic, in the sense that one can't understand hammers unless one also practically understands nails, boards, houses, and an open-ended, indeterminately large group of tools that provide the context for hammering.

Typically, Heidegger puts these points in terms of necessary features of the entity that is understood when there is a practical understanding of tools, rather than in terms of necessary conditions for understanding how to use those tools. As a practical understanding of a tool, for Heidegger, is just the practical understanding of how to use it or of how to perform its defining function, and as to be a tool of a certain type is just to be useful in a given type of practical activity, the two kinds of condition are easily convertible. First, Heidegger claims, there is no such thing as a single item of equipment. To be a given tool is to be capable of serving along with other equipment in contexts of use. There can be things that are hammers only if there are things that are nails. "Taken strictly, there 'is' no such thing as an equipment. To the being of any equipment there always belongs a totality of equipment, in which it can be this equipment that it is. Equipment is essentially 'something in-order-to'. . . . A totality of equipment is constituted by various ways of the 'in-order-to' such as serviceability, conduciveness, usability, manipulability."[28] If to be a hammer is to be useful for hammering, and if hammering is a range of activities that need to be performed on nails, boards, and the like if we are to reach various ends, then there can't be any hammers unless there are nails, boards, and the like. If no things were nails and boards, there could be no hammers. Similarly, and even more significantly from Heidegger's perspective, a practical understanding of hammers presupposes (1) that there are such things as ends and (2) that anyone who has a concrete practical understanding of how to hammer in a given situation has an

28. *B.T.*, p. 97/68.

implicit understanding of that for the sake of which the hammering is to be done.

The first point follows from the fact that there is no appropriate time or way to hammer if there are no ends to be attained. The second point is a consequence of the fact that knowing how to hammer is at least knowing when to hammer, and knowing when to hammer involves at least knowing what is to be accomplished with the hammering. Heidegger puts these points in ontological language. "With any such entity [tool] as entity, there is some involvement. The fact that it has such an involvement is ontologically definitive for the being of such an entity . . . with this thing, for instance, which is ready-to-hand, and which we accordingly call a 'hammer', there is an involvement in hammering; with hammering there is an involvement in making something fast; with making something fast, there is an involvement in protecting against bad weather; and this protection 'is' for the sake of providing shelter for Dasein—that is to say, for the sake of a possibility of Dasein's being."[29]

Hammers are only hammers if they can be used for hammering. Hammering is only hammering if it is used in order to make things fast. Two things are made fast, in the context of building a house, only if they are held together sufficiently to provide shelter, and they are to be made fast only in order to provide shelter. Shelter is provided for the sake of keeping some Dasein warm and dry. With this 'for-the-sake-of' we have forged a link between Heidegger's analysis of self-understanding and his analysis of the practical understanding involved in understanding how to use tools, perform actions, and cope with situations.

For Heidegger, understanding—both the self-understanding of Dasein itself as an end to be realized and the understanding of how to use something, which is central to the practical understanding of tools as tools—is essentially concerned with possibility. To understand myself as existing is to understand myself as an end that is not yet actual but that I grasp as my possibility. To understand a tool practically, I must understand what it is capable of: that is, its possibilities for use. How are these two kinds of possibility related?

To understand myself it is necessary that I intend myself as a possible end to be realized. To understand myself as a philosopher is, for Heidegger, to have as the purpose of my actions that I philosophize. I am aware of myself as the one who, for example, is to be in class on time. This does

29. *B.T.*, p. 116/84.

not mean, however, that in order to be aware of myself or to have self-understanding I must adopt a specific self-conscious plan of action or that I am explicitly focusing upon the end I am attempting to realize. On the contrary, I understand myself primarily precisely insofar as I do not think about the end I am trying to accomplish or the sort of person I want to be. "We say that the Dasein does not first need to turn backward to itself as though, keeping itself behind its own back, it were at first standing in front of things and staring rigidly at them. Instead, it never finds itself otherwise than in the things themselves, and in fact in those things that daily surround it. It finds itself primarily and constantly in things because, tending them, distressed by them, it always in one way or another rests in things. Each of us *is* what he pursues and cares for. In everyday terms, we understand ourselves and our existence by way of the activities we pursue and the things we take care of."[30] In other words, the purpose of my actions, which is my self-understanding, is not identical with any thought I might have of myself as being in a certain way in the future or with any mental intention on my part. But then what is it for me to be an end for myself, and what is Heidegger talking about when he speaks of the self-understanding of Dasein?

Heidegger's term for the structure of existential (that is, self-)understanding is projection (*Entwurf*).[31] Projection "has nothing to do with comporting oneself towards a plan which has been thought out," and Dasein, in order to be Dasein, must always already have projected itself. Understanding as projection projects (throws ahead of itself) possibilities. "Projection, in throwing, throws before itself the possibility as possibility, and lets it be as such. As projecting, understanding is the kind of being of Dasein in which it *is* its possibilities as possibilities."[32] But as we have just seen, to project possibilities is not to 'grasp thematically' that which is projected: that is, possibilities. "Grasping it in such a manner would take away from what is projected its very character as a possibility, and would reduce it to the given contents which we have in mind."[33] Rather, Dasein projects possibilities in that and precisely insofar as it has a practical understanding of those tools which surround it and which it uses. As the foregoing quotation attempts to express, our self-understanding is, for Heidegger, our practical understanding of things; and the

30. *B.P.*, p. 159/226.
31. *B.T.*, p. 184/145.
32. *B.T.*, p. 185/145.
33. *B.T.*, p. 185/145.

end that we understand ourselves as is the end that is implicit in the activities in which we are engaged.

This is the point of Heidegger's distinction between projecting possibilities as possibilities and a possibility as actual, as a 'given content we have in mind'. If the intentions that, for Heidegger, I am were a thought or a representation that I am currently intending, then such a purpose could be at most a present modification of myself as a thinking substance. To be a thinking substance is to be a substance whose qualifications consist in the thoughts, representations, or ideas that it intends. And insofar as I specifically intend my purpose to be realized, the thought of that intention is an actual modification of myself as thinking substance. My activities with and on things, however, themselves betray an intentional pattern, regardless of whether or not I am explicitly conscious of the end I am pursuing in those actions. My actions 'project' a 'possible' end, are an intending toward such an end, in themselves. To exist, to be a Dasein with self-understanding, involves being purposive, being capable of engaging in purposive activity; it is in this sense that each of us "is what he pursues and cares for." And it is because the end for which such activity is instrumental is not actual or present in any sense, not even as my thought of what I want to accomplish, that Heidegger speaks about the projection in understanding of possibilities as possibilities rather than as actualities.

To be Dasein, to exist, involves an understanding of oneself as an end. But to have such an understanding is for one's actions to be, in themselves, directed toward that end, regardless of what one is thinking about. To have an understanding of oneself as end is to be able to perform actions for the sake of that end, for the sake of coming to be in the manner of that end. In acting for the sake of the realization of a purpose, I am projecting a possibility of myself as a possibility. But when is it the case that a thing's actions are so related as to be directed in themselves toward an end, and thus for the thing itself to have an existential understanding of itself in a projection of possibilities?

We saw above that the possession of a practical understanding of a tool is identical with an understanding of how to use the tool and with an understanding of how to perform the actions for which that tool is suited. We also saw that if one has a practical understanding of a tool, then it is also the case that (1) there is a purpose in the service of which the tool is to be used and that (2) the one who understands the tool has an implicit understanding of the purpose that is the end of the series of activities in which the tool has its function. The very existence of things such as tools, and the actuality of practical understanding of tools, demands that action be directed toward ends and that those who know how to do things appropriately implicitly understand those ends. That is, for Heidegger, insofar as Dasein has a practical understanding of equipment, it also has an existential understanding of itself as the purpose implicit in its activity with the tools. As Heidegger says, "we understand ourselves by way of the activities we pursue and the things we take care of." To project oneself as a possibility is to understand oneself as a for-the-sake-of, and to do this is for one to have a practical understanding of equipment.

Practical understanding of a tool is the capacity to use the tool in a variety of practical contexts for a variety of practical ends. Insofar as someone understands tools, she also has the ability to use other tools in order to realize her ends, and she has the further ability to act coherently for the sake of those ends. The capacity to act in such a way is part of what it is to be Dasein, and every actual Dasein, as Dasein, is always actually acting coherently in some way or another so as to achieve some end or another. It is thus always displaying its practical understanding of tools, its practical understanding of how to reach its ends, and its existential understanding of itself as an end to be realized. This is no accident. All of these determinations are essential to what it means to be Dasein: that is, a self-intending being. When Heidegger says that, in understanding, what we have competence over is being as existing, he is indicating this complex structure. We understand ourselves as end insofar as we are competent to reach ends, and we are competent to reach ends insofar as we understand how to use tools. Practical understanding and self-understanding must occur together.

This claim should not be thought of as suggesting that there are two entirely different events, the practical understanding of tools and a self-understanding, that happen to be constantly conjoined or to be causally related. Rather, for Heidegger, the relation between the two sides is a logical one. Self-understanding as projection of a possible future for oneself is an aspect of the practical understanding of tools. When I use a pen appropriately to write with and thus display a practical understanding of this thing as a pen, part of what it means to say that I understand it is that I use the pen as a part of a series of activities that have an identifiable end or purpose. That my actions have such a purpose is part of what it means to say that I am Dasein or that I understand myself as an end which is possible and to be attained. But if none of my actions ever displayed such understanding, I would not be Dasein at all. Self-understanding as purpose and practical understanding of the capabilities of things are just two sides of the same coin, a coin that consists in the ability to use things to bring about ends.

We noticed above another constraint on practical understanding, in addition to the necessity that such understanding implicitly involve an understanding of the purposes for which tools are instrumental. I must not only understand what hammering is for the sake of, if I am to have a practical understanding of hammers; I must also have a practical understanding of nails, boards, and a whole host of other implements. Heidegger develops this constraint in the assertion that Dasein is 'being-in-the-world' (*In-der-Welt-sein*). We turn now to this claim and to Heidegger's conception of the world.

World: Being in the World

The Heideggerian concept of 'world' can be comprehended only in relation to 'being-in-the-world', another of Heidegger's characterizations of Dasein's mode of being, or existence. "The Dasein exists in the manner of being-in-the-world, and this basic determination of its existence is the presupposition for being able to apprehend anything at all."[34] We can work backward toward the concept of world from the second clause of this assertion, that being-in-the-world is a necessary condition for our ability to understand—indeed, to apprehend—anything at all.

As we have already seen, the early Heidegger contends that the kind of 'awareness' involved in the exercise of our practical abilities with things is the primary and basic mode in which we intend them. Strictly, in order to demonstrate this proposition, one would need to show that (1) there is no 'understanding-that' without an 'understanding-how', but not necessarily the reverse, and that (2) there is no awareness of things other than Dasein without some understanding of them. In Chapters 4 and 5 we will construct an argument in favor of these claims. Heidegger himself moves toward (1) and (2) in two ways. First, he argues by way of a phenomenological description of how we ordinarily live in an 'everyday' manner, a manner that he sees as primarily involving a practical understanding of things. Second, he proceeds in the way in which we have

34. *B.P.*, p. 164/234.

proceeded here. There is no apprehending of things, he argues, without self-understanding. There is no self-understanding apart from practical understanding. Therefore, there is no possibility of awareness of things other than Dasein apart from the practical understanding of things. So to say, as Heidegger does, that being-in-the-world is necessary for the possibility of apprehending individual things is tantamount to saying that being-in-the-world, whatever it is supposed to be, is either a necessary condition for practical understanding or another necessary condition for intentionality entirely separate from practical understanding. But that being-in-the world is meant as a condition for or of the complex of self-understanding and practical understanding that we have been analyzing is immediately apparent from Heidegger's texts. "The Dasein exists in the manner of being-in-the-world and as such it is for the sake of its own self."[35]

We discover which necessary condition being-in-the-world is supposed to be as soon as we look at Heidegger's definition of 'world': "World is that which is already previously unveiled and from which we return to the beings with which we have to do and among which we dwell. . . . We always already understand world in holding ourselves in a contexture of functionality [*Bewandtniszusammenhang*]."[36] For Heidegger, "that which is already previously unveiled" is just such a context of functionality. "The functionality contexture is not a relational whole in the sense of a product that emerges only from the conjoint occurrence of a number of things. The functionality whole, narrower or broader— room, house, neighborhood, town, city—is the prius, within which specific beings, as beings of this or that character, are as they are and exhibit themselves correspondingly. . . . A specific functionality whole is preunderstood."[37]

Since in the context of these assertions we are dealing with the practical understanding of tools, the "functionality contexture" which is necessary for things to have the character they have and the understanding of which is necessary for them to exhibit themselves as they are (that is, for us to understand them) is a context that is presupposed in both the practical understanding of tools and in the tools being the tools they are. But this is just the context comprising the practical interrelations among a variety

35. *B.P.*, p. 170/242.
36. *B.P.*, p. 165/235.
37. *B.P.*, p. 164/233.

of tool types, all of which have their appropriate uses, within practical projects of a given kind. To be a hammer is just to be an instrument for driving nails into boards. All of these kinds of equipment function together in contexts of building; that is, hammers are a kind of tool which, along with nails and so on, are for building. "We say that an equipmental contexture [*Zeugzusammenhang*] environs us. Each individual piece of equipment is by its own nature equipment-for—for traveling, for writing, for flying. Each one has its immanent reference to that for which it is what it is. . . . The specific structure of equipment is constituted by a contexture of the what-for, in-order-to."[38]

So, an equipmental contexture is a context of use in which a variety of tools are encountered through each having a specific functional relation with the others and through all of these functional relations being oriented toward the realization of some kind of end. A hammer is for driving nails into boards; this operation is performed in order to build; and hammers, boards, and nails are equipment for building. None of these functional objects could be what it is unless the others were what they are also—no thing could be a hammer unless there were the 'nail kind of thing'—and none could exist unless there were activities directed toward the end of building. Similarly, insofar as one practically understands hammers or understands something as a hammer, one must also practically understand nails, and so on, and have a practical understanding of what it is to build: that is, of the activities that are for the sake of building. To understand hammers practically is to be capable of using them appropriately, which entails both an ability to use other kinds of instruments appropriately and an understanding of what the tool can be used for. The practical understanding of any single instrument, the ability to use it appropriately, is always part of an ability to engage in a teleologically ordered pattern of action; as such, it entails both a practical understanding of a whole range of other tools with which it functions and an understanding of what can be accomplished with these tools. These two, the practical understanding of a range of equipment (or rather, of equipment types) and the self-understanding of the purposes to which they can be put constitute the two sides of Heidegger's 'being-in-the-world': the understanding of 'significance' and the understanding of the for-the-sake-of-which.

Before we go on to 'world' we should clean up the terminology we

38. *B.P.*, p. 163/233.

have been using. Strictly, for Heidegger, the term 'equipmental contexture' [*Zeugzusammenhang*] refers to individual structures of defining relations among tools and purposes in terms of which individual tools can be encountered as the things they are. The equipmental contexture is a context of things, or entities. In coping practically I encounter things as equipment, and in doing so I deal with them as related to one another in a reciprocal, mutually supporting, instrumental way. The hammer and nails 'go together', and to encounter the hammer is to encounter it as equipment for hammering nails. Both are encountered together with other things in a context of equipment for building, an 'equipmental contexture'. Insofar as such tools can be thus encountered, they are encountered as having a specific function. They are 'for' something; they are 'in order to do' something. But no one thing can be what it is, can be 'in order to' as it is, unless its function has been defined and determined in terms of a variety of other functional roles. Each function occurs only within a whole context of mutually supporting functional roles. Such a context is called by Heidegger a 'functionality contexture' [*Bewandtnis-zusammenhang*]. An 'equipmental contexture', then, is a context of things or entities, a group of tools that go together. A 'functionality contexture' is a context of functional roles in and through which individual functions are defined, functions in terms of which particular entities—hammers, for example—can be what they are.

To "hold ourselves in a contexture of functionality" is to use the tools that operate in that context for the purposes for which they are designed. It is nothing more or less than having, and exercising, skills in regard to the tools themselves. Such skills are always holistic in that to understand one tool we must also understand others, and in order to understand any tool practically, one must be capable of practical activity that uses those tools and is directed toward some end. 'The world' is the most general and all-encompassing field of functional relations in terms of which we practically understand each thing we encounter. The world is, as it were, the functionality contexture of all functionality contextures, the whole in which specific equipmental contexts have their place. Its structure is the structure of functional relations as such—a structure that is also the structure of existential self-understanding. Insofar as Dasein understands itself, it understands itself as an end to be accomplished, a for-the-sake-of, or a for-which. But to understand oneself in this way is also, necessarily, to understand the capacities of a variety of tools. One can't do this, however, unless one also has a practical understanding of a whole host of additional tools and of the functional contexts in which they are all defined. Heidegger calls the formal structure of this holistic practical understanding 'significance'. "The 'for-the-sake-of-which' signifies an 'in-order-to'; this in turn a 'towards-this'; the latter an 'in-which' of letting something be involved; and that in turn a with-which of an involvement. These relationships are bound up with one another as a primordial totality; they are what they are as this signifying in which Dasein gives itself beforehand its 'being-in-the-world' as something to be understood. The relational totality of this signifying we call 'significance'. This is what makes up the structure of the world."[39]

We display our understanding of significance whenever we display our practical understanding of things, whenever we use them appropriately. This is also the field in which we understand ourselves as ends to be accomplished.

> Because as existents we already understand world beforehand we are able to understand and encounter ourselves constantly in a specific way by way of the beings which we encounter as intraworldly. The shoe-maker is not the shoe; but shoe gear, belonging to the equipmental contexture of his environing world, is intelligible as the piece of equip-ment that it is only by way of the particular world that belongs to the existential constitution of the Dasein as being-in-the-world. In under-standing itself by way of things, the Dasein understands itself as being-in-the-world by way of its world. The shoemaker is not the shoe but, existing, he is his world, a world that first and alone makes it possible to uncover an equipmental contexture as intraworldly and to dwell with it. It is primarily things, not as such, taken in isolation, but as intra-worldly, in and from which we encounter ourselves.[40]

Heidegger considers this many-sided structure of practical activity—which is at one and the same time (1) the demonstration and realization of our practical understanding of tools, (2) the exercise of our under-standing of how to do things with tools, (3) the field in which we understand ourselves as ends, and (4) the demonstration of our under-standing of the context of functional relations in terms of which tools operate—to be a unitary phenomenon. He calls this phenomenon 'being-in-the-world' and says that it is the being of Dasein, or what it is to exist. In fact, these various determinations are nothing other than delin-

39. *B.T.*, p. 120/87.
40. *B.P.*, pp. 171/243–244.

eations of what is necessarily involved every time an entity acts in a purposeful way to realize some end or other. To act purposefully, one must demonstrate a capacity to use a number of tools together so as to accomplish an end of one's own, and to do so is to understand the significance each of these things has as a tool of a certain type, a significance each has only in relation to the others and the end to which they are all put. To be Dasein, to be a being in the world, is to act purposively.

We can now recapitulate the results of this section. The self-understanding of Dasein and Dasein's practical understanding of tools are two aspects of a unitary phenomenon. The capacity to act coherently for the sake of ends is the fundamental trait of Dasein. The ability to use tools together to achieve ends is the sine qua non of practical understanding. One cannot have the one ability without exercising the other. Finally, to say, as Heidegger does, that Dasein is 'being-in-the-world' is to say that Dasein can't understand itself or any single tool unless it understands a whole range of tool types, the functional relations among those types, and the purpose to which those types of tools are to be put. Practical understanding, which is necessary for self-understanding, is holistic.

The World Is a With-World

At least since Descartes, the standard way to interpret the person has turned on variations on the theme of the 'subject'. Initially, the notion of the subject was tied to the grammatical subject, that which is qualified by the predicate. The subject is that, whatever it is and however it is understood, which remains the same throughout changes in its modifications. Since for a person the modifications in question are thought of as experiences, the person is the selfsame bearer of those experiences. That is, the subject is thought of as a special kind of substance.

Heidegger, however, thoroughly rejects this ontological concept of the person as substance. He replaces it with Dasein, which is thought of as a certain kind of happening rather than as any sort of substance. To be Dasein, to exist, is to be capable of engaging in ordered, goal-oriented behavior. It is to know one's way around a practical field of instrumentalities, where instruments have functional relations to one another and to the ends for which they are designed. To be in this way is to 'be-in-the-world'. Dasein's being is characterized by (1) self-understanding, which is accomplished by and through (2) an understanding of oneself as end to be accomplished, which in turn is always embodied in (3) a practical understanding of tools and a practical capacity to realize a variety of ends with those tools. But not every being that can correctly be interpreted as acting purposively thereby counts as Dasein. A tiger, for example, is not Dasein even though it does act for ends. In short, Dasein is a particular, definite species of purposively acting beings. What is distinctive about Dasein as a species of purposive beings is that the activities those beings perform for ends are (4) *socially* regulated activities adjusted in such a way that Dasein make use of socially standardized tools, in socially sanctioned ways, to attain socially recognized and useful ends. Dasein, as beings that act in communities in this way are also beings which, in acting to attain a definite end, act so as to become some definite *kind* of Dasein. In acting in order to make shoes within some society (that is, using socially standardized tools to reach a socially standardized end), the person acts in such a way as to *be* a shoemaker.

Heidegger's way of describing Dasein sometimes makes it seem a radically individual sort of being. After all, that there is a purposive pattern to *x*'s behavior is (or seems to be) a function only of that entity's activity itself.[41] No one would doubt, for example, that a tiger's behavior can be properly described in teleological terms, even though tigers are, by and large, solitary animals. There would be no contradiction in speaking of a single tiger as purposive, even if—contrary to physical possibility—it were the only tiger ever to exist. Nevertheless, to distinguish Dasein from other purposive beings, the early Heidegger holds two important theses in regard to the essential sociality of Dasein or, as he puts it, the claim that "Dasein is essentially being-with."[42] First, "the world is always the one I share with others. The world of Dasein is a with-world [*Mitwelt*]."[43] Second, "Dasein is for the sake of the 'they' in an everyday manner, and the 'they' itself articulates the referential context of significance."[44] When we understand these theses, we will come to see that they add two crucial determinants to the being of Dasein.

We can come to comprehend these aspects of Dasein if we focus on Dasein who belong to a different community from the one to which we belong. Imagine a being that engages in purposive action with tools but does not understand tools in the same way we do. Something can act

41. E.g., the early Sartre, who is usually quite derivative from the early Heidegger, draws this conclusion.
42. *B.T.*, p. 156/120.
43. *B.T.*, p. 155/118.
44. *B.T.*, p. 167/129.

purposively with a hammer, after all, without understanding hammers, nails, and boards and without even understanding that they are all equipment for building. It is easy to imagine such a being. The plot of a South African movie, *The Gods Must Be Crazy,* turns on a Bushman's discovery of a Coca-Cola bottle that had been thrown from a passing plane. The Bushmen immediately take the bottle to be a tool, and they use it successively as a hammer, a rolling pin, a pestle, and a weapon. Later, the discoverer decides that the bottle is dangerous and becomes determined to throw it away. As it is a gift from the gods, however (it fell from the sky, after all), it must be treated in a properly respectful way. He therefore decides to throw the bottle off the edge of the earth and proceeds to do so. This person is clearly acting purposively, and just as clearly he is in a world of purposes, instruments, and so on. Nevertheless, we have a practical understanding that he lacks. How should we describe this difference?

The Coke bottle is both an implement and an artifact. It is useful and has been made, by people, in order to be useful. But in general, those who make the implements we use are not those who use them. One person, or a group, acts on the physical world so as to bring about a result that will be the means to other people's ends. That is, the artificer can, and usually does, have as the purpose of his act that other people might become capable of performing certain kinds of activity. His product is adjusted to the needs of others.[45] For me to make something for the purpose of someone else's use, however, if the tool is to be made efficiently and successfully, requires that I have a practical understanding of my end, which in this case is just that others be able to use in a particular way the thing I am making. That is, I must have a practical understanding of how and for what purposes others will use what I am making. It is thus necessary that there be a certain standardization of ends and of ways of reaching those ends which we share or, at least, which the artificer takes into account in his work.

For a tailor to make a suit successfully is for the tailor to produce something that can be used in a given determinate way, generally by

---

45. There is, of course, an alternative, non-altruistic description of this situation in which my end is, e.g., the obtaining of food; then the making of a car to be driven, a bottle to be used as a container, or a book to be read and dissected is merely instrumental to that end. For our purposes here, one description is as good as the other. What is important in this situation is the mutual adjustment of means to ends within a human community, and the 'selfish' description contains this feature to the same degree as the 'altruistic' one does.

someone else. To understand suits is to understand how the suit is to be used, to understand that this thing has a determinate role in an already established equipmental context with a determinate structure. This context is practically understood in common by a group of people whose purposive actions all presuppose this same equipmental contexture. Similarly, to understand cars as cars is to understand what is to be done with cars, to understand the region of practical activity in which they are designed to function (they are equipment for traveling) and the role cars play within that context. The Bushman has *some* understanding of the Coke bottle: he understands it as a tool. But he does not understand it, practically, as a bottle. That is, he doesn't understand how *it is to be used*, even though he understands quite a bit about how *it can be used*. The cash value of this 'to be used' is the use the thing has within the shared equipmental context for which it was made and in which it is made to function.

Heidegger calls the entire field of functional relations 'the world'. But as we have just seen, the world is *typically* organized, insofar as a number of Dasein can and do engage in common projects and projects whose proximate ends are for the sake of each other's future actions. That is, under these conditions, the world is organized into standard types of instruments and ends for which they are designed to be useful. Every object is, strictly, capable of an indefinite number of applications, as demonstrated by the Bushmen's use of the bottle. Nonetheless, there is a 'correct' way to understand (that is, to use) most implements and the vast majority of implements that are also artifacts: the way in which these tools function within shared patterns of use and, if they were made, the way in which they were designed to be used. (These two criteria of correctness can, on occasion, conflict.) This correct way to be used defines what sort of tool a given tool is.

From the fact that tools belong to types in this way, and are understood as belonging to types (they are, by and large, used correctly, and Dasein that use them in some other manner are 'corrected' in their use) Heidegger draws a series of implications. First, insofar as an individual Dasein uses most tools in the world according to established type and thus behaves in a way that is purposively integrated with the purposive activity of other Dasein, she is not only understanding these tools in the same way as others do but is also sharing a world with the others. A world is a structure of functional relations establishing a set of instrumental roles for attaining ends and the ends that are to be attained. The fact that someone understands how to use some tools correctly implies that she understands how to use other tools correctly and has an understanding of the standard ends for which these tools are designed. I have no practical understanding of a hammer as a hammer unless I also have a practical understanding of nails as nails, and so on, and a practical understanding that they are all tools for building. But the hammer is a hammer, as opposed to a paperweight, for example, only insofar as it has a proper and correct use and is properly used within a standard equipmental context, and such propriety obtains only if there is a community of persons for whom the hammer is used in this way. Only the standardization of means, procedures, and ends across a group of people enables the distinction of one use from other potential uses as the correct one. Therefore, correctness of use—that is, typification of instruments in terms of standardization of function—entails commonality of world among several Dasein.[46]

But who are the members of such a community? They must act purposively, but not all purposive agents qualify. They must be Dasein and thus belong to some community in virtue of which there are proper ways to do and use things, but not all Dasein qualify. I have a different relation with the Bushman in the story than I do with my colleagues. The others with whom I share a world are those who are like me. As we are both Dasein, for them to be similar to me is for them to act like me, and for them to act like me is for them to use things as I use them and do things as I do them. "By 'others' we do not mean everyone else but me—those over against whom the 'I' stands out. They are rather those from whom, for the most part, one does not distinguish oneself—those among whom one is too."[47] "In that with which we concern ourselves environmentally the others are encountered as what they are; they are what they do."[48] All of us, however, in doing the same sorts of things with the same sorts of tools, are both accepting and helping to establish norms for the use of things, norms that in turn establish an instrumental sorting of things. Such norms are our common product and are embodied both in the ways

46. It is legitimate and important to ask further what could count as evidence that there is a shared world among individuals in this sense; i.e., when are we entitled to judge that a commonality of world and functional types obtains? Heidegger doesn't really address this issue, but it is already clear that the answer turns on the purposiveness of activity across individuals, which is evident in the artificer-user complex described earlier.

47. *B.T.*, p. 154/118.

48. *B.T.*, p. 163/126.

in which each person's purposive behavior relates to and serves to aid the actions of all the others and in the design of our common implements. In that we all use cars in more or less the same ways, in more or less the same equipmental context, we also establish norms for the proper use of cars as cars, which in turn specify how cars ought to be made so as to fulfill their function. Things that have many potential uses come to have *a* use. And insofar as they have a use, they need not be merely discovered in the prehuman environment; they can be designed and made specifically to fulfill their unique function.

We are now in position to interpret the twin Heideggerian assertions that (1) Dasein is essentially being with others and that (2) the world is always a shared world. A world is shared insofar as there are typical and proper uses for tools, typical and proper equipmental and functional contextures, and interlocking social patterns of purposive activity in which means and ends are purposively integrated across a group of individuals. To say, as Heidegger does, that the human world is always a shared world is just to say that nothing can count as Dasein unless it engages in purposive behavior *and* that behavior fits into a wider structure of purposive action on the part of a number of individuals, a structure sufficiently detailed to establish what is to be done with the tools the individual Dasein uses to reach its own ends. To say that Dasein is essentially 'being with' is to say that every individual Dasein, in order to be Dasein, must as a logical necessity inhabit a shared world; and that insofar as it acts in a way appropriate for its community, it has an implicit practical understanding of the other members of that community as purposive agents who also use things as they ought to be used. I am with others insofar as my behavior is proper within my community. When I use things in the appropriately typical way and my actions are integrated with those of others, I am implicitly understanding the others as Dasein and as authorities in relation to my own utilization of things. I practically understand things as they are to be understood: that is, as 'they' understand them.

Whatever plausibility this account of the essentially social nature of Dasein has arises from our sense that human beings not only are capable of using things in the world in purposive and instrumental ways but also work together and share and coordinate purposes and ways of doing things. This is the key to comprehending the apparently opaque claims that "Dasein is for the sake of the 'they'" and that "the 'they' articulates the referential context of significance." The 'for-the-sake-of' is the end or purpose that both organizes the goal-directed activity of Dasein and embodies the self-understanding of Dasein. The "referential context of significance" is the structured context of instrumentalities, purposes, and procedures that constitutes the world of any Dasein and is the field in which it exercises its abilities for purposive action. But what is the 'they' that Heidegger speaks of here? "Dasein's everyday possibilities of being are for the others to dispose of as they please. These others, moreover, are not definite others. . . . What is decisive is just that inconspicuous domination by others which has already been taken over unawares from Dasein as being-with. . . . The others . . . are those who proximally and for the most part 'are there' in everyday being with one another. The 'who' is not this one, not that one, not oneself, not some people, and not the sum of them all. The who is the neuter, the 'they'.[49]

The 'they' is the putative subject that determines the typical correct ways of behaving, use of instruments, and ends to be achieved. The 'they' is the embodiment of the norms for correct use and behavior which every member of a community accepts insofar as he or she belongs to that community. And we are members of that community insofar as we know how to function in the world established within that community. "In utilizing public means of transport and in making use of information services such as the newspaper, every other is like the next. . . . We take pleasure and enjoy ourselves as they take pleasure; we read, see, and judge about literature and are as they see and judge; likewise we shrink back from the 'great mass' as they shrink back; we find 'shocking' what they find shocking. The 'they', which is nothing definite, and which we all are, though not as the sum, prescribes the kind of being of everydayness."[50]

But then, of course, the "referential context of significance" in which we all operate *qua* members of a community is articulated by the 'they'. This claim merely states that all proper uses of things and proper ways of doing things must be established communally, and that in order to be Dasein a being must be capable in some appropriate way of belonging to some community of Dasein. And finally, to say, as Heidegger does, that Dasein is for the sake of the 'they' is just to assert that for humans the purposes that orient their individual behavior, by being a goal, are purposes that function within a wider community context and count as purposes of a given type only as social. I am writing a book. Insofar as my

49. *B.T.*, p. 164/126.
50. *B.T.*, pp. 164/126–127.

actions make sense as purposive, they are oriented toward the goal of there being a book and my being its author. But to be a book is to be a kind of thing; something counts as a book only if it is to be used and responded to in some appropriate way; and this reaction, which in this case involves communication, is precisely what I am aiming for in writing the book. My end, the for-the-sake-of of my behavior, is impossible as an end unless I belong to a community and the end is a type of end within that community, an end that in turn performs an instrumental role for others within that community. My for-the-sake-of, that I am to write a book, is for the sake of the readers, and unless there were the roles of author and reader, I could not intend to write the book. As Dasein I am for the sake of the 'they'.

In writing a book I am producing a socially recognized and standardized product. Books are to be used in certain ways by the members of the community, although not everyone must use every individual book or, indeed, any individual book. Not all members of a Dasein community act so as to bring about this generally useful type of end. To produce books in a society is to *be* an author, that is, a Dasein that acts in a particular standardized way so as to bring about a definite kind of socially standardized end. In acting in order to bring about that end, a Dasein is also acting so as to be an author; for a Dasein to act for the sake of an end is also for it to choose a certain socially sanctioned role and thereby choose a certain possible way for itself to be. This way of being itself, the Dasein's role, is itself part of the overall pattern of integrated purposeful activity of the community of which the Dasein is a part. That is, to be an author is to perform acts that have as their result products that can be used in certain ways by any other Dasein, by the 'they'. Being an author, then, is being for the sake of the 'they'. Not only are the products of my acts for the sake of the 'they', but my being and acting as I am and do is also for the sake of the 'they'.

2 Interpretation, Meaning, and Assertion

We are now in position to begin our interpretation of Heidegger's analysis of understanding *that* something is the case. Heidegger tends not to use the locution 'understanding (believing) that' something is the case; instead, he speaks of what we believe or understand to be the case in terms that are somewhat object-oriented. For Heidegger, when I hold to the truth of an assertion or proposition, I am understanding some being *as* something, because what is believed true—the assertion of a 'that' clause—is itself analyzed as a 'taking of something *as* something'. "The latter [*Aussage* = assertion] consists in saying something about something: the body is heavy, the triangle is equilateral, Kant died in 1804, 'king' is a substantive noun, nature is objectively present. Such assertions express a determining something as something, a determination. We call this determining 'thinking'."[1] 'Understanding that' in the sense of holding to the truth of a proposition, is for Heidegger a species of 'understanding *x* as . . .'.

It is important to emphasize that 'understanding that', insofar as this is thought to involve the occurrent propositional attitude of belief toward some propositional and/or linguistic content, is only one kind of taking-

1. *M.F.L.*, p. 1/1. Translation modified. 'Aussage' is always translated as 'assertion'. Heidegger's traditional analysis is going to get into serious difficulties, e.g., with multiplace predicates. As Ernst Tugendhat (in *Traditional and Analytic Philosophy*, trans. P. A. Gorner [Cambridge: Cambridge University Press, 1982]) has pointed out, Heidegger's fixation with objects (as opposed to events or states of affairs) and words (as opposed to assertions) is at best unfortunate. In his early period, however, Heidegger does, as we shall see, place substantial weight on assertions as the primary form of language, and his object fixation causes only minor problems.

52

something-as-something, for Heidegger. He thinks there is another species of 'taking as' that is entirely independent of both linguistic competence and belief that any propositional content obtains; that is, someone can take something as something in a nonpredicative manner. We are thus forced into a terminological decision. Either we can reserve 'understanding that' for the kind of 'taking as' that involves the occurrent acceptance or the believing true or asserting of propositional contents, or we can use 'understanding that' as a term for the genus 'taking as' of which the propositional 'taking as' is a species. Since Heidegger himself avoids the phrase 'understanding that', the texts place little restriction on our choice. We will, then, stipulate that 'understanding that' will be used as synonymous with 'understanding as' or 'taking as' in the broad sense. Hence, there is no a priori semantic reason not to say of some entity without language that it understands that '*x* is dangerous' or to say of some persons to whom the thought has never occurred that they believe zebras don't wear underwear. (There may, of course, be other sorts of reasons for denying either or both of these possibilities.)

Heidegger's word for our 'understanding that' (the taking of something as something in general) is 'interpretation' (*Auslegung.*) He holds in regard to interpretation that (1) all interpretation is 'grounded in' understanding (where 'understanding' means the sort of practical understanding we have already discussed); (2) all interpretation stands under three necessary conditions, which he calls 'fore-conditions'; (3) meaning (*Sinn*) is what is articulated in an interpretation; and (4) assertion is a particular variety of interpretation such that to believe the truth of an assertion is to accept and engage in a certain kind of interpretation.

This chapter considers only linguistic and nonlinguistic forms of interpretation which involve taking something as a tool of a given type.

Interpretation Is Grounded on Understanding

"That which is disclosed in understanding—that which is understood—is already accessible in such a way that its 'as which' can be made to stand out explicitly. The 'as' makes up the structure of the explicitness of something that is understood. It constitutes the interpretation."[2] Someone understands, in Heidegger's sense, a hammer. This means that she knows how to use this tool, along with other tools, to accomplish the

2. *B.T.,* p. 189/149.

types of ends for which the hammer is designed. Such understanding is a capacity embodied in and exemplified by a disposition to use this thing in appropriate ways in goal-directed activity. In selectively using this tool for some task that is defined functionally within a functionality context, the person is demonstrating both her understanding of how to hammer and her understanding of this thing as a hammer. She could have driven the nail with a book, a screwdriver, or her shoe. All are, roughly, capable of being used successfully in that activity. But she uses this thing for hammering and thereby takes it as a thing that is in order to be hammered with. She has discovered the use for the thing, discovered what it is for.

"All preparing, putting to rights, repairing, improving, rounding-out, are accomplished in the following way: we take apart in its 'in-order-to' that which is circumspectively ready-to-hand, and we concern ourselves with it in accordance with what becomes visible through this process. That which has been circumspectively taken apart with regard to its 'in-order-to', and taken apart as such—that which is explicitly understood—has the structure of something as something. The circumspective question as to what this particular thing that is ready-to-hand may be, receives the circumspectively interpretive answer that it is for such and such a purpose."[3] This interesting passage points to an apparent ambiguity in Heidegger's treatment of the relation between understanding and interpretation. At times he speaks as if an interpretation requires some sort of additional act or event in addition to the kinds of activities and capacities in which practical understanding consists. First, it seems, we have a practical understanding of the world in which a hammer functions, and then we come to an explicit understanding of this thing as being functional as a hammer. Some sort of temporal priority appears to be assigned to understanding over interpretation. "To say that 'circumspection discovers' means that the world which has already been understood comes to be interpreted. The ready to hand comes explicitly into the sight which understands."[4] Yet Heidegger is abundantly clear that to interpret x as y requires no special act over and above those acts that demonstrate our practical understanding of x (and thus of the world in which x functions). "In dealing with what is environmentally ready-to-hand by interpreting it circumspectively, we 'see' it as a table, a door, a carriage, or a bridge."[5]

3. *B.T.*, pp. 189/148–149.
4. *B.T.*, p. 189/148.
5. *B.T.*, p. 189/149.

(The scare quotes around 'see' are crucial to the comprehension of this and the following passages. They indicate that the kind of 'seeing' involved here is not a perceptual act, but rather the sort of 'seeing' involved in 'seeing' what to do and how to do it. Heidegger calls such sight 'circumspection', and it is, of course, demonstrated in our concrete activity with and on things.) "Any mere pre-predicative seeing of the ready-to-hand is, in itself, something which already understands and interprets."[6] "This grasping which is free of the 'as' is a privation of the kind of seeing in which one merely understands. It is not more primordial than that kind of seeing, but is derived from it."[7] "Interpretation is carried out primordially not in a theoretical statement but in an action of circumspective concern—laying aside the unsuitable tool, or exchanging it, 'without wasting words'."[8]

This apparent ambiguity is resolved as soon as we realize that 'understanding how' is a capacity phrase. To understand how to use a hammer is to have the ability to use it appropriately. That ability—and one's understanding—is demonstrated in one's purposive actions: unless one engages in the right sort of actions, we have no evidence of the ability. But what we assign with the words 'understand how' is a latent capacity. Whenever one engages in concrete purposive actions of the sort that the presence of understanding implies the ability for, the capacity has been exercised, and the understanding of some thing as a tool of a certain sort has been made explicit. At this first level, to interpret x as a hammer is just to use x as a hammer. That a given act is in fact a use of x as a hammer, that it is an interpretation of x as a hammer, implies that we already had the capacity to use it thus, that we already knew how to hammer before our actual appropriately purposive action with the hammer (and all that we have found such an action to entail).

As the foregoing quotations from Heidegger make clear, however, there is a second way in which an interpretation, as an articulation of a functionality contexture, can be carried out. When one works on some entity in such a way as to 'repair' it or 'improve' it or 'set it to rights', one always does so in light of some end to be accomplished, and that end is that the entity be better capable of fulfilling some function. For example, when a hammer is repaired, it is acted upon in such a way as to make it

6. *B.T.*, p. 189/149.
7. *B.T.*, p. 190/149.
8. *B.T.*, p. 200/157.

better capable of fulfilling the functional role of hammering. To act on an entity in such a way is to take it as, interpret it as, a hammer in that the repair is made in order to make the entity better capable of being used in order to hammer. The act of improving the object treats the object as something which is to perform a function and as such can do it more or less well. Notice that in this case one can interpret *x* as a hammer without actually using it as a hammer, although using *x* as a hammer can also count as such an interpretation. Needless to say, every act of such 'second-order' interpretation must itself count as a purposive act within a world; nothing can count as 'repairing a hammer' unless it is performed in order to improve a hammer in order to drive nails . . . for the sake of some standardized possibility of Dasein.

To interpret something, *x*, as something, then, to understand it as a *y* in this nonlinguistic sense, is either simply to use it as a *y* or to act on it in order to make it better able to fulfill the role of being a *y*. This means that for someone to understand *that x* is a *y*, in our broad sense, all that is required is that he use *x* as *y*'s are used or that he make *x* better able to function as a *y*. But what is necessarily involved in 'using *x* as *y*'? The answer to this question follows directly from our previous analysis of understanding-how. For any act to count as using a tool of a given type, it must be part of a teleologically ordered sequence of actions that use a variety of instruments to reach subordinate goals, which in turn are what they are as instrumental to a further end, or 'for-the-sake-of'.

To say of some entity that it is using a hammer, or using something as a hammer, then, implies that it at least has the capacity to perform a string of actions for a particular purpose: the purpose to be achieved, partially, through hammering. In Heidegger's language, this amounts to an understanding of 'the totality of involvements', or functionality contexture, in which hammers function and are hammers. Someone can use and interpret something as a hammer only if she is able to use nails and boards in order to build, not because such an ability is causally necessary to hammering but because to say of someone that she hammers or uses a thing as a hammer necessarily implies a capacity to use the hammer in building (or picture hanging, or whatever). This is so because the definition of hammering is functional (hammering is an activity performed in order to accomplish such and such a purpose): a behavior counts as hammering only if it is performed in order to realize that sort of purpose; and to count it as attempting to realize that purpose, we must presumptively assign appropriate capacities to use other tools to the agent of the hammering activity.

Similarly, to count what a being p is doing as, for example, repairing x so that it can better function as a y presupposes that p understands how y's are to be used: that is, that p has a practical understanding of y's. To repair a y, such as a hammer, is to act in order to make this thing a better y. And that one is acting in order to do that, as opposed to anything else, involves the 'repair' in an ongoing sequence of activities within the functionality contexture of building, which in turn necessarily involves understanding and being capable of appropriately dealing with boards, nails, and the like. Heidegger puts this holistic 'understanding how' condition on understanding something as something by saying that interpretation is 'grounded on' a 'fore-having'. That is, in order to interpret x as y, we must understand x in its involvements: we must have the capacity to use x, along with a, b, and c, in order to achieve ends. "The ready-to-hand is always understood in terms of a totality of involvements. This totality need not be grasped explicitly by a thematic interpretation. Even if it has undergone such an interpretation, it recedes into an understanding which does not stand out from the background. And this is the very mode in which it is the essential foundation for everyday circumspective interpretation. In every case this interpretation is grounded in something we have in advance—in a fore-having [*Vorhabe*]"[9]

This presupposed understanding consists in a capacity to use something in a variety of appropriate ways. Whenever someone actually uses or improves a hammer—that is, interprets or takes something as a hammer—he does so for a purpose. This isn't an accident. To count as hammering, an act must be performed for the sake of reaching one of the ends that hammering accomplishes. The fact that it is an attempt to realize that end in a particular way is what makes it an instance of hammering. And to count as repairing a hammer, an act must be performed for the sake of one of the ends such a repair could be performed for. So any actual interpretation of something as a hammer implies that the agent has 'sighted' in advance or intended some end in that interpretation of the thing as a hammer. That is, interpreting something as a hammer implies a particular purpose for that act of interpretation on the part of the agent, and it is in light of that purpose that the behavior is an interpretation of x as a hammer. Heidegger calls this condition 'fore-sight' (*Vorsicht*). "When something is understood but is still veiled, it becomes unveiled by an act of appropriation, and this is always done

9. *B.T.*, p. 191/150.

58   Heidegger's Pragmatism

under the guidance of a point of view, which fixes that with regard to which what is understood is to be interpreted. In every case interpretation is grounded in something we see in advance—in a fore-sight."[10]

Heidegger's third 'fore-condition' for interpretation is 'fore-conception' (*Vorgriff*). The idea here seems to be that every interpretation involves an 'anticipation' of what the thing is capable of doing: that a hammer is usable for the driving of nails, for example. Someone who is truly hammering with a thing must at least believe that the thing is capable of being used in hammering. And someone who is repairing a hammer must at least interpret the thing as potentially capable of being made usable as a hammer. He can, of course, be wrong. "In such an interpretation, the way in which the entity we are interpreting is to be conceived can be drawn from the entity itself, or the interpretation can force the entity into concepts to which it is opposed in its manner of being. In either case, the interpretation has already decided for a definite way of conceiving it, either with finality or with reservations; it is grounded in something we grasp in advance—in a fore-conception."[11]

Heidegger speaks of the way in which interpretation is grounded on each of the 'fore-conditions' for interpretation. He also says more simply that "all interpretation is grounded on understanding."[12] We can now see that 'to be grounded on' in this sense is a particular sort of relation: x is grounded on y if x could not be unless y also is; to be grounded on a condition is to have that condition as a necessary condition. There cannot be an interpretation of something as something unless there is also an understanding, on the part of the interpreter, of that thing: an understanding of the world in which that thing functions, of the purpose to which it is put, and of the capacities of the thing to be instrumental to that end. But in the simplest case, to interpret x as y is to use x as y. So all these conditions must be seen as conditions for such use. They are not, however, meant by Heidegger to be causal conditions. Rather, they are formal conditions. If it is true to say of someone that she concretely uses x as a y and thus interprets x to be a y, this by itself implies that (1) she has the capacity to use a variety of other tools along with x to reach a variety of ends; (2) she is using x as y in order to achieve one of those ends; and (3) she has a practical understanding of x

10. *B.T.*, p. 191/150.
11. *B.T.*, p. 191/150.
12. *B.T.*, p. 195/153.

as being capable of being useful in achieving that end. All of this follows, for Heidegger, because to use x as y includes all this practical understanding, while practical understanding is evidenced and realized only in acts of interpretation. In the next simplest case, that of action performed to make an object capable of fulfilling a functional role, interpretation necessarily presupposes understanding because no action can count as an interpretation of x as y unless it is part of an ongoing series of acts that demonstrate the capacity of the agent to deal with the functional contexture in which y's have a role, and no one can do this without thereby fulfilling conditions (1), (2), and (3).[13]

Meaning and Intelligibility

Given the fact that the German word *Sinn* and the English word 'meaning' have been central to almost all the philosophical debates and projects of the twentieth century (including the work of Heidegger's mentor, Husserl), it is surprising how little the early Heidegger actually uses or discusses the word. This lack is especially noteworthy in light of Heidegger's official formulation of his overall project at this period as a concern with the question of the meaning of being. Part II analyzes the import and point of this question in detail, but if we are to make any headway with Heidegger's views in regard to the linguistic form of 'understanding-that', it is important to understand the little that he does explicitly say concerning 'meaning' in general.

Things in the world, objects and events, have meanings. In fact, of course, they can have meaning in several different senses. A memento of some special occasion can be meaningful (in the sense of important or significant) for a person in virtue of its association with that occasion. The meaning of such a keepsake would seem to be either the event with which the memento is associated by the person or the emotional state evoked in the person by the presence or thought of the thing. In either case it is clear that the meaning of the thing here is a three-place property that relates the thing, that with which the thing is associated, and a person. The memento has a meaning for a person.

A natural event that is causally linked with another natural event (for example, the south wind with an impending storm) can also be meaning-

---

13. For the implications of all this on Heidegger's analysis of the famous "hermeneutic circle," see the appendix to Part I of this book.

ful. In this case the presence of the meaningful event indicates the presence or impending presence of the second event, and its meaning is the occurrence of that second event. As opposed to the first case, however, it seems that here one can mistake the meaning of the meaningful event; one can 'misread' the signs. That is, the natural event can either have a meaning or fail to have a meaning for some individual; if it has a meaning for an individual, the event itself can either have or fail to have the meaning that the individual takes it to have, depending upon the actual causal nexus in which the event stands.

This is also true of conventional signs. A highway stop sign, for example, has a meaning, though its meaning is not another object or event with which it is causally linked. Rather, it seems, someone has understood the meaning of the sign when he knows what to do relative to the sign. In this case, he understands the sign's meaning if he understands that when he sees it in a certain position, he is supposed to stop. He understands the meaning of the stop sign if he has interpreted it as a directive to stop in certain situations.

But what is it to interpret the sign: that is, to understand its meaning? According to the discussion above, to understand x as y where y is a tool type, to interpret x as y, is in general to use x as a y or to operate on x so as to make it a better y. This second possibility is clearly irrelevant here, so to understand some thing as a stop sign is to use it as a stop sign: that is, as a piece of equipment with a certain determinate function. The function of the stop sign is to communicate to drivers a certain orientation in their activity of driving; that is, it is equipment for getting drivers to stop, in order that all drivers will correlate their actions in such a way that all arrive safely. Stop signs are equipment for traveling, and one interprets the thing as a stop sign if one does what it indicates ought to be done in order to reach one's destination: if one stops. The meaning of the sign is what it directs one to do, which in this instance is the proper interpretation of this thing as an item of equipment. Once again, one can misunderstand or fail grasp this meaning. The meaning thereby achieves a certain objectivity, arising out of the standard patterns of instrumental action and purpose that are established along with the public, interpersonal structure of the 'with-world'.

The primary use Heidegger makes of the word 'meaning' (*Sinn*) is related to this last usage but is somewhat simpler. It is simpler because signs are a special sort of equipment, while Heidegger uses 'meaning' to refer to that *as* which any piece of equipment is interpreted to be, or properly interpreted to be. This thing I am currently using 'has' a meaning, for Heidegger: its meaning is being a pen. This other thing over here also has a meaning: it is a desk. The meaning of *x* in general for Heidegger is just that as which it is interpreted. "That which has been articulated as such in interpretation and sketched out beforehand in the understanding in general as something articulable, is the meaning."[14] In an odd way, then, meaning is use; to interpret *x* as *y* (where *y* is the meaning of *x*) is to use *x* as a *y*. As we have just seen, to use *x* as *y* implies a multiplicity of other talents and capacities, which together can appropriately be seen as understanding how to cope with the context in which something can function as a *y*. Within that context, *x* has the implicit meaning of being a *y*, a meaning articulated and made explicit in the act of using *x* as a *y*. "That which can be articulated in a disclosure by which we understand, we call 'meaning'."[15] Insofar as it is possible to understand some thing—that is, insofar as it is possible to understand how to use that thing—the thing has an implicit meaning that allows it to be understood. This meaning allows for such understanding in that it consists in the possibility for use which this thing has, and understanding the thing consists in an agent's having the capacity to use the thing as it is capable of being used. The meaning of this *x* is that it is a hammer: that is, it is possible and appropriate to hammer with it. What I understand when I understand how to use this thing is, among other things, this possibility of the thing. That I can understand how to use the hammer depends, among other things, upon what the thing is capable of. When I interpret *x* as a hammer—that is, actually use it as a hammer—I am 'articulating' this capacity through the activity itself. "In the projecting of the understanding, entities are disclosed in their possibility. The character of the possibility corresponds, on each occasion, with the kind of being of the entity understood. . . . When entities within-the-world are discovered along with the being of Dasein—that is, when they have come to be understood—we say that they have meaning. But that which is understood, taken strictly, is not the meaning but the entity, or alternatively, being. Meaning is that wherein the intelligibility of something maintains itself."[16]

This relation between the meaning of *x* and what the possibilities for

14. *B.T.*, p. 195/153.
15. *B.T.*, p. 193/151
16. *B.T.*, pp. 192–193/151.

use of x are in fact supplies one element of the objectivity of the 'meaning of x': x can't have the meaning of being a hammer unless it is actually capable of being used in hammering. The very attempt to use x as a hammer implies that it is being interpreted as a hammer: that is, that x is interpreted as having the meaning of being a hammer. The interpretation could be wrong, however. It is wrong if the interpretation (the act of hammering) fails because of the incapacity of the thing to be used in that way—if, for example, the 'hammer' is made out of pasta.

A second way in which an interpretation or taking-as can be mistaken and a meaning misinterpreted can be grasped by returning to our example of the conventional sign. If a tool has an established unique or preferred use within a social world of practices, ends, and procedures, then to use it in some other way is to 'misinterpret' its meaning, even if it is physically capable of such use. Conventional signs—that is, equipment for communicating 'correct' modes of behavior or correct interpretations of the things around us—can function *as* signs *only* if they are interpreted as having the unique use of being a sign of a certain sort. Regardless of the physical possibilities for use of the stop sign (I suppose it could be used as a shovel, for instance), it is usable as a *sign* only if it is interpreted in a particular way. To interpret it as any other sort of sign—that is, to act in response to it in any other functionally defined way—is of necessity to misunderstand its correct meaning as a sign.

To this point we have been speaking as though the proper—indeed, sole—use of 'meaning' is in the locution 'the meaning of x', where x is some thing other than Dasein. In this use, the meaning is that which x is correctly interpretable as (in this context, used as). Heidegger, however, while using 'meaning' in just this sense, also claims that "meaning is an existentiale of Dasein, not a property attaching to entities, lying 'behind' them, or floating somewhere as an 'intermediate' domain."[17] To be an *existentiale* of Dasein is not to be a property of Dasein; it is to be a way in which Dasein is, comparable to 'being such as to have a quality' rather than 'being white'. To say that meaning is an *existentiale* of Dasein, then, is to say that Dasein is such as to be, or live, in terms of meaning. It 'has' meaning insofar as other entities are understood along with its self-understanding. "Dasein only 'has' meaning, so far as the disclosedness of being-in-the-world can be 'filled in' by the entities discoverable in that disclosedness. . . . That is to say, its own being and the entities disclosed

17. *B.T.*, p. 193/151.

with its being can be appropriated in understanding."[18] The self-under-standing of Dasein is being toward an end, or purposiveness, and it is only in terms of such purposes that entities other than Dasein can have a meaning in the sense in which we have been using the term. If the meaning of x is what x can be correctly interpreted to be; if what x can be correctly interpreted as being is what x can be used for, and appropriately used for, within some community of Dasein; and if the use of something for something is necessarily the use it has for realizing some purpose or other, then if there were no purposes and no socially standardized pur-poses—that is, no Dasein—there could be no meaning. Even though meanings can be objective in the sense that they are not relative to the opinions and interpretations of an individual, there could be no mean-ings at all, even objective ones, without Dasein. That anything has a meaning thus implies that it is understood within some practical context of Daseinish activity.

Heidegger also uses the word 'meaning' for that structure of purposive-ness without which there could be no meaning at all; that structure which is identical with Dasein's self-understanding as end and its practical understanding. "The concept of meaning embraces the formal existential framework of what necessarily belongs to that which an understanding interpretation articulates. Meaning is the 'upon which' [*Woraufhin* = 'toward which'] of a projection in terms of which something becomes intelligible as something; it gets its structure from a fore-having, a fore-sight, and a fore-conception."[19]

Thus 'meaning' has at least two uses in early Heidegger. The meaning of x is what x is (correctly) interpretable as, what x can be used for and ought to be used for within some with-world. But 'meaning' is also the transcendental condition for any x to have a meaning—that there be a being that is socially purposive and thus has a practical understanding of things other than itself. In the first sense, 'meaning' qualifies some x that is understandable and interpretable within some with-world as fulfilling a unique functional role. In the second sense, 'meaning' is roughly equiv-alent to 'meaningfulness', or the character of a being for whom there are meanings in virtue of its practical social understanding. The structure of such meaningfulness is just the 'fore-structure' of understanding and interpretation. In addition, when used in relation to the functionality

18. *B.T.*, p. 193/151.
19. *B.T.*, p. 193/151.

context of intelligibility, 'meaning' has a particular as well as general ontological use for Heidegger. The 'meaning' of some entity, let us say a hammer, is the specific type of functionality context and horizon in terms of which things can be hammers. Meanings in this sense get their determinacy from the for-the-sake-of toward which such contexts are oriented. This use is related to the ordinary nonphilosophical use in which we talk about the meaning of acts; the meaning or significance of the act of hammering is that there is building going on and that the hammerer intends to build.

Assertion Is a Derivative Mode of Interpretation

Heidegger's position can't be criticized on the standard grounds for attacking logical behaviorists, such as Gilbert Ryle. For Heidegger, a 'belief that' is never identical with a disposition to behave in a certain physically described way, no matter how complicated that disposition is thought to be. Rather, he holds that one can attribute beliefs only insofar as one attributes ends to a thing's behavior and only in terms of those ends; and to attribute purposes, one must also attribute beliefs. That is, it is built into Heidegger's view of understanding that beliefs and desires must be ascribed together. This is the ultimate point of claiming that only Dasein (that is, purposive beings) understand and that all Dasein (as purposive beings) understand. One can't act purposively unless one takes things as such and such, and one can't take things as such and such unless one engages in purposive behavior. An activity therefore counts as an interpretation, or an understanding-that, only if it is part of a teleologically ordered sequence of activities: that is, only if the agent wants something and is acting so as to get it. An understanding-that can never be defined in terms of dispositions to behave apart from purposive contexts and independently of ends. But this is what the logical behaviorists unsuccessfully attempted to do.

There are two major difficulties for this Heideggerian position in regard to 'understanding that', however. First, it is clear that most of what we understand, in the sense of 'understand that', most of what we believe, does not have the form of 'understanding that x is a tool of a certain sort'. I understand that Kant died in 1804, that grass is green, that $2 + 2 = 4$, that Charlotte is beautiful, that Jane desires Jack, and even that this pen weighs one ounce. None of these understandings appears to be even remotely related to tool-using contexts, let alone analyzable in terms of use for a purpose or repair and putting to rights, as the simple form of the Heideggerian theory suggests. The first difficulty, then, consists in seeing how Heidegger proposes to account for 'understanding that' when what is understood is not some thing that can properly be used in some way for some purpose: that is, as a tool of a given type. In Heideggerian language, the problem consists in giving an analysis of understanding entities whose being is not ready-to-hand, beings that are, as Heidegger puts it, 'meaningless' (not understood within an equipmental context), 'lacking in [practical] intelligibility'.

Second, Heidegger interprets one kind of taking-as, or interpreting, as characterizable in terms of overt practical activity with things. But what does this have to do with the other form of taking-as, the overt or covert acceptance or belief in the truth of a linguistic assertion? The second problem amounts to the question of how Heidegger proposes to account for assertion, or the linguistic form of taking-as, and on what grounds he claims that assertion is itself properly seen as a form of interpretation in his sense.

As it turns out, the two issues are intimately linked in Heidegger's thought and can be most profitably dealt with by considering the second. What is an assertion and what is it to assert something? The remainder of this chapter considers this issue in regard to assertions concerning the functional properties of tools.

It is significant that the early Heidegger usually uses the word *Aussage* (assertion) in his discussions of the primary form of linguistic statements. When I believe that something is true, what I believe true is an *Aussage*. Like the English word 'assertion', *Aussage* refers etymologically to an overt activity in which something is expressed, or said out. And, again like the English word, *Aussage* is ambiguous between the activity of asserting and whatever is asserted in the asserting. "Assertion has the characteristic double signification that it means both asserting and asserted. Asserting is one of Dasein's intentional comportments. In essence it is an asserting about something and thus is intrinsically referred to some being or beings."[20] As asserting, an assertion is something that one does. But what does one do when one asserts? The primary sense of 'assertion' is the act of engaging in an overt linguistic performance of some type, whether it is oral, written, in sign language, or whatever. But such a performance counts as an asserting only if what is 'expressed' in

20. *B.P.*, p. 207/295.

and by the linguistic performance is an 'assertion'. Not all vocalization, or even language use, counts as asserting, because not all of what is vocalized counts as assertion. I can promise, question, or simply make noise, as well as assert. Then which linguistic performances are assertions? Assertions (what is asserted in an asserting) as a class can themselves be defined functionally, and this is what Heidegger attempts. What it is to be an assertion is thus characterized in terms of what assertions (not assertings) do, what is accomplished through them; to be an assertion is to be a very special type of tool. To be an asserting is to be an actual use of a tool of this kind.

What kind of tool is an assertion? Heidegger suggests three differentiae. An assertion (1) is a pointing-out that (2) gives a definite character to the thing pointed out by assigning a predicate to it and (3) communicates this 'exhibitive disparting' and determination: "We may define 'assertion' as a pointing out which gives something a definite character and which communicates."[21] Let us begin with the last: how is an assertion (proposition) in itself, apart from any actual asserting of it, a tool for communicating? We have already encountered such tools; conventional signs are equipment for communicating. What is communicated by such signs is that if one is engaged in a certain kind of activity with a certain sort of goal, (for example, driving for the sake of reaching a destination), one ought to engage in that activity in a certain way (for example, stop at the corner). The force of this 'ought' is that to act in this way is instrumental to the achieving of the end of the activity. It is instrumental to act in this way because the sign serves to standardize the behavior of a number of people so as to avoid problems that would otherwise arise through the interference of their various projects (one driver's car colliding with another) or because of obstacles to their projects in the natural world (driving off a curved road). The meaning of the sign is what it is properly taken as—for example, a sign for communicating that the road ahead is curved and that this should be taken into account in a determinate way in one's projects. So what is communicated by such signing tools is a conditional of the form: 'If one wants x, then one ought to do y'. 'To do y' is both to take the sign as the sign which it is (to slow down in the face of a curved-road sign, under the circumstances, is to take it as a curved-road sign) and to take some other feature of the world as a certain kind of thing (to slow down, given the end and the

21. *B.T.*, p. 199/156.

circumstances, is to take the road as both curved and dangerous). The sign communicates that way of taking-as: if one is driving, then one can and should take this road as dangerous. The meaning of the *sign* is that it is to be interpreted as a tool for communicating a way of interpreting the *road* and *its* meaning, or what the road is to be taken as.

Assertions, like conventional signs in general, are equipment for communicating. An assertion, Heidegger tells us, communicates our 'being toward' what is referred to in the assertion. "Letting someone see with us shares with the other that entity which has been pointed out in its definite character. That which is 'shared' is our being towards what has been pointed out—a being in which we see it in common."[22] This characterization of what is communicated in assertions leads us to the other two differentiae of assertion, pointing-out (apophansis) and predication. What is communicated is that some entity (what is pointed out or referred to) can be appropriately taken as of some type (the class to which the predicate assigns it). The assertion 'this is a hammer' is, according to Heidegger, a kind of equipment that could be used in asserting an assertion and is 'designed' to be used in that way. In the same manner that the hammer itself is a tool for hammering—that is, it could correctly be used to hammer with, is designed for hammering, and has a specific socially standardized utility in a socially standardized practice of building—the assertion 'this is a hammer' can be used to communicate (that is, assert) that this thing could be used for hammering, is 'designed' to communicate this, and has a socially standardized role within some socially standardized practice. In other words, what assertions communicate are understandings of this as that. In the case of 'this is a hammer' what may be communicated with the assertion is that if one wanted to build something, then this thing could be used in hammering.

The meaning of the assertion is that it is a communicating that the meaning of this thing is to be interpreted as being that of a hammer. As all assertions have the function of communication, the meaning of *this* assertion as assertion is fixed solely by the particular interpretation it communicates. In light of this, its 'meaning' is fully specified if we say simply that its meaning is *that* this thing is a hammer. This is the connection between meaning in Heidegger's practical sense (which we will name 'meaning$_h$') and meaning in the more philosophically familiar intentional or linguistic sense of the semantic content of a mental act or

22. *B.T.*, p. 197/155.

assertion (which we will term 'meaning$_i$'). An assertion is a tool for (has the meaning$_h$ of) communicating that this thing can be used as (has the meaning$_h$ of) a hammer. Any assertion that has this relation of communication to some meaning$_h$ can be said to mean$_i$ that the thing picked out by that assertion has the meaning$_h$ the assertion says it has or, more simply, that the thing is of some ready-to-hand kind: that x is a y.

Since assertions are equipment for communicating an understanding of things, Heidegger considers assertings to count as a kind of interpretation: that is, as a taking-as or understanding-that. One who actually asserts that 'this is a hammer' is explicitly warranting that, should the occasion arise, this thing could in fact function in hammering. Making such a statement is just as much a taking of this thing as a hammer as is using it as a hammer or repairing or improving it, because the use of the assertion implies that the speaker would use this thing as a hammer, were she to have a need for a hammer. Assertions introduce the subjunctive, as it were. Even if an assertion is used in order to deceive, it counts as that assertion and can be used to deceive only insofar as it itself implies that the thing can be taken in the way that the assertion says it can be taken. One couldn't even lie unless assertions implied such understandings of things as . . .

What assertions have that practical interpretations lack is the capacity to take something as something without actually using it. This they share with repairing or improving behavior, which can thus be seen as transitional forms. Such behavior doesn't use an x as a y, but it does operate overtly on or with x. Assertions concerning x neither use nor work on or with x, in virtue of their role in communicating conditional understandings. The assertion communicates that if one were building a house, then one could use this thing as hammers are used. What is communicated is that the thing is serviceable as a hammer, that the thing has the capacity to be used in hammering: that is, that the thing has the meaning of being a hammer. We would say that someone understood the meaning of this assertion (that is, took the vocalization of 'this is a hammer' as an asserting of the communicative tool 'this is a hammer') if, when he wanted to build, he attempted to use this thing as a hammer. (This is far too simple, of course; in fact, most of our evidence that someone understands the meaning of some assertion comes from that person's linguistic responses to the assertion. We deal with these connections in the next chapter.) In the same way that slowing for a curved-road sign counts at one and the same time as interpretation of the sign as a curved-road sign and of the road as curved, the actual use of this thing as a certain type of tool after an assertion to that effect is asserted counts as both an interpretation of the thing as a type of tool and an interpretation of the asserting as an asserting of the assertion in question; that is, as having a certain meaning.[23]

We ascribe beliefs (understandings-that) to various Dasein in two different ways. When someone uses a tool in a given manner or operates on it so as to make it better able to perform a given functional role, we think of such activity as good evidence that the person understands or believes that it is that sort of tool. For Heidegger, such interpretation actually consists in that sort of activity. The early Heidegger also thinks that we can assign interpretations, or understandings-that, on the basis of what people assert and communicate in those assertions. If someone says that x is a hammer, we have good reason to think that she understands x as a hammer, and the asserting counts as an explicit interpretation of x. In this case, however, understanding x as a hammer, the explicit interpretation of x, consists in the actual appropriate use of the *assertion* 'x is a hammer'. And when we ascribe such use of the assertion, we are also implicitly ascribing whatever else is necessary for such correct use.

An *asserting* is of a particular type, it has a particular meaning, if it is useful as a tool for communicating a particular interpretation. Let us use the same example, a vocalization that is correctly interpretable as an asserting of 'this is a hammer'. What else do we thereby ascribe to the person who made this assertion? First, we ascribe a desire to communicate and indeed to communicate something in particular. Insofar as the speaker is communicating the assertion 'this is a hammer', we can infer that she wants to communicate that it is appropriate to interpret this thing as a hammer; that is, she wants us to take this thing as a hammer. We must also ascribe to the asserter at least the understanding that what she says counts as an assertion of 'this is a hammer'; otherwise, it makes no sense to say that she is attempting to assert this assertion. Parrots and computers can utter sounds that we might take to be assertions of 'x is a

23. Obviously, one can use a thing in a certain way without understanding the corresponding assertion, even when one uses the tool directly after an attempted communication. While a great number of such correct behaviors count as important evidence in favor of the ascription of understanding of assertions (consider speechless people), we ordinarily don't ascribe such understanding unless the persons are capable of using the assertion type appropriately either by making correct assertions themselves or by drawing correct inferences from the assertions of others.

How about bels?

logical
spoken
relations

hammer', but when we discover that a parrot or simple computer uttered the sound, we revise our estimate and say that no assertion was made. The reason parrots can't make assertions is that an act to which one assigns the desire (to communicate that *x* is a hammer) and the understanding (that to say just this is to say that *x* is a hammer) integral to the purposive act of asserting must itself fit into a wider teleologically ordered context of behavior and, indeed, a socially standardized context. The behavior of the parrot doesn't fit such a context well enough to count.

In addition, as we see in the next chapter, that someone makes an assertion is usually sufficient evidence to warrant an understanding on our part that the asserter takes the thing he is speaking about as he communicates it to be. Ordinarily, that is, he not only understands what he says as a communication of a given assertion; he also understands the thing referred to in the assertion as the assertion says it is. This need not be the case, however. The intent to communicate that 'this is a hammer', which is essential to there being an assertion of 'this is a hammer', itself counts as such within a further context of teleologically organized activities in which it functions as a subordinate end. I can want to communicate that this is a hammer for your benefit (I'm teaching you English), or in order to get your approval (I'm a small child), *or* in order to deceive you (you are blind and I wish to play a cruel joke on you); in the last case the fact that I assert that this is a hammer in no way implies that I take this thing as a hammer. But in none of these cases can I attempt to communicate that this is a hammer unless I have an understanding of what it is to be a hammer and what hammering consists in. To use the assertion 'this is a hammer' correctly is to use it in order to communicate a taking-as, and one can't attempt to communicate a taking-as unless one is at least capable of understanding the thing as that sort of thing. In the case of tools, to do that is to understand how that type of tool is used.[24] To assert that '*x* is a hammer', one must at least know how to use '*x* is a hammer'; and to understand how to use '*x* is a hammer', one must at least know how hammers are used. This in turn implies the presence of exactly the same kind of fore-having, fore-sight, and fore-conception that we found were required for simple practical interpretation. "The pointing out which assertion does is performed on the basis of what has already been

24. We take the overwhelming verbal competence of the physically disabled as a replacement for actual physical competence.

disclosed in understanding or discovered circumspectively. Assertion is not a free-floating kind of behavior which, in its own right, might be capable of disclosing entities in general in a primary way: on the contrary it always maintains itself on the basis of being-in-the-world. . . . Any assertion requires a fore-having of whatever has been disclosed; and this is what it points out by way of giving something a definite character."[25]

It is of course possible for someone to assert, and to assert correctly, that 'x is a computer' without knowing how to use x or even understanding what computers are used for: that is, without understanding the functional role of computers. We will contrast two cases: (1) a Dasein who has no understanding of the practical role of a tool (what it is for) and (2) a Dasein who understands how it is to be used (what one does with computers, what they are for) but not how in particular to use it to perform that function. For Heidegger, assertions made by people in the first situation should not be seen at all as interpretations of the things referred to as having a specific functional property, or even as interpretations of the things as ready-to-hand. Rather, people who are capable of the correct use of such assertions understand how to use the assertion in question to communicate that this thing has some extant property in virtue of which it is usually appropriate to say that things having that property are computers. That is, such an extant property correlates more or less well with the functional character of being a computer. In short, such a Dasein knows what computers 'look like' (or smell like, or whatever) without knowing what it is to be a computer. That a Dasein without any practical understanding of the role of computers cannot correctly assert the assertion that 'x is a computer', where the thing is taken as ready-to-hand as a computer, is indicated by the fact that such a person has no possible grounds for distinguishing real computers from mock-ups of computers, or for recognizing that something may indeed be a computer even if it lacks the right 'look'. Indeed, the consistent failure to make such verbal discriminations is excellent evidence that certain Dasein understand neither what it is to be a computer nor 'what they are talking about' when they assert that something is a computer.

A Dasein can genuinely assert that something is a computer without understanding how to use it as a computer or even understanding how to use any computer. He can do so, however, only if he has a practical understanding of what computers *qua* computers are useful for or of how

25. *B.T.*, p. 199/156.

and for what they are to be used. Such an understanding can be demonstrated in several ways. First, a person can actually use computers appropriately: that is, interpret things correctly as computers in his actual practice. Second, someone can show himself capable of integrating the activity of computers into his own ongoing projects. An executive who has no actual computer competence but is aware of and indirectly uses (through the mediation of other people) the capabilities of computers fits this case. Third, someone who for physical reasons is incapable of actual performance with computers may be capable of a wide and full range of verbal performance concerning computers, a range comparable with that demonstrated by other experts on computers. In all these cases, then, we would ascribe an understanding or belief that 'this is a computer' to a Dasein who understands what computers are for and how and for what they are to be used, even if he does not actually understand how to use them. For a person to be incapable of any of these actions is just for that person to lack any understanding of the role of computers. And we would consider such a person incapable of genuine understandings that some entity has a functional property and is ready-to-hand as a given sort of tool.

The practical competency, the understanding-how, required for assertoric understandings-that in regard to tools, then, is not an ability actually to use the tool in question. Rather, it is the practical ability to understand how a thing can or is to be used, which in turn involves the ability to make use of the use of that thing or, in extreme cases, the ability to speak correctly concerning the thing in question in a range of circumstances and contexts. The first kind of case is what Heidegger means by a fore-having of some thing or an understanding of the world in which the thing operates. Such understanding is evidenced in the actual practical activity of a Dasein. The second kind of case provides a bridge to the analysis of our assertoric understanding that some thing has some natural or extant property, because, as we shall see, Heidegger holds that such understanding and interpretation is possible only as assertion.

By using an assertion to communicate a taking-as, we substitute a virtual taking-as for an actual one and thereby become capable of taking something as what it can potentially be used for, as opposed to what it is at present being used for. In addition, it becomes possible to ascribe an interpretation of something to somebody even if that person is not actually using the thing in that way, or indeed operating on or with the thing at all. Finally, this kind of interpretation allows for the possibility of deception, because it is ordinary but not necessary for an asserter to understand as she communicates, even though the assertion remains an interpretation in accordance with the communication. For Heidegger, both the simple practical form of interpretation and the assertoric form, however, stand under the same formal conditions of possibility. If x is a tool, one can neither interpret x as y nor assert that x is y unless one understands how x is to be used as a y, which in turn implies an understanding of how to use a whole host of tools to realize a variety of ends within a common with-world. This is why Heidegger says that at least in regard to tools the second kind of understanding-that, asserting-that, is (1) a form of interpretation and (2) derivative from understanding how. Assertions in regard to tools are derivative from understanding how, for Heidegger, insofar as every use or understanding of an assertion, every verbal understanding that x is y, presupposes and implies that the Dasein understands how and for what y's are to be used.

This second claim, however, has been derived, and indeed is plausible, only for a very restricted class of assertions, the ones whose meaning is most obviously related to contexts of purposive use. We obviously believe in the truth of many assertions that neither concern tools nor assign functional properties to entities; nevertheless, Heidegger holds that all assertions are derivative forms of interpretation, are grounded in understanding how, and thus stand under the formal fore-conditions for all interpretation. The next chapter examines Heidegger's view that all understanding is derivative from understanding how and thus, ultimately, depends upon self-understanding.

3 Understanding the Extant: Truth

The Extant Is the Specialty of Assertion

What is it and how is it possible to understand that some thing has some property, where that thing is not a tool and that property is not functional? And how are we to interpret Heidegger's reiterated claims that it would be impossible to understand in this way unless we understood how to do things and that this understanding-that derives from understanding how? The key to comprehending Heidegger's answers to these questions is to recognize that for him, all understanding of 'the extant' (non-equipmental, natural beings) is realized through the acceptance and use of assertions, and assertions themselves are considered to be a special kind of tool: they are tools for communicating interpretations.

As opposed to tools, which belong to classes in virtue of their functional roles, many entities are understood as having nonfunctional determinations and non-functional essential determinations. In addition to Dasein itself, there are, for example, aesthetic objects (works of art, which at some points Heidegger considers to belong to a separate class of being) and, most prominently, natural objects and things considered as having natural determinations. Heidegger calls such beings 'extant' *(vorhanden)* and names their being 'extantness' *(Vorhandenheit)*. (This chapter deals with the extant entity, which is understood as extant. Part II treats the issue of the being of the extant entity, its 'extantness', at length.) His discussion of them turns on two features: such beings are perceivable, and they are causally efficacious. We will deal with perceivability first.

74

The extant is the perceivable, what is capable of being perceived. While we discover tools by using them and thereby discover their potential utilities, we discover extant beings by perceiving them and thereby discover their possibilities for perception. "In accord with its directional sense, perceiving intends the extant in its extantness."[1] "This leveling of the primordial 'as' of circumspective interpretation to the 'as' with which extantness is given a definite character is the specialty [*Vorzug*] of assertion. Only so does it obtain the possibility of exhibiting something in such a way that we just look at it."[2] If we ignore for the moment the reference to the role of assertion in the second of those two passages and focus on the results of its action, we can notice two things about the intending of what is extant. First, the extant being is supposed to be the intentional object of perception; it is the thing insofar as it is capable of being revealed in a perceptual encounter. Second, such perceptual encountering is not considered by Heidegger to be a giving of blank, indeterminate sensation. Rather, even to perceive is to perceive something as something; for Heidegger, all perception involves understanding.

This understanding has two sides. When I hear, for example, I am not perceptually given a group of noises, which I then judge to be produced by some object. Rather I hear the object itself; I hear the noise as the sound of some thing. "What we 'first' hear is never noises or complexes of sounds, but the creaking wagon, the motor cycle. We hear the column on the march, the north wind, the woodpecker tapping, the fire crackling."[3] Such perceiving already contains an implicit understanding of the perception as of one kind or another. But notice, the kind Heidegger thinks perceptual experiences belong to as perceptual also contains a reference to the thing I am perceiving in the perception. I hear the fire crackling; I see things that are red, not red patches. To perceive is to perceive something as having some perceptual determination. "In conformity with its sense of direction, perception is directed toward a being that is extant. It intends this precisely as extant and knows nothing at all about sensations that it is apprehending."[4] Heidegger is insisting on the classical distinction between perception and sensation and specifying that (1) perception is the normal apprehending state, and (2) the intentional object of

1. *B.P.* p. 71/100.
2. *B.T.* p. 201/158. Translation modified.
3. *B.T.* p. 207/163.
4. *B.P.* p. 63/88.

perception is the extant. Sensation is merely a phase of perception, abstractly considered apart from its perceptual context, where it can never actually exist as sensation. There are sensations only as aspects of perception. So, for Heidegger, to perceive is to perceive some thing as having some determination. Perception has the structure of understanding and interpretation built into it.

But what sort of objects do we perceive, and what sort of determinations do they have? The fast and flip answer to this question, of course, is that we perceive objects that are capable of being perceived and we perceive them with perceptual determinations. But what is it to have a perceptual determination? Does my seeing that the desk is square imply that I am currently sensing a square ocular pattern, and if I am currently sensing such a pattern, does it follow that the desk is square? The answer to both these questions is 'no'. Once we concede to Heidegger (along with Kant and against Hume) that we perceive objects as having perceptual determinations, then we are perceiving an object as having a certain capacity to affect us perceptually in various ways, depending upon the perceptual situation. To see the desk as square is to see it as capable of affecting us visually and tactilely in certain determinate ways, ways that vary as a function of (among other things) the angle from which it is seen. To see an object as yellow is to perceive it as able to affect us in determinate ways that vary as a function of the lighting, among other things. So when we perceive x as y, the y, the property of the thing we perceive, must be understood in terms of the pattern of effects the thing would have on us if certain other conditions were fulfilled.

That is why our perception can be mistaken. I can perceive x as y, though x might not be y, as I find out when I get into another situation vis à vis x. But then, to be an x, to be a being capable of being perceived, is to be such that it would affect us in determinate ways were we in certain situations relative to it. To perceive some thing is to perceive it as such that it is a standing possibility for bringing about perceptual effects in me (via sensations), effects that vary and that I take as varying (insofar as I perceive the thing as having a natural determination) as a function of the natural context of the perceptual event. To see something as red is to see it as such that were I to look at it in yellow light, one sensation would occur; if in blue light, another. To take something as extant in perception is to interpret it as a being that operates on our perception according to counterfactual, condition-laden rules.

There is, of course, a sense in which the cognitive understanding of a tool as belonging to some functional type also consists in a grasp of counterfactual conditionals: to understand something as a hammer is to intend it as such that if one wanted to do x in situation y, then one could use this thing in way z for a whole series of x's and y's. What is distinctive about the conditionals governing the understanding of extant entities, however, is that they make no reference whatsoever to any possible ends. Extant entities, as extant, are—as Heidegger says—meaningless. To interpret something as extant is not to interpret it as useful; it is to determine it independently of any meaning$_h$.

Many things that we understand to have natural determinations and to be extant cannot be directly perceived at all. Such 'theoretical' entities as electrons are posited, with their determinations, through the final determination of the extant which we have just discovered. To be extant is to be able to effect some change; it is to fulfill some system of counterfactuals of this form: Were x in situation s, it would bring about a new state of affairs s*, and the particular properties of x are fixed by just which values s and s* take. To understand theoretical entities is to take them as performing some role in a chain or nexus of such conditionals, which ultimately brings about some identifiable perceptual event or pattern of events. That is, the efficacy of the extant comes to be taken as its fundamental determination, and we come to understand theoretical objects as causing changes in other extant entities, which cause . . . , which eventually cause perceptual changes in us. Given what it is to be extant, it is difficult to conceive of what it would mean even to think that there is some extant being totally incapable of making any difference, no matter how indirect, to us.[5]

To be extant, then, to be actual, is to be capable of operating on or affecting other extant beings. "In the modern period it is customary to interpret the concept of actuality and the actual in another way. It is taken in the sense of that which influences, that is, acts or works inwards upon the subject or as that which acts or works on another, stands with another in an interconnection of efficacious action. The actuality of things consists in their exercising the action of forces on each other."[6] When I

5. In this 'verificationism', Heidegger is merely following Kant and Husserl (see Chapters 5 and 6).

6. *B.P.*, p. 104/147. Heidegger is here contrasting a modern conception of actuality with an earlier teleological conception that he finds in Aristotle and scholasticism. As we will see in Part II, early Heidegger thought that the modern understanding of extantness or actuality in terms of perception was derived from the ancient doctrine of *ousia* and

perceive, I perceive something as extant and as determined as extant, as having natural determinations. As Heidegger puts it, the mere fact that I am perceiving in this sense implies that I am understanding what I perceive as extant, as a being capable of effecting changes in me and in other natural beings. "This understanding of extantness is present beforehand as pre-conceptual in the *intentio* of perceptual uncovering as such."[7]

In perceiving, I also understand the extant being as having definite determinations. For Heidegger, such understanding always involves or consists in a disclosure of what the thing understood is capable of, of what it would do were it in various situations. "In the projecting of the understanding entities are disclosed in their possibility. The character of the possibility corresponds on each occasion, with the kind of being of the entity which is understood."[8] The difference between tools and extant things is thus a difference between the kinds of properties they have, which in turn is a difference in the kind of possibilities they are disclosed or understood as having. To be a tool of a certain type is to be capable of a certain sort of utility; to be a certain type of extant being is to be capable of affecting us and other extant beings in certain determinate ways.

Now, Heidegger holds that it is impossible to understand extant beings without having an understanding of how to do things and a self-understanding exemplified by an understanding of oneself as an end to be accomplished. He does not hold that there would be no extant beings without such understanding; Heidegger is not an idealist. "Extant things are beings as the kind of things they are, even if they do not become intraworldly, even if world-entry does not happen to them and there is no occasion for it at all. Intraworldliness does not belong to the essence of extant things as such, but it is only the transcendental condition . . . for the possibility of extant things being able to emerge as they are. And that means it is the condition for existing Dasein's experience and comprehension of things as they are."[9]

---

thereby from a practical horizon of activity. For now, what is significant is how *we* understand what it is for extant entities to be; and early Heidegger doesn't deny, indeed he affirms, that this fundamentally Kantian understanding of the extant entity in terms of perception is our own.

7. *B.P.*, p. 71/100. Heidegger goes on to explain that this 'beforehand' should not be understood in a temporal sense; such understanding is a necessary feature of perceptual intentionality.

8. *B.T.*, p. 192/151.

9. *M.F.L.*, p. 194/251.

How is an understanding that some thing is extant and is extant as such and such possible? It looks as if the answer to this question is straightforward. According to Heidegger, when we perceive, we perceive and understand that which we perceive as extant. So, perception supplies the possibility of understanding the extant: insofar as we perceive, we understand the extant as extant. The causal conditions for perception are whatever science discovers them to be. Nevertheless, Heidegger maintains that "the 'as' with which extantness is given a definite character *is the specialty of assertion*" and that "only so does it obtain the possibility of exhibiting something in such a way that we just look at it." That is, Heidegger claims that being able to use assertions is a necessary condition for understanding something *as extant* and that the kind of perception that specializes in perceiving things as extant is possible only for a being with the capacity to use language. Whatever kind of perception animals have (the most likely candidate is the kind of circumspective concern exhibited when we 'see' that something can be used for some end), Heidegger thinks they are incapable of perceiving things as extant with purely natural, non-instrumental determinations.

There is an extremely complex nexus here. According to Heidegger, to interpret something as extant, it is sufficient to perceive it as extant. We can also interpret something as extant 'theoretically', insofar as we intend it as causing the state of some extant being we *can* perceive. But, also according to Heidegger, the making of assertions is necessary for the ability to understand the extant and, indeed, for the ability to perceive. This will seem less odd if we remember what it is to perceive. To perceive is to intend some object in a very particular way. One must have a current, 'sensed' giving of the extant. In addition, the entity must be interpreted as acting according to a whole series of counterfactual conditionals whose antecedents are entirely separate from the ends of the one who understands. In Husserl's language, if we are to perceive *x,* we must intend a sensation as fulfilling the meaning of the empty intention with which we intend the object *x.*

We can approach an interpretation of this claim by asking under what conditions it would be true to say that some being has an understanding of some extant being as having some natural determination. In the case of tools, we have a perfectly good touchstone of 'understanding as' in how a being uses a thing. Similarly, there are occasions when we have reason to think that the agent believes there is some causal or logical relation between a thing with a natural property and some functional determination. Thus a rat can be trained to strike only red levers, which leads us to say that it understands those levers as red. Our grounds for ascribing such understanding, however, are essentially identical to those we use in ascribing ordinary interpretive 'understanding as' of ready-to-hand things, and being red in this case really is a functional determination of a piece of equipment. That is, the rat is treating the red levers as pieces of equipment for obtaining food, and we can assign an understanding of those levers only if we assume that the rat in fact desires or intends to get food.

In a similar fashion, we may say of some person that he believes it is raining and that umbrellas protect against rain (the first is an understanding of an extant determination, the second of a ready-to-hand determination) on the basis of his act of carrying an open umbrella. To do so, however, is to presuppose some end on the part of the person (to stay dry) for which umbrellas are instrumental and rain is detrimental. What is demonstrated here is his understanding of the rain as detrimental, not that something has some natural property. That is, such understanding necessarily involves a holistic grasp of the situation in which various things are understood as pieces of equipment or at least ready-to-hand (they could be detrimental) in light of some end or other.

In fact, the overt behavior of a purposive being in relation to things can count only as an interpretation of something as useful or detrimental for some end, because it counts as intending some thing at all only insofar as it is part of a pattern of activity that amounts to an intending to realize some end. Even interpretation by way of improvement presupposes that that which is improved is improved as a tool fulfilling a functional role. There is no improvement without a standard of what would be good, and there are no standards in this sense without ends. But the whole difference between the extant and the ready-to-hand resides in the different sort of possibility the extant is understood to have insofar as it is extant. There can't be tools without Dasein, not because there would be no one to make them (there are natural tools, after all) but because nothing can be a tool except for a purpose.[10] There are extant things without Dasein, however, because to be extant is simply to be capable of causing change. But if no overt purposeful activity can count as an interpretation of something as extant, what can count as such an interpretation?

---

10. Remember, to misconstrue a tool is either to take it as a piece of equipment for a job for which it is unsuited or to miss its 'standardized' function within a community.

Heidegger's answer is that only the final kind of interpretation, assertion, is capable of being an interpretation of something as extant. Assertions are capable of such interpretations because of their double aspect. They are tools for communicating interpretations. To say that someone asserts that 'the desk is square' is to interpret her utterance as being used in order to communicate the understanding of the desk as square. In other words, we interpret her act as a use of a tool for a particular purpose, and her asserting as the use of an instance of an assertion type. But insofar as the act is successful, she has communicated an understanding, the understanding that the desk is square. And as such, her act is both an interpretation of the assertion as a tool of a certain sort and an interpretation of the desk as square. To interpret some thing as extant, it is sufficient to make an assertion to that effect. (All that is at issue here is that assertions accomplish this task, not how they do so.) What assertions are used for (communicating understanding) and what they say or assert (an understanding of some thing) do not in general correspond. What is asserted is thereby freed from the context of activity, and assertions thus become capable of interpreting things independently of the actual or potential use of the thing interpreted. And since any overt behavior with the thing would count as an interpretation of the thing as useful, symbolic expression of extant determinations via assertions is the only way in which such interpretation can be carried out. Assertions are necessary for interpreting things as extant.

As the reader will certainly have noticed, this discussion slips between what is necessary if there is to be evidence that some being understands some thing as extant—as in principle open to perceptual encounter in a certain way—and what is necessary for that understanding itself. We can know or have evidence that some being is actually taking something as extant in a particular way, that it is perceiving it in that way, only if it can say that it is. Moreover, there can be no possible evidence for the perception of anything extant apart from the ability to make assertions. But Heidegger goes further and claims that such understanding and perceptions themselves are impossible without assertions. This follows only on the basis of some strong variety of verificationism. And, as we shall see in Chapter 4, such a verificationism is a presupposition necessary to the structure of Heidegger's overall argument.

It will be useful to quote in full the passage in which Heidegger makes these claims.

The entity which is held in our fore-having—for instance, the hammer—is proximally ready-to-hand as equipment. If this entity becomes the 'object' of an assertion, then as soon as we begin this assertion, there is already a change-over in the fore-having. Something ready-to-hand with which we have to do or perform something, turns into something 'about which' the assertion which points it out is made. Our fore-sight is aimed at something extant in what is ready-to-hand. Both by and for this way of looking at it, the ready-to-hand becomes veiled as ready-to-hand. Within this discovering of extantness, which is at the same time a covering-up of readiness-to-hand, something extant which we encounter is given a definite character in its being extant in such-and-such a manner. Only now are we given any access to properties or the like. When an assertion has given a definite character to something extant, it says something about it as a 'what'; and this 'what' is drawn from that which is extant as such. The as-structure of interpretation has undergone a modification. In its function of appropriating what is understood, the 'as' no longer reaches out into a totality of involvements. As regards its possibilities for articulating reference-relations, it has been cut off from that significance which, as such, constitutes environmentality. The 'as' gets pushed back into the uniform plane of that which is merely extant. It dwindles to the structure of just letting one see what is extant, and letting one see it in a definite way. This leveling of the primordial 'as' of circumspective interpretation to the 'as' with which extantness is given a definite character is the specialty of assertion. Only so does it obtain the possibility of exhibiting something in such a way that we just look at it.[11]

It is important in this context to recall the relations between understanding and interpretation. 'Understanding how' is always a capacity phrase. To say that some Dasein understands how to do something is to say that he is capable of doing it. To interpret something as something always involves engaging in a purposive activity. If to interpret x as y, where y is extant, is to assert that 'x is y', then to understand the assertion 'x is y' is to have a practical understanding of how to use the assertion so as to communicate that x is y. To believe that x is y, however, is actually to take x as y: that is, to assert that x is y. Now, of course, we ascribe many beliefs to people in regard to extant entities even in the absence of their making assertions about those entities. To accommodate these cases, it is best to think of belief itself in terms of a possibility, by way of counterfactual conditionals: to understand that x is y, where x is extant, is to be such

---

11. *B.T.*, pp. 200–201/157–158. Translation modified.

that one would assert or assent to 'x is y' were one queried on the subject. What one believes when one believes that x is y, on the other hand, is that x is capable of the variety of perceptual effects on us and causal effects on other extant entities which amount to its being a y. Unless one knew how to use an assertion with the meaning$_h$ of being a tool for communicating that x is a y, one would be incapable of the belief, or the perception, that x is y, but the content of that belief is 'x is y', or the interpretation the assertion 'x is y' is a tool for communicating. This is the meaning$_i$ of this assertion.

So, when Heidegger says that understanding the extant is the prerogative of assertion, he is saying that the only way to interpret something as extant is to make (or at least believe) assertions in regard to it. This formulation of course leaves a whole host of important, indeed crucial, issues entirely up for grabs. Nothing in the early Heidegger can count as a fully (or even adequately) developed philosophy of language. He says very little about the relation between word meaning and assertion meaning, or the relation between assertions and other kinds of sentences. He leaves an even more serious gap by his failure even to consider how assertions are capable of making claims about extant entities. It is also disturbing that he gives very little consideration to the question of how the practice of making assertions is related to Dasein's overall project, which can always be formally described as intending a possibility of itself.

From what we do have, however, it is clear why Heidegger holds that unless Dasein did have some such self-understanding, and thus some understanding of how to do things, it could not understand that any thing had natural, or other, determinations. To interpret something as a tool, one can either use it or improve it or make functional assertions concerning it. To interpret something as having any other sort of being or any other sort of property, one can only make assertions. But to make an assertion is to do something, specifically, with language. Unless we understood how to use language to make assertions, for various purposes, we could not interpret things as extant. So, once again, to count as 'understanding that', even in the case of understanding some thing as having a nonfunctional determination, one must be Dasein, a being who acts within a society in a rational manner for the sake of accomplishing ends. This seems a weak conclusion, comparable to saying that we couldn't assert things unless we understood how to make assertions. To see how Heidegger uses this conclusion, we must look at what assertions are: equipment for communicating understanding.

What Assertions Are Used For and What They Say

What is the relation between the primary practical function of assertions, to communicate interpretations, and their semantic content, what they communicate? In general, on the view we are ascribing to the early Heidegger, this relation can be expressed by saying that an assertion can communicate an interpretation only because, if it is to be the tool it is at all, it must be used mostly in a particular range of initial conditions to bring about a particular kind of end. These conditions are determined only by the linguistic practices of some community of Dasein. In other words, the semantic capacity of assertions depends upon their communicative function, which is impossible except insofar as they are used within some speech community in particular kinds of already current situations for some definite end.

Assertions have a double aspect. On the one hand, assertions express come content; they say of some thing that it has some determination. Insofar as it does this, an assertion has a semantic content; what it interprets the thing as can be true or false. On the other hand, assertions are themselves tools that are useful in performing a certain job, precisely the job of communicating the interpretations they express. It is Heidegger's position—in that he holds that an assertion is "a pointing out which gives something a definite character and which communicates"[12] and that the interpretation of things as extant is the specialty of assertion— that only insofar as assertions can and do perform their functional role of tools do they become capable of expressing some semantic content.

How do assertions function as tools? As with any other piece of equipment, an assertion is the sort of equipment it is within an equipmental context. Tools are used in definite situations in order to achieve results that are in turn preconditions for performing other acts so as to ultimately achieve the end for the sake of which the series of purposive activities takes place. What is the result that the use of assertions is to bring about and that serves to define assertions as a class of equipment? To this point we have blandly characterized the function of assertions as that of communicating interpretations. But what does that purposive action consist in, under what conditions is it appropriate, and for what is it carried out? What are we doing when we communicate interpretations?

In an early section of *Being and Time* Heidegger raises the question of the equipmental character of signs, such as highway signs. Highway

12. *B.T.*, p. 199/156.

signs, like assertions, communicate interpretations, but at this point in the exposition Heidegger has not introduced the notion of interpretation. Instead, he directly discusses the point of signs, the context in which they are used, and what is brought about through their use. A curved-road sign is placed by the side of a road. It warns people who are driving that if they want to arrive safely at their destination, they ought to slow down and respond to the road as hazardous. The sign serves a very definite function, the function of 'drawing our attention to' an aspect of the equipmental context in which the sign itself stands and which we might be using; further, it orients us to that context in a particular way. It communicates: If you want to stay alive, pay attention to the road as something that is potentially detrimental and needs some definite response in order to avoid danger. The sign is a piece of equipment that is used to get us to use an equipmental context in a definite way and in doing so to practically understand some item of equipment as having some ready-to-hand determination. It allows us to get practical understanding of our environment; it directs us in how to use things in the world so as to attain our ends, whatever they should happen to be.

"Signs of the kind we have described let what is ready-to-hand be encountered; more precisely, they let some context of it become accessible in such a way that our concernful dealings take on an orientation and hold it secure. A sign is not a thing which stands to another thing in the relation of indicating; it is rather an item of equipment which explicitly raises a totality of equipment into our circumspection so that together with it the worldly character of the ready-to-hand announces itself."[13] Signs are necessary and useful for pointing out some ready-to-hand determination of some entity and thereby orienting our behavior within an equipmental context. In fact, the bringing about of this orientation is what the sign is for. "Such a sign addresses itself to the circumspection of our concernful dealings, and it does so in such a way that the circumspection which goes along with it, following where it points, brings into an explicit 'survey' whatever aroundness the environment may have at the time. This circumspective survey does not grasp the ready-to-hand; what it achieves is rather an orientation within our environment."[14] What the sign does is show us how to act in order to achieve an end. It does this by showing us how some thing is to be dealt with in reaching that end. The

13. *B.T.*, pp. 110/79–80.
14. *B.T.*, p. 110/79.

road, the sign says, is to be taken as dangerous, to be interpreted as curved, which in context requires caution.

Assertions concerning the ready-to-hand are like highway signs. Their primary function is to orient us within a particular equipmental context and thereby show us how to achieve some end by using some items of equipment. Insofar as assertions 'point out a definite character' of some thing, the equipmental potentials they draw our attention to are useful in standard ways of reaching communally recognized and standardized ends. The functional role of such assertions is to coordinate activity. When I say 'there's a curve ahead' in the context of driving (or backseat driving), it serves the function of drawing the driver's attention to the ready-to-hand context in which she is operating and orienting her in that context to deal cautiously with an obstacle. Of course, if the person isn't driving, if she is not using the equipmental contexture set up for traveling in cars, then the assertion is so much idle talk; it doesn't help the one to whom it is communicated to deal effectively with her world. Nevertheless, if the assertion is true, it does communicate a conditional orientation: if one were using the equipmental contexture of traveling in cars, then at this point one should use the brakes. Similarly, if an assertion of 'this is a hammer' is true, then if I were building, I should approach and use this as a hammer.

It is no accident that at this point we start discussing 'truth'. What is communicated in the assertion, the interpretation that it communicates and thus its meaning$_i$, is just a certain conditional whose antecedent is specified by an end or ends and some set of already present conditions, and whose consequent specifies the capacity of some thing to be used in a certain way, in those conditions, to reach that end. For the assertion to be true is for the thing really to have that capacity, which is discovered when we use it in the way indicated. Another way of putting this is to say that what the assertion communicates, the interpretation it expresses, is the conditions that must be met if the assertion is to be true. The assertion communicates its own truth conditions. How can it do this?

We will deal with this question for the special class of assertions that communicate interpretations of the extant. We do so because we are ultimately concerned with what it is to understand that some entity has some extant determination, and in the last section we discovered that, for Heidegger, only beings who assert such determinations can understand that some thing has those determinations.

We need a better understanding of the unique status, for Heidegger, of assertions concerning the extant. Proximally, of course, such assertions are tools for communicating interpretations of the extant. In addition to having a functional role, they also express a set of truth conditions. In this case, however, the truth conditions cannot be established in the assertion in the same way as in assertions concerning the ready-to-hand. The whole difference between the ready-to-hand and the extant is that to be an extant being of a certain type is to be capable of effects that make no reference to potential ends. The capacities that define the extant are not instrumental, so what it is for such an assertion to be true is not statable in conditions of practical success or failure. Something is a hammer if it can be used in given situations to hammer with, and the function of hammering makes sense only in terms of ends to be accomplished. But for this thing to weigh two kilos has to do, among other things, with what would happen were it to be put into a balance—with what, ultimately, we would perceive were this done. The truth conditions here thus involve perception rather than practical success. The question we need to ask, then, is not how Heidegger thinks perceptual assertions concerning the extant are made true or false by practical success or failure; they aren't, and Heidegger doesn't think they are. Rather, our questions concern how and why Heidegger holds (1) that there can be no such perceptual truth conditions established for assertions concerning the extant except for and by beings who are Dasein, that only purposive beings of a social sort can understand assertions concerning the extant and thus believe that some thing is extant and has some natural determination; (2) that for a wide range of cases, which assertions concerning the extant are true will depend in some way upon what practical interests Dasein has, even though whether perceptual assertions concerning the extant are true or not is entirely independent of the interests of Dasein; and (3) that this in no way implies any vicious kind of relativism or undercuts the objectivity of truths concerning the extant.

In order to approach the issue of the relation between the functional meaning_h of assertions and their semantic content, we must remember that actual assertings of assertions are themselves used for some purpose, but that to be so used they must be active responses to some state of things in the world. To use a thing as a hammer presupposes both a current state of affairs which is altered in some way through the intervention of the hammering and that for the sake of which the intervention occurs; in the same way, to use an assertion is to do something for the sake of communicating but is also an action performed in and on some already constituted situation. Assertions, as socially constituted tools, are in fact limited severely,—in both their purpose and their initial conditions of use—by their routine function within a community. The dominant purpose for using an assertion is to communicate some interpretation of some entity. If we assume this purpose, it is appropriate to use this tool only in severely limited conditions, however, and it is possible to use such a tool only if its use within a society mostly follows upon those conditions. To see what sorts of conditions of use are relevant to assertions, and how these are related to the truth conditions fixed in and by the assertions concerning the extant, let us perform a little thought experiment.

Consider the case of someone using something as a hammer. He is engaged in building the frame of a house, which involves placing boards together in a certain way, striking nails with the instrument, and so on—all done in the extended context of engaging in activities which together amount to activity for building. What if this person in this context chooses, for an activity that for all the world looks like hammering the nail into the boards, an instrument that is altogether unsuitable for doing so—say, a piece of wet pasta. Upon failing to drive the nail, our carpenter looks annoyed and puzzled, lays down his noodle, picks up a more suitable tool, and proceeds to drive the nail. We would routinely conclude that the person had taken the pasta to be a hammer but had been mistaken; it wasn't one. His initial act, however, would still be a hammer interpretation: that is, the taking of something as a hammer.

Now, let's vary the story slightly. Instead of laying down the pasta upon failing to drive the nail, our carpenter turns to other presumptive hammering situations and continues to 'use' the pasta hammer as he goes through the motions of building a house. But of course, if he always uses the pasta to hammer with, it is very quickly going to become impossible to go on even trying to build the house. His other activities are no longer going to count as activities for building. Whatever this person is intending to do, it's not building houses, because in virtue of what we take to be the consistent and obvious failure of his 'hammering', we find it difficult to believe that he is interpreting the pasta as a hammer, and his activities no longer make sense as building.

Now, consider a final case. A person frequently picks up an actual hammer and goes through hammering motions with it but does so with no apparent relation to the situation in which he does so. He never uses boards or nails in his hammering; his hammering never successfully takes two things that are apart and fastens them together—indeed, it may break one thing into many. Once again we would say that whatever this person is doing, it's not hammering; and however he is interpreting this thing, it is not as a hammer.

The moral of these little stories is clear. Because to hammer is to engage in a certain functionally defined activity, it is to perform an action in a given circumstance so that a given end results. If a being consistently fails to achieve that end or even make progress—according to our lights—toward that end, or consistently fails to perform the activity in the correct circumstances (and thus also consistently fails to achieve the end) and performs it in other, inappropriate circumstances, then that being no longer counts as even attempting to perform that type of activity. If someone tries to hammer once with a noodle, he is indeed taking the noodle as a hammer; the action is a hammer interpretation, albeit false (unsuccessful). If someone hammers with a hammer once in an unsuitable set of circumstances, then he is still hammering, albeit unsuitably, and interpreting the instrument as a hammer. But if he consistently 'hammers' in inappropriate conditions, then he no longer counts as interpreting the thing as a hammer or attempting to hammer at all.

The inverse of these results also holds. What distinguishes the conditions under which it is correct or appropriate to hammer? First, those conditions are conditions relative to an end to be realized. If one wants to build, then it is appropriate to hammer in this circumstance, and this, and this. If the class of hammering activities is the group of activities performed in a functionally defined situation to achieve a functionally defined end, it is equally true that the situations that call for hammering are just those that can be transformed so as to achieve a functionally defined end through the intervention of the activity of hammering. All the elements—the already given situation, the action performed, and the end to be accomplished—must be so related that the act is performed on a situation so as to reach the end if the act is to have the meaning which it has, if the end is to be the end of the act, and if the situation is to be one in which it is appropriate to perform the act. A localized failure of any one of these elements to be adjusted to the others allows the act to count as continuing to be performed for the sake of the end, although unsuccessfully; the act is still performed in order to reach the end. But a massive and global alteration of this adjustment, through the consistent inappropriateness of the act to the situation and the end, destroys both the sense in which the act is performed in a situation in order to realize the end and the sense in which the situation is one that (given the end) calls for the act, because in this case nothing is done for the sake of the end.

Let us consider how all of this applies to the purposive activity of making assertions in order to communicate interpretations of the extant. If someone wants to communicate the interpretation that 'this thing is red', she makes use of a tool, the assertion type 'this is red'. There can be a variety of reasons why she wants to communicate this interpretation, (which we will consider in a moment), but since doing so is a purposive activity, there must be some reason why she does so. But, again as a purposive activity, the act of using an assertion to communicate an interpretation is an act performed in a set of initial conditions, the situation that 'calls for' the asserting. What those conditions are will vary as a function of the ultimate end of the asserting. It would, in general, be inappropriate to say to one's driver 'it is red' concerning some car that is about to strike a car in which one is traveling—even if the other car *is* red. It probably is appropriate to say of some car 'it is red' to a person one is for some reason trying to deceive, even if the car is green and only if it is not red. Nevertheless, as socially defined tools, assertions have standard functions and thus standard initial conditions of use, which are defined in terms of that standard function. And in just the same way that a hammer is no longer being used as a hammer if it is consistently used in unsuitable contexts, an assertion ceases to be used as the assertion it is socially if it is consistently used in unsuitable contexts. Someone who uses 'this is red' completely inappropriately ceases to assert 'this is red'. He doesn't know the meaning of the words, that is, his failure in use is correlated with an ascribed failure to know which conditions are picked out by the assertion. As standardized tools, assertions must be used for some privileged purpose within a society, a purpose relative to which initial conditions of use are determined. It is these normative conditions of use, fixed in relation to a preferred end, that fix and identify which assertion an assertion is and, giving it an identity, permit it to be used in other situations in order to achieve other ends. These other ends, such as deception, trade on and presuppose the standard function and thus the standard conditions of use.

What is the standard use of assertions, and what sort of initial conditions of use does this standard function fix? Because assertions are primarily tools for communicating interpretations, they are fundamentally useful for inferring. If I say that 'this is red', then you are also entitled to assert that 'this is red': that is, to interpret this thing as red. To say that the assertion communicates the interpretation is to say that the asserting allows you to come into the very same relation to the thing that I am in, to interpret it as I do. In the interpretation that the assertion expresses, I take the thing as something definite. "Asserting is a way of being towards the thing itself that is."[15] The assertion is primarily a tool for allowing you to enter into that same interpretive relation with the thing. "Assertion communicates entities in the 'how' of their uncoveredness. . . . This uncoveredness is preserved in what is expressed. What is expressed, becomes, as it were, something ready-to-hand within-the-world which can be taken up and spoken again."[16] For you to interpret an asserting as an assertion that communicates an interpretation of a given type is just for you to adopt or take over that very same interpretation which you take the assertion to be communicating, on the basis of that asserting. For you to interpret it as a given assertion is for you to infer an interpretation of some thing in the world from that assertion, and that you come to do so is what the assertion is primarily useful for.

What sort of initial conditions of use are fixed relative to this primary communicative function of assertions, this function in immediate inference? On one level the answer to this question is clearly just the truth conditions for the assertion. An assertion can be used for communicating interpretations—that is, ways of taking a thing—only insofar as it is primarily used when the thing has the determination the assertion takes it as having. If the 'assertion' is used randomly, relative to that determination, it would be impossible to use it to infer the presence of that determination; it would no longer be the assertion of that determination of that thing. The situation would be analogous to a 'hammer' that is used randomly, relative to its initial conditions of use. Just as the 'hammer' is no longer being used as a hammer, and the act of use is no longer an act of using the thing as a hammer, the 'asserting' of the assertion would no longer count as a use of that assertion. In the case where what is asserted is a ready-to-hand determination, the assertion communicates that interpretation only if it is mostly used in situations in which the thing pointed out as useful within a purposive context can actually be used within that context in the way indicated. When the assertion asserts, for example, 'this is red', it can be used to communicate this interpretation only if it is mostly used in communication when *this is red:* that is, in

15. *B.T.,* p. 260/218.
16. *B.T.,* p. 266/224.

situations when the thing can be appropriately interpreted as red. The initial conditions of appropriate use of an assertion and the truth conditions expressed by the assertion are identical. If they were not, the assertion would cease to be usable in communicating this interpretation; it would lack any communicative function. In having a functional utility, in having the meaning$_h$ that it does, an assertion also specifies the conditions under which it is true: that is, its meaning$_i$. If it weren't mostly used, when used to communicate, in situations in which it is true, it would have no meaning at all; in lacking function, it would lack semantic content.

As we have repeatedly stressed, if what is communicated is an assertion that concerns the ready-to-hand, what the assertion communicates is that if this thing were used appropriately in some specified equipmental context, given some initial conditions, then it could be used successfully to accomplish the end implied in the determination or predicate of the assertion. The initial conditions of standard use for the assertion and the truth conditions specified by the assertion are both defined relative to some practical end, context, and understanding; both the use and the meaning of the assertion are possible only in light of that practical context. How do matters stand, then, in regard to assertions concerning the extant? That is, what is it for the assertions to be true and the initial conditions of their appropriate communicative use to be met?

Heidegger says that the extant is the specialty of assertion. What this means is that the use and meaning of the assertions concerning the extant are fixed only relative to the communicative act of assertion itself. For assertions concerning perceptual determinations, something is red, for example, if within some community the thing is such that most members of the community would say it was red were they in the appropriate perceptual circumstances relative to that thing. That is, what it is for the thing to be red, for the assertion 'it is red' to be true, is that the members of the community would agree that it was red were they in the same perceptual situation as the speaker. In this case, the purposive context in which the initial conditions of proper use of the assertion, and thus the truth conditions of the assertion, are made determinate is the communally purposive situation of language use itself. If the assertion can be meaningful only if it is used to communicate assertions only when mostly true, it is also the case that what it is for the assertion to be true is that the members of a community agree that, in this situation, it is appropriate to use this assertion in order to communicate. The purposive context of communication within a language group thus provides the context in which an assertion concerning the extant can pick out initial conditions of correct use and truth conditions for what the assertion says. Outside such a social context of agreement on ascription within a community, it is impossible for any assertion concerning the extant to pick out any determination at all, even though the determinations thus picked out are not themselves ready-to-hand determinations. Perceptual truth conditions for assertions can be fixed only for and by the linguistic practices of some group of Dasein. This is the first claim that we ascribed above to Heidegger.[17]

But why would any group of Dasein be at all interested in using assertions to communicate such perceptual conditions, such interpretations of extant determinations? After all, the fact that these things are such as to have extant determinations, that they are such that they can be responded to appropriately with a given assertion within a community, involves no direct practical serviceability. And, for Heidegger, Dasein always acts for a purpose. What is the purpose of assertions concerning the extant? To answer this question, we need to make a slight detour and consider our ability to talk intelligibly about nonperceivable extant entities and nonperceivable determinations of beings. Remember, assertions are instruments that are useful in drawing inferences. It is in general not only possible to infer another asserting of the same assertion from a single asserting of it but also to infer different assertions from it. If we have 'reason to believe' (that is, initial conditions for proper use of the assertion), for example, that x is red, either through perceptual means or because such a belief has been suggested by a previous assertion, we also have the initial conditions for the assertion 'x is colored'. The acceptance of one or more assertions as being used with the proper communicative function can itself be a sufficient initial condition for an appropriate

---

17. Notice, as assertions concerning the extant concern what would happen were the thing perceived in a variety of different situations (i.e., involve a range of counterfactuals), the judgment could still ultimately turn out to be false (i.e., in other circumstances we could all see that the thing only appeared to be red) even though it had the meaning 'x is red'. What is necessary here for the assertion to be meaningful is that in these circumstances it is appropriate to assert or assent to 'x is red'. The 'seems' locution undoubtedly has its origin in this gap between the grounds on which it is proper to assert a perceptual assertion concerning the extant and the grounds on which the assertion can be seen to be true. The gap in turn derives from the fact that what is intended in a perception is an extant being, which as extant continues over time and thus is in principle available for multiple perceptions, while the assertions expressing that some thing has a given perceptual determination may be used properly on the basis of a very limited range of the possible perceptual encounterings of the thing.

asserting of some other assertion. This can occur even when there are no possible perceivable conditions for correct asserting of some assertion, where the assertion itself picks out no perceivable truth conditions. In these cases, the meaning$_i$ of such assertions is fixed entirely by the practical role they fill in chains of inferences among assertions, which assertions or groups of assertions it can properly be inferred from, and which assertions it can properly be used—together with which other assertions—to infer. Indeed, since most of the assertions we use concerning the extant (as well as most of our assertions concerning other ontological types, such as works of art and even Dasein) lack definite perceptual conditions of proper use (and thus perceptual truth conditions), most assertions have their meanings fixed in this way.

'Inference' here must be conceived broadly. Deductive inference is the strongest case and the paradigm. In true logical inference the presence of initial conditions of proper use (that is, truth) of an assertion or assertions guarantees the truth of the assertions that are based upon them. But in many other cases the inferential chains are such that we are generally entitled to assert communicatively some assertion, given acceptance of some other assertions (on whatever grounds), even though, given the character of the inferences involved, those conditions provide only a provisional license to assert the assertion communicatively. The license can be removed, even if all the other conditions continue to obtain, if new circumstances present themselves. This would seem to be the situation with induction, for example.[18]

When it is proper to draw an inference, as when it is proper in general to use an assertion with a communicating function, is always decided by the normal and standardizing practice within a society. It is only the standardized use of assertions as tools for communication among a group of Dasein that gives them any meaning$_i$ at all, because it is only so that initial conditions of their appropriate use can be established. This may seem to imply that the structure and links of the chains of those assertions which have neither direct perceptual nor instrumental initial conditions of use or truth conditions are entirely matters of convention, having no relation to the world. After all, the conditions of use of such assertions are

18. That some group of assertings have a 'routine' or 'standardized' use need not mean that they are habitually used in some way. The assertion may be standardized with a potential usability, even if it has never been used in that way, in virtue of certain relations between its internal structure (the words that compose it) and the internal structure of assertions that are habitually used in some way.

purely linguistic. Their only initial conditions of use are that other assertions have been used and that practice within this society prescribes that whenever the first assertion is used, the second can also be used. To infer this, however, would be to confuse meaning$_i$ and truth. The conditions under which it is appropriate to use such assertions are proximately entirely linguistic, and the meanings of these assertions are fixed by intralinguistic conditions. But whether in any particular case the assertion is true depends on whether the use of that assertion was in fact appropriate in that case, which in turn depends upon whether some other assertions were used appropriately. The appropriateness of the use of any given assertion finally depends on two sorts of factors. It depends on whether or not the nonlinguistic conditions for appropriate use of some group of assertions are in fact met, and whether the practices governing inference are in fact *possible*.

Chains of inference governing assertion connection are semantically anchored in two places. First, at some point in the series one comes to assertions whose initial conditions of use are instrumental or perceptual conditions, conditions in the world which, if met, sanction the use of particular assertions. It is always the case that in order to be meaningful, most of the communicative uses of these assertions must be in situations in which they are true. The second anchoring can occur in either of two ways. The practices governing the inference of assertions may eventually generate some assertion which itself is about the perceivable extant, making it possible to check whether these perceptual conditions of appropriate use are really present; if they aren't, it becomes necessary, as they say, to revise the theory, either by reviewing the initial 'evidence' on which the inference was based or by revising the practices governing the appropriate use of assertions. Or, the inferential chains may eventually result in some assertion concerning the ready-to-hand capacities of things, assertions that have initial conditions of use tied to some practical context of purposes; in other words, assertions concerning the extant can have practical implications. In that case we can check the assertions against their standard initial conditions of use: we do what the assertion says can be done and see if it works. If it does, well and good. If it doesn't, it's time to change practices again.[19]

19. This sort of holistic view of theoretical assertions has been worked out in far more detail by W. V. O. Quine and others than it ever was by Heidegger. Cf. W. V. O. Quine, *Word and Object* (Cambridge: MIT Press, 1960). As Robert Brandom points out, however (see n. 20), it is implied by much of what Heidegger has to say.

But now we also know what, according to the early Heidegger, this whole elaborate linguistic construction dealing with the extant is for. Once the system is established, it is possible for Dasein to develop an interest in the extant as such. In that case the point of the system is to generate new, unexpected, and previously unobserved determinations of the extant. It is even possible to use language in order to come to an interpretation of language, odd as that may seem. Clearly, however, the main point of using language about the extant is to generate successful new ways of coping practically with things in order to attain practical ends. In this, linguistic practice has been wildly successful. As Robert Brandom puts this Heideggerean point: "Assertions about the present at hand [= extant] can be practically relevant. We can use information about the merely present at hand properties of things, such as the heaviness of the hammer. Without the possibility of language exits through non-assertional performances, theoretical or intralinguistic inference would lose much or all of its point."[20]

If this is the case, if making assertions about the extant is ultimately done in order to realize practical ends, then which perceptual conditions it is important to pick out will vary as a function of the ends to be ultimately served by the talk; and which of the possible practices for generating inferential chains of assertions ought to be adopted within a society will also vary as a function of those ends. Not every conceivable perceptual determination of the extant is picked out by the proper use of assertions in any language. Which determinations are so exalted is some rough function of what the group using the language has a practical interest in: remember the famous nineteen flavors of white among Eskimos.

Perhaps more interesting, however, are the implications of this view of assertion for the status of theoretical language.[21] As we have seen, not

20. Robert Brandom, "Heidegger's Categories in *Being and Time,*" Monist 66 (July 1983), 406. In general, the interpretation of Heidegger on assertion that I offer here is similar to the one suggested by Brandom in this excellent article but differs in several crucial respects. Brandom holds that, for Heidegger, all assertions concern the extant, that to respond to a situation linguistically is to respond to the extant as such. In light of what Heidegger says (e.g., at *B.P.,* p. 211), this is clearly false. Brandom also interprets 'interpretation' rather differently than I have done, and this leads him to a somewhat different interpretation of the relation between the communicative function of assertions and their semantic content.

21. In fact, as many have pointed out, the perceptual-theoretical distinction as applied to language is artificial. Even 'perceptual' assertions concerning the extant usually have linguistic as well as nonlinguistic initial conditions of appropriate use. I have presented the two classes as sharply distinct solely for the sake of simplifying the exposition.

every set of linguistic practices for relating assertions is practically possible. Some ways of relating assertions will never yield any practical fruit. Others would lead to assertions that would need to be rejected, on perceptual grounds, within the speech group. And if some group of Dasein were to use such contradictory practices, we would be hard put to find any initial conditions of proper use at all in what they say; that is, what they do would cease to be linguistic communication at all. But having said this, we still find a wide field of possible variations. For example, a 'discipline' can countenance the existence of a class of extant entities that some other discipline, which claims to give a complete list of such entities, fails to acknowledge. If the ultimate constraints on systems of inferential assertions are in some sense practical, then it is a practical matter whether we need to adopt just one of them. That is, the unity of science becomes a practical suggestion rather than a methodological requirement. Which possible systems of practices of inference are adopted, and thus which theoretical assertions are taken as true, will vary as some complex function of the interests of the Dasein community that uses those assertions. This is the second Heideggerian position we stressed above. Whether it counts as a 'relativism' in any vicious sense, we will consider in the second half of this book.

At this point, we need to know more about Heidegger's views of truth and being and how they relate to the truth of assertions.

The Truth of Assertions and the Truth (Unveiling) of Beings

Throughout his work, Heidegger offers an idiosyncratic definition of truth, which is associated with a curious argument in regard to the 'primordial' character of truth. He tells us that "being-true ('truth') means being-uncovering."[22] He tries to support this definition with an appeal to the etymology of the Greek *aletheia* (truth), which is a privative of *lethe* (whose root means 'hidden'); therefore, it is the not-hidden, the uncovered. But beyond this, in a wide variety of texts, Heidegger offers an argument meant both to develop this notion of truth and to relate the truth of assertions with the practical understanding inherent in being in the world.

In Heidegger's later work, *aletheia* becomes a crucial term, especially in relation to the phrase 'the truth of being'. Part II of this book is largely

22. *B.T.*, p. 262/219.

concerned with interpreting this phrase and the notion of 'truth' associated with it. At this point we introduce *aletheia* merely to aid in the comprehension of the early Heidegger's view of language and assertions concerning beings.

Every assertion is a determination of something as something; it both communicates such an interpretation and itself counts as an instance of such an interpretation. As such, an assertion is a way of grasping some thing, and an asserting is a way of actually intending the thing or an interpretation of it as determined. Every assertion is a tool for communicating. What it communicates is its meaning$_i$, a determinate way of interpreting some other entity. The assertion itself has the function of communicating its meaning$_i$ and thus has the functional meaning$_h$ of being that kind of tool. Assertion as interpretation is a specific manner in which we intend things. "Asserting is a way of being towards the thing itself that is."[23] "An assertion lets that which is talked about in it be seen in the way of determinative predication; assertion makes that which is talked about accessible."[24] Insofar as an assertion is understood—that is, insofar as it is taken as having the meaning it has—we take the thing indicated in the assertion as it is determined to be by the assertion. To understand an assertion is to come to interpret the thing in the very way in which the assertion says it can be interpreted. "In understanding the communicated assertion, the hearer is not directed towards words or meanings or the psychical processes of the communicator. Instead, so far as the assertion is on its own part in keeping with the thing, the hearer is directed from the very beginning in his understanding of it toward the entity talked about, which should then come to meet him in its specific being."[25]

If this is what an assertion is, then what is it to say of some assertion that it is true? The obvious and traditional thing to say is that an assertion is true if and only if what it takes the thing as is a way in which the thing is. If a statement asserts that a thing is red, it takes that thing as red. It is true if what it says of the thing, what it takes it as, corresponds with the way the thing is: that is, if it really is red. This is the origin of the traditional correspondence theory of truth. Although early Heidegger doesn't consider this view ultimately adequate as a complete theory of

23. *B.T.*, p. 260/218.
24. *B.P.*, p. 215/306.
25. *B.P.*, p. 215/306.

truth, he does hold that, properly understood, it is perfectly acceptable as a theory of propositional truth. 'Correspondence' can't mean a similarity between two extant things, however; an assertion isn't at all like a coin, for example. Rather, what corresponds in a true assertion is the way the thing is taken or presented in and by the assertion with the way the thing is. "The assertion regarding the coin relates 'itself' to this thing in that it presents it and says of the presented how, according to the particular perspective that grounds it, it is disposed. What is stated by the presentative statement is said of the presented thing in just such manner as that thing, as presented, is."[26] But if an assertion is an interpretation of some thing which presents the thing to us as having a determinate character, then for the assertion to be true is for the assertion to present or reveal the thing as it is.

Heidegger emphasizes the active, intentionally directive, and revealing character and function of assertion. Assertions show us how things are to be taken, and they are true if they uncover a thing as it is. To be true, an assertion must uncover a thing as it is; and the being-true, or truth, of an assertion is its successful performance of its uncovering function, its 'being-uncovering'. "To say that an assertion 'is true' signifies that it uncovers the entity as it is in itself. Such an assertion asserts, points out, 'lets' the entity be seen in its uncoveredness. The being-true (truth) of the assertion must be understood as being-uncovering."[27] "Exhibition has the character of unveiling, and it can be determination and communication only because it unveils. This unveiling, which is the basic function of assertion, constitutes the character traditionally designated as being-true."[28]

Understood in this way, assertions aren't the only things that are true. If truth is essentially the activity of revealing something as being of a certain character, as having some determination, then nonlinguistic actions can and do also perform this activity. When, for example, one uses a thing successfully as a hammer, one is revealing it to be a hammer. Practical acts of interpretation, as well as assertions, can be true. For such an act to be true it must succeed in using the thing as the thing it is attempting to use it as. If the act succeeds, the thing is revealed to be as it has been taken to be in the practical activity.

---

26. *O.E.T.*, pp. 123/183–184. Translation modified.
27. *B.T.*, p. 261/218.
28. *B.P.*, p. 215/306.

It is immediately obvious from this that, and why, there can be no truth in this sense without beings who are Dasein, or at least beings who act in a purposive manner. To reveal something is to reveal it as something; the successful practical act reveals the thing with, as Heidegger calls it, the hermeneutic 'as'.[29] It is the success of the act as the kind of act it is, however, that uncovers the thing as having the ready-to-hand determination (as Heidegger puts it, the hammering reveals the hammer), and an act is the kind of act it is only in terms of the practical end it serves; acts are fundamentally functional. So no thing can be revealed as some thing, there can be no hermeneutic truth, apart from the structured purposive activity of Dasein. It is also clear that in this case the truth—the uncovering performed by the act, and through it, what the thing revealed is revealed to be, the truth concerning it—is both completely objective and also relative to the end and context of activity. The truth is relative to the end and context in that only as functioning within a particular practical context and for a particular practical end can the act be as it is, and the successful performance of the act can reveal the thing as functional for the act, as having the ready-to-hand determination it has. Yet the capacity the thing is revealed as having really does belong to the thing itself. Because of what it is, the hammer is capable of being used in hammering. In no way is this capacity a product of the practical interpretation. All that the purposiveness does is provide the context in which things can show themselves as they are and, in doing this, provide the terms in which the capacities of the thing can be revealed in a determinate way.

But how is the practical truth contained in the practical activity of unveiling things related to the kind of unveiling that happens when an assertion is true? Heidegger holds that only because and insofar as things are revealed practically can they be revealed linguistically. Practical truth is a necessary condition for semantic truth, but not vice versa. This means that the being of Dasein as purposive is for Heidegger a necessary condition for all truth. As such, he considers it suitable to say that the being-purposive of Dasein is that which is true in the most basic sense. "Being-true as being-uncovering, is a way of being for Dasein. What makes this very uncovering possible must necessarily be called 'true' in a still more primordial sense."[30] This claim, that the being of Dasein is

29. *B.T.*, p. 201/158.
30. *B.T.*, p. 263/220.

'true' in a more original sense than assertions can be true, is examined in detail further on. For now, it is sufficient to comprehend why and how early Heidegger thinks that Dasein is necessary for truth in the usual sense.

But how does Heidegger support his contention that propositional truth is dependent on practical truth? It is at this point that he interpolates what I have called his 'curious' argument.[31] The prototype for this argument, in *Being and Time,* is stated rather cautiously. (In succeeding years, Heidegger makes increasingly extreme use of it.) In *Being and Time* he associates the truth of an assertion with knowledge, which at first seems fair enough. He then goes on to ask about "the kind of being which belongs to knowledge itself"; that is, he questions what it is to know. In the course of the analysis he asks, "When does truth become phenomenally explicit in knowledge itself?" That is, what is it to come to know the truth of an assertion, or that the assertion is true? Unsurprisingly, he finds an answer in confirmation or demonstration: "It [truth] does so when such knowing demonstrates itself as true. By demonstrating itself it is assured of its truth."[32] Demonstration of the truth of the assertion occurs only when there is evidence of that truth, when the thing shows itself to be as the assertion says it is. "What is to be demonstrated is solely the being-uncovered of the entity itself—that entity in the 'how' of its uncoveredness. This uncoveredness is confirmed when that which is put forward in the assertion (namely the entity itself) shows itself as that very same thing. 'Confirmation' signifies the entity's showing itself in its self-sameness. The confirmation is accomplished on the basis of the entity's showing itself."[33] There is thus confirmation or verification of the truth of an assertion only when a thing shows itself to be as it is said to be in the assertion.

In *Being and Time* this argument fragment is used to support the definition of truth as uncovering. The strategy is to discover what it is 'to be true' by uncovering the conditions under which we would know that an assertion is true. That is, Heidegger hopes to define truth by examining the verification conditions for the assertion 'assertion *x* is true'. We have knowledge concerning the truth of an assertion, of course, only insofar as we have evidence in regard to its truth. But the evidence for the

31. The argument appears in slightly different forms in at least *B.T., B.P., M.F.L., The Essence of Reasons,* "What Is Metaphysics?" *O.E.T.,* and "Origin of the Work of Art."
32. *B.T.,* p. 260/217.
33. *B.T.,* p. 261/218.

truth of an assertion is identical with the evidence for what that assertion says about some thing. To know the truth of an assertion is just to know that the thing is as the assertion says it is, to know the thing as such and such. What we know when we know is convertibly that some thing has some property or that some assertion is true; the evidence for one is always and equally evidence for the other. The evidence for the two can in principle be identical if and only if what it is for the assertion to be true is just for the thing to be as it is said to be. Assertions are tools for communicating interpretations: we know them to be true, we have evidence for their being true, whenever we have evidence for the thing being as the assertion says it is; so a true assertion is an interpretation that is and communicates a taking of a thing as it is. But an interpretation that takes a thing as it is is a revealing or uncovering of what that thing is capable of, a revealing of what it is. Just as successfully using a tool as a hammer 'reveals' the thing as capable of being used in hammering, a true linguistic interpretation, an assertion, reveals what a thing is capable of and thus what it is. The being-true of an assertion thus amounts to the being-uncovering of the assertion in the sense that the assertion successfully reveals how the thing it refers to is. Being true is being uncovering.

The major presupposition of this argument is clearly just the standard verificationist principle "that the meaning of a sentence turns purely on what would count as evidence for its truth,"[34] but its use here is distinctive in two respects. First, following Husserl, Heidegger invokes this principle in the objective case: what it means to be x turns solely on the conditions that must obtain if we are to know (that is, have evidence for the truth) that something is an x. Second, Heidegger applies the principle reflexively in order to determine what it is for a sentence to be true; that is, he assumes a kind of verificationism in regard to meaning in order to ground a variety of disquotationalism (that is, the doctrine that the sentence "'x is y' is true" is true just in case x is y) in regard to truth. Whether this procedure is acceptable stands or falls wholly on whether or not verificationism is acceptable, and the argument in this form presents no special problems. (The entire question of the status and role of Heidegger's verificationism is considered in the next chapter.)

After *Being and Time,* however, Heidegger appears to use this argu-

---

34. W. V. O. Quine, "Epistemology Naturalized," in *Ontological Relativity and Other Essays* (New York: Columbia University Press, 1969), p. 80.

ment in an altogether different way in order to ground an entirely different proposition, the proposition that "an assertion can finally be true, be adequate in propositional content to that about which the statement is made, only because the being it speaks of is already in some way disclosed."[35] This seems to suggest that in order for assertions to be true in the appropriate sense of correspondence, it is necessary that what the assertion speaks about must already be revealed as having the property in question. The argument in this new guise seems to run as follows: (1) the truth of assertions consists in the revelation of things as they are; (2) in order for us to know that an assertion is true, we must have some 'standard' or 'measure' against which we check to see whether the thing really has the determination the assertion says it has—that is, we need evidence for the assertion's truth; thus, (3) unless things are revealed to us in some way other than in the assertion, the assertion can't be true. The argument is then extended to conclude that (4) this other way of un-covering things is our practical dealings with things, so a practical under-standing-how is necessary for truly understanding that some particular thing has some property. "If truth means correspondence, adequation to beings, then this assertion measuring itself on beings is evidently founded on the fact that, in our intercourse with beings, we have already, as it were, come to an understanding with beings; beings not ourselves, with which we in some way deal, are disclosed to us. So an assertion can finally be true, be adequate in propositional content to that about which the assertion is made, only because the being it speaks of is already in some way disclosed. That is, an assertion about x is only true because our dealing with that x has already a certain kind of truth."[36] "An assertion is invested with its correctness by the openness of comportment; for only through the latter can what is opened up really become the standard for the presentative correspondence."[37] "The being-true of assertions is not primary but is founded upon the disclosure in our being-by-things, in our having to do with things."[38]

What is odd about the argument in this form is just that it is such a bad one. The fact that I can only *know* an assertion to be true if I have evidence for it (which is useful in determining what it *is* for an assertion to be true), and thus that the thing it refers to must be given to me in some other way

35. *M.F.L.*, p. 127/158.
36. *M.F.L.*, pp. 126–127/158. Translation modified.
37. *O.E.T.*, p. 124/185. Translation modified.
38. *M.F.L.*, p. 128/160. Translation modified.

than in the assertion if I am to know the assertion's truth, indicates nothing in regard to whether I must at present have that evidence in order for an assertion to be true. After all, an assertion can in fact be true even if no one now knows it to be true, and even if there is currently no evidence for its truth and thus no disclosure that currently gives the thing as it is indicated to be. Even extreme verificationists must admit this much. The problem is that for an assertion to be true is for it to reveal a thing as it is, and the thing is as the evidence would reveal it to be were that evidence available to us, not what we currently have evidence of its being. The 'argument from the conditions for confirmation', which Heidegger presents in *Being and Time* and later adapts to argue that the truth of assertions is founded on a practical uncovering of the specific thing the assertion is about, can't be used to show that for an assertion to be true we need current evidence of its truth. The third planet circling Alpha Centauri can be verdant, even though no evidence is currently available in regard to it, and even if the only way we can intend that planet is linguistically, through having a propositional attitude toward some propositional content.[39]

The ultimate point that Heidegger tries to make in this regard concerns the relation between the truth of assertions and a more 'primordial' truth, the uncovering of which is accomplished in and through Dasein's being in the world. As we have seen, he wants to maintain that without Dasein's being in the world and operating in a context of purposeful action, assertions couldn't be true. Propositional truth, for Heidegger, needs the disclosiveness of practical Dasein. "Newton's laws, the principle of contradiction, any truth whatever—these are true only as long as Dasein is. Before there was any Dasein, there was no truth; nor will there be any after Dasein is no more."[40] To maintain this position, however,

---

39. Heidegger sometimes puts his point by saying that we must intend a thing in some other way than linguistically if we are to be able to make an assertion concerning it. See, e.g., *B.P.*, p. 208/296: "In order for something to be a possible about-which for an assertion, it must already be somehow given for the assertion as unveiled and accessible. . . . Some being must be antecedently given as unveiled in order to serve as the possible about-which of an assertion." This claim seems to me plainly false. We can refer to entities that are intended in no other way than linguistically, and we can make intelligible assertions concerning them. The later Heidegger gives up this claim that language has a strictly secondary unveiling status, for example in *L.H.* and the various essays of *On the Way to Language*. Unfortunately, in those contexts he emphasizes the role of the word almost to the exclusion of the assertion. As Tugendhat (see note 1, Chap. 2), among others, has emphasized, this is another error.

40. *B.T.*, p. 269/226.

does not require the extreme view that Heidegger attempts to support using the argument from the conditions for confirmation. That argument as he sometimes uses it, suggesting that for any given assertion to be true we must already have available to us the particular evidence that confirms it, goes in the face of the way in which we use the word 'true' in relation to propositions.

To show that there is no truth of propositions without Dasein's being in the world, one need only posit (1) that propositional truth as such demands the *possibility* of evidence and (2) that the possibility of evidence demands Dasein. In order for 'the third planet circling Alpha Centauri is verdant' to be true, it would at least be necessary that there could be evidence in support of that proposition, but that evidence need not be currently available to us. And, for there to be the possibility of such evidence, it would at least be necessary that there be the situation in which alone there can be evidence, the situation in which things are given or presented as having the determination the assertion says they have. Such a presentational situation would be a transcendental condition for there being anything like evidence at all, and thus for the possibility of evidence in regard to Alpha Centauri. The thing itself, the planet of Alpha Centauri, need not be given to us. But—this view holds—for the assertion to be true, *things* must be given, and given as determined; and we must know what in particular would need to be given were this assertion to be true (that is, the assertion must have some identifiable meaning). The final conclusion, that truth of assertions demands the practical uncovering of Dasein, would then follow if it could be shown that there is no evidence, in the sense of an actual presentational giving of a being as determined, without Dasein's practical understanding.

This, I suggest, is the appropriate structure with which to interpret Heidegger's argument from the conditions for confirmation. In the many places in which he discusses these issues, Heidegger rarely asserts that a proposition concerning a thing can't be true unless we are already presented with the evidence for its truth. Rather, he typically maintains that no assertion can be true unless we already are with and by things, beings, or being as such, through having practical dealings with things. But how can one argue for this more moderate form of pragmatic verificationism? In fact, Heidegger does have an argument strategy available to him.

The first part of this argument, that there can be no truth without the possibility of evidence, follows directly from the definition of truth embodied in the argument from the conditions for confirmation. If for an assertion to be true it is necessary that, were we in a certain situation vis-à-vis the thing spoken of in the assertion, we would be given evidence that confirms the assertion, then unless there is the possibility of evidence as such and at least the logical possibility of being in the situation specified, there could be no truth. Thus, anything that is a transcendental condition for the possibility of evidence is a necessary condition for the possible truth of assertions. But how can one argue that the practical activity of Dasein is a necessary condition for the possibility of evidence as such?

The obvious counterexample to this claim is the evidence provided in and through perception, which since antiquity has been considered the paradigm of evidence as such and independent of any actual purposes on Dasein's part or even the possibility of Dasein's acting in a purposive manner. The arguments of the last two sections, however, have given us reason to believe that this traditional dogma of the independence of the possibility of perceptual evidence from all praxis has been misconceived. According to those arguments, a mere content of sensuous input or even a difference between sensory inputs, while necessary for perceptual evidence (that is, the actual perceptual presentation of something as something), is insufficient for it. In addition, if one is to have a perception, a sensory giving of some thing as having extant determinations, it is also necessary that the thing be given to one as such that, were one wishing to communicate, these sensory conditions would be recognized as initial conditions for appropriately making some definite assertion within some Dasein speech community. For us to perceive that some thing is red, it is necessary that the thing be given to us as such that in these circumstances it would be appropriate to assert or assent to 'this is red' if we intended to communicate. For Heidegger, beings without the ability to use language to communicate cannot perceive something as something, even if they are capable of discriminatory behavior in the face of different stimuli. Such beings are thus also incapable of having perceptual evidence. But no beings can use language to communicate unless they (1) do things for purposes and (2) do so within a shared social with-world. Beings who meet conditions (1) and (2) are Dasein. So the socially purposive, practical activity of Dasein is a necessary condition for the possibility of perceptual evidence, as it is for any conceivable evidence that is not an immediate instance of a successful use of some thing for some practical purpose. That is, the practical activity of Dasein is a necessary condition for evidence as such. And, given the foregoing argument, it follows that no assertion can be true apart from the possibility of the practical activity of Dasein.

It is for this reason that Heidegger says, "Truth exists only when the Dasein exists."[41] If there were no Dasein, no purposive activity, no assertion could be true or false. It even follows—given that truth is an uncovering in the sense of a revealing of a thing as it is—that if an assertion is true, then there must in principle be some evidence that would show it to be true. It does not follow from any of this, however, that for an assertion to be true the being it refers to must already be uncovered in some way other than by the assertion. Indeed, given the holistic character of inferential language use, there is no necessity that we can even intend an entity about which we are making a true assertion in any other way than linguistically. All that is necessary for an assertion to be true is that there be some activity (defined by act, circumstances, end, and so on) that is communicated and that could be successfully or unsuccessfully performed; that the practical context of that activity be rich enough to distinguish between success and failure; and that were this action in fact performed, it would lead to success. This last condition simply amounts to some thing in fact having some determination and there being some way, in principle, for our coming to know that it does.

Nor does it follow that what the extant is revealed to be in the perceptual evidence is not fully objective. The thing given in perceptual evidence is revealed as actually having a particular capacity, the capacity to effect changes in us and other beings, which are extant. The context of Dasein's practical linguistic activity is necessary to fix the definite conditions that must be fulfilled if a thing is to have a particular determination. The practical activity of Dasein fixes what it is to be an x, not whether some thing is an x. The projects and purposes of a linguistic community fix meaning, not whether a being is. "World-entry and its occurrence is the presupposition not for extant things to become first extant and enter into that which manifests itself as its extantness which we understand as such."[42] "Intraworldliness does not belong to the essence of extant things as such, but it is only the transcendental condition, in the primordial sense, for the possibility of extant things being able to emerge as they are."[43]

41. *B.P.*, p. 223/318.
42. *M.F.L.*, p. 195/251.
43. *M.F.L.*, p. 194/251.

But, to speak again with Heidegger, what is the status of the meaning of *being*? What is the status of what it is to be and to be of a definite ontological type at all? Is 'to be' something that varies as a function of the purposes of a community of Dasein, and would there be any being (or being such and such) if there were no Dasein? The capacities of things (the determinable), which we determine as such and such in and through our practical activities, are independent of those activities, but those determinations themselves are not independent. Is the being of things independent in this way of practices, or not? For example, would things have natural determinations at all, regardless of which particular ones they can be determined as having, and would there be extant beings at all if there were no Dasein?

Well, yes and no, and which it is depends upon what we mean by things 'having determinations' and things 'being' at all. On the one hand, which determinations extant beings have, among any possible set of determinations (a set made definite by the practices of Dasein), is entirely independent of Dasein and its purposes and practices. On the other hand, that there is a determining of them—their 'being determined'—needs Dasein, as does their being determined as extant. "If . . . one lets this word [reality] have its traditional signification, then it stands for being in the sense of the pure extantness of things. . . . No matter how this being of 'Nature' may be interpreted, all the modes of being of entities within-the-world are founded ontologically upon the worldhood of the world, and accordingly upon . . . being-in the-world. . . . In the order of the ways in which things are connected in their ontological foundations and in the order of any possible categorial and existential demonstration, reality is referred back to the phenomenon of care. . . . Of course only as long as Dasein is (that is, only as long as an understanding of being is ontically possible) 'is there' being. When Dasein does not exist, 'independence' 'is' not, nor 'is' the 'in itself'. . . . In such a case it cannot be said that entities are, nor can it be said that they are not. But now, as long as there is an understanding of being and therefore an understanding of extantness, it can be said that in this case entities will still continue to be. As we have noted, being (not entities) is dependent upon the understanding of being; that is to say, reality (not the real) is dependent on care."[44]

Extantness cannot 'be' unless there is an understanding of extantness;

44. *B.T.*, pp. 254–255/211–212. Translation modified.

nothing can 'be' extant unless there is an understanding of what it is to be in such a way. In general, there is no being without an understanding of the meaning (or truth) of being, yet individual determinations of entities do not depend upon an understanding of being. What can all of this mean? We haven't come far enough to disentangle this mass of claims about the relations among being, beings, the understanding of being, and the meaning of being, but we have come far enough to identify the problem this thicket of concepts is meant to deal with: what are the relations among (1) the determinations that a thing 'in itself' really has, (2) the sorts of determinations it has (instrumental, natural, aesthetic, or whatever), (3) the understanding of that thing as having those particular determinations, and (4) the understanding of that thing as having that ontological sort of determination? The second half of this book interprets Heidegger's thinking about this problem.

Before turning to the difficult job of interpreting Heidegger on being, however, we must ask whether there is reason to think that Heidegger's convoluted doctrine concerning understanding—which these chapters have been attempting to explicate—might be true. The next two chapters construct one possible line of argument in favor of Heidegger's position, a line implicit but never clearly spelled out in his work.

4 Phenomenology and the Verificationist Principle

One of the most striking things about the way in which the early Heidegger presents his views of understanding, and indeed all his views, is his seeming lack of concern for argument. The noteworthy thing is not that he presents weak arguments to support his views but that at first sight he appears not to offer any arguments at all. Instead, he seems to advance a series of descriptions. Heidegger describes objects, the being of objects, everyday experience of objects in practical and perceptual activity, everyday experiences of ourselves and of our understanding, and so on. It is clear that these descriptions are meant to be persuasive; we are supposed to recognize what is described and be persuaded by the perspicacity of the description. But it is not at all clear how the conclusions suggested by these descriptions, and the descriptions themselves, are meant to be warranted. How do we know that these descriptions—these interpretations, in Heidegger's sense—are either adequate to what is being described or uniquely adequate to it?

In this chapter and the next we reconstruct—in some measure, construct—the argument implicit in what Heidegger says, the order in which he says it, and the way in which he says it. In short, we attempt a 'rational reconstruction' of the early Heidegger on understanding. In general, I claim that the argument structure of Heidegger's early work is 'verificationist' to the core. To be a verificationist, in the sense in which I use the term here, is to hold, as Quine says of Peirce, "that the meaning of a sentence turns purely on what would count as evidence for its truth."[1]

1. W. V. O. Quine, "Epistemology Naturalized," in *Ontological Relativity and Other Essays* (New York: Columbia University Press, 1969), p. 80. As Quine points out, this

For an argument to be verificationist is for it to use this principle as an essential premise. My claim is that Heidegger both accepts this principle and must accept this principle and make use of it if his assertions in regard to understanding are to be warranted and cogent.

At first sight this suggestion must seem a bit bizarre. After all, the Vienna Circle was active during the period we have been discussing, and Heidegger's attitude toward it (and its attitude toward him) was markedly hostile. The style, substance, and tone of these two kinds of philosophy, as well as their aims and the range of problems they seriously consider, could not be more different. In fact, the metaphysical question 'what is the meaning of being?' which supplies the *raison d'être* for Heidegger's work in this period was considered meaningless by the verificationists within the Vienna Circle. In addition, the early Heidegger sees himself as following a different and well-defined method, the method of phenomenology as developed by Husserl and modified by himself. How is this self-proclaimed phenomenological method related to the verificationist procedure and principles that I claim are central to Heidegger's method and argument?

Husserl's Phenomenology

Throughout the period we have been examining, Heidegger remained a self-ascribed phenomenologist, and he understood himself as following the phenomenological method. Even though there are serious and important differences between Heidegger's method and that articulated by Husserl (we will look at the most important of these), and though the publication of *Being and Time* marked something of a break in the long personal and professional relationship between the two, the book is dedicated to Husserl "in friendship and admiration," and Heidegger boldly maintains in it that "only as phenomenology, is ontology possible."[2] A year later, in *The Basic Problems of Phenomenology* (its problems are the basic problems of ontology and thus the basic problems of all philosophy) Heidegger maintains simply that "phenomenology is the name for the method of scientific philosophy in general"[3]: that is, of philosophy as such. What is the phenomenological method that Heidegger considers so important, and how does he practice this method?

principle need not imply that every meaningful sentence has a unique range of evidence that would verify it, as the Vienna Circle thought. Cf. the previous discussion concerning the holistic character of the fixing of the meaning$_i$ of assertions.

2. *B.T.*, p. 60/35.

3. *B.P.*, p. 3/3.

It is striking that the three terms systematically related in Quine's formulation of the basic verificationist principle—truth, meaning, and evidence—are also key terms in Husserl. In Quine these terms are related so as to define one of the three, 'meaning' (in particular, the meaning of a sentence); in Husserl they are also related so as to define one of the three, 'truth'. As early as the Sixth Logical Investigation, Husserl stresses this relationship, and he never gives it up. "The epistemologically pregnant sense of self-evidence [*Evidenz*] is exclusively concerned with this last unsurpassable goal, the act of this most perfect synthesis of fulfillment, which gives to an intention, e.g., the intention of a judgment, the absolute fullness of content, the fullness of the object itself. The object is not merely meant, but in the strictest sense given, and given as it is meant, and made one with our meaning-reference. . . . Self-evidence itself, we said, is the act of this most perfect synthesis of fulfillment. Like every identification, it is an objectifying act, its objective correlate being called being in the sense of truth, or simply truth."[4] As this passage should make clear, however, Husserl doesn't mean quite the same thing by these words as Quine does. In particular, Husserl's use of the German word '*Evidenz*', which carries connotations of certainty and infallibility that the English word 'evidence' lacks, should alert us that the kind of experience that counts as evidential for him is different from those that have evidential weight for Quine and the Vienna Circle.

In the First Logical Investigation, Husserl makes a series of distinctions among the (intending) meaning of an expression (he quickly extends this analysis to include the meaning of intentional mental acts), the object meant, and the fulfilling meaning of that expression. The distinction between the meaning and its object is roughly the same as Frege's distinction between the sense [*Sinn*] and reference [*Bedeutung*] of a referring expression,[5] although Husserl doesn't use this terminology. "An expression only refers to an objective correlate because it means something, it can rightly be said to signify or name the object through its meaning. An act of meaning is the determinate manner in which we refer to our object of the moment, though this mode of significant reference and the meaning itself can change while the object of the reference

---

4. Edmund Husserl, *Logical Investigations,* trans. J. N. Findlay, vol. 2 (London: Routledge & Kegan Paul, 1970), p. 765. Henceforth cited as Husserl, *L.I.*

5. Gottlob Frege, "On Sense and Meaning," trans. Max Black, in *Philosophical Writings of Gottlob Frege,* ed. Peter Geach and Max Black (Totowa: Rowman & Littlefield, 1952), pp. 56–78.

remains fixed."[6] Husserl advances two grounds for this distinction. First, as for Frege, two expressions can have the same reference and yet differ in meaning. Husserl's example is the difference in meaning between 'the victor at Jena' and 'the vanquished at Waterloo'. Second, an expression can have a meaning, and we can intend and be in relation to that meaning, in one or another intentional attitude (Husserl's term is 'quality' of the intentional act), even if the object referred to through that meaning doesn't exist.

Because Husserl admits mental acts as having a meaning, insofar as they are intentional, he also needs a distinction between the 'fulfilling meaning' of an intention and, on the one hand, its 'intending meaning'; on the other, the object itself. "Relation to an actually given objective correlate, which fulfills the meaning-intention, is not essential to an expression. If this last important case is also taken into consideration, we note that there are two things that can be said to be expressed in the realized relation to the object. We have, on the one hand, the object itself, and the object meant in this or that manner. On the other hand, and more properly, we have the object's ideal correlate in the acts of meaning-fulfillment which constitute it, the fulfilling sense. Whenever the meaning-intention is fulfilled in a corresponding intuition . . . then the object is constituted as 'given' in certain acts, and, to the extent that our expression really measures up to the intuitive data, as given in the same manner in which the expression means it."[7] When I actually perceive, for example, this piece of white paper, I see it as a piece of white paper. That is, I intend it as having that meaning. As opposed to the *expression* 'this piece of white paper' (or the mere thinking of this paper), however, the perception intends the object as 'actually given' in the perception, while the expression 'merely' intends the meant. In the actual intuition the fulfilling meaning coincides with the intending meaning; that is, the paper is meant just as it is given. "In the unity of fulfillment, the fulfilling content coincides with the intending content, so that, in our experience of this unity of coincidence, the object, at once intended and 'given', stands before us, not as two objects, but as one alone. The ideal conception of the act which confers meaning yields us the Idea of the intending meaning, just as the ideal conception of the correlative essence of the act which fulfills meaning, yields the fulfilling meaning."[8]

6. Husserl, *L.I.,* vol. 1, p. 289.
7. Ibid., p. 290.
8. Ibid., p. 291.

Husserl's notion of evidence is essentially dependent on his notion of meaning fulfillment. To have evidence in regard to an intention is to have that which is merely meant in an intention with a certain meaning actually given to us intuitively as it is meant in that intention; the evidence is the fulfilling of the intention. The connotations of certainty and infallibility attaching to the word 'evidence' arise out of Husserl's way of analyzing the variations among the different ways in which we can have fulfillment of an intention. When I actually see a piece of white paper, and it is given to me as white and as paper, it is given to me as fulfilling the meaning 'white paper' but as doing so incompletely and inadequately. For something to be a sheet of white paper means that it will appear a certain way at a certain time in a certain light, and this thing does appear in that way to me now. But the meaning intention contained in 'white paper' also intends a certain continuity of appearance over time and across conditions, and a single intuitive presentation can never adequately fulfill this aspect of the intention.

For Husserl, *Evidenz* applies only to "this last unsurpassable goal, the act of this most perfect synthesis of fulfillment, which gives to an intention . . . the absolute fullness of content, the fullness of the object itself."[9] To have evidence in regard to a meaning intention is to have an adequate (complete) or apodictic fulfillment, or both, of that intention. As we have just seen, it is hard to imagine genuine evidence, in this sense, in regard to spatially and temporally extended physical objects; nevertheless, Husserl feels that there are some intentions that can be fulfilled in such a way as to provide us evidence in the strong sense, and, as we shall see, this is the evidence that stands as the basis of all scientific knowledge. "Judging is meaning—and, as a rule, merely supposing—that such and such exists and has such and such determinations; the judgment (what is judged) is then a merely supposed affair or complex of affairs: an affair, or state of affairs, as what is meant. But, contrasted with that, there is sometimes a pre-eminent judicative meaning, a judicative having of such and such itself. This having is called evidence. In it the affair, the complex (or state) of affairs, instead of being merely meant 'from afar', is present as the affair 'itself' . . . the judger accordingly possesses it itself. . . . This conversion is inherently characterized as the fulfilling of what was merely meant, a synthesis in which what was meant coincides and agrees with what is itself given."[10]

9. Ibid., vol. 2, p. 765.
10. Edmund Husserl, *Cartesian Meditations*, trans. Dorion Cairns (The Hague: Martinus Nijhoff, 1960), pp. 10–11. Henceforth cited as Husserl, *C.M.*

Evidence, then, is given in an intuition that fulfills an intending meaning, and is intended as doing so. Beginning early in his phenomenological career, Husserl correlates the notions of 'truth' and 'being' and relates both of them with meaning fulfillment. "Self-evidence itself . . . is the act of this most perfect synthesis of fulfillment. Like every identification it is an objectifying act, its objective correlate being called being in the sense of truth or simply truth."[11] 'Truth' and 'being' are distinguished in that the former is a character of the intentional acts that are fulfilled in evidence, while the latter is applied to the objective correlate of such acts.[12]

But, as we will see in detail in Chapter 6, neither the being of the entity nor the truth of an intention or assertion is straightforwardly identified by Husserl with the fulfillment of an intention or the intention's being fulfilled. Rather, Husserl suggests that there is an intentional act that intends the identification of what is meant emptily in the intention and what is actually given in intuition, and both being and truth are understood by way of the object intended in *this act of identification*. Nevertheless, there can be no fulfillment of the act that intends the identification unless there is in fact evidence, or fulfillment of the first-order act, that intends some being. As both being and truth are essentially defined in terms of evidence, then, what it is to be true and what it means to be are essentially determined as related to evidence. There is neither being nor truth independent of the (possible) evidence in which intentions directed toward beings are fulfilled. "Whatever we assert then concerning objects—provided we speak reasonably—we must submit, whether as meant or spoken, to 'logical grounding', 'proof' . . . 'that which truly and really is' and 'that which is rationally demonstrable' are intrinsically correlated."[13] "The Eidos True-Being is correlatively equivalent to the Eidos Adequately given-being and being that can be posited as self-evident."[14]

For Husserl, the idea of science is fundamentally dependent upon the notion of the evidential grounding of knowledge. We know scientifically insofar as what we know is grounded in an evidential giving of what is meant in the assertions we claim to know. "The scientist intends not merely to judge, but to ground his judgments. Stated more precisely: He

11. Husserl, *L.I.,* vol. 2, p. 765.
12. Ibid., p. 768.
13. Edmund Husserl, *Ideas,* trans. W. R. Boyce Gibson (London: Collier-Macmillan, 1962), p. 350.
14. Ibid., p. 367.

intends to let no judgment be accepted by himself or others as 'scientific knowledge', unless he has grounded it perfectly and can therefore justify it completely at any time by a fully actualizable return to his repeatable act of grounding."[15] The positive sciences (physics, mathematics, and the like) are scientific only to the degree to which they realize this ideal.

But what distinguishes philosophical science, or phenomenology, as a science? What sort of science is philosophy? For Husserl, phenomenology as science has two essential differentiae. First, it is an 'eidetic' science. It is not only possible to intend particular objects (this table, this material object); it is also possible to intend what it is to be those objects insofar as they are intended as having some definite character (what it is to be a table or a tool, a natural object, a mathematical object). "It belongs to the meaning of everything contingent that it should have some essential being and therewith an Eidos to be apprehended in all its purity. . . . An individual object is not simply and quite generally an individual, a 'this-there' something unique; but being constituted thus and thus 'in itself' it has its own proper mode of being, its own supply of essential predicables which must qualify it, if other secondary relative determinations are to qualify it also. . . . Whatever belongs to the essence of the individual can also belong to another individual, and the broadest generalities of essential being . . . delimit 'regions' or 'categories' of individuals."[16] When I intend the 'idea' table, I am not intending a particular table. Rather, I am intending what it is to be a table: that is, what it is that is meant insofar as something is meant as a table, and what meaning must be fulfilled if a thing is to count as a table.

As with any other intention, for Husserl, the intentions that intend essences can also be 'empty' or fulfilled: they can be a mere meaning of the essence or a giving of the essence itself. "The essence is an object of a new type. Just as the datum of individual or empirical intuition is an individual object, so the datum of essential intuition is a pure essence. . . . Essential insight is still intuition, just as the eidetic object is still an object."[17] So it is possible to have pure sciences of essence, or scientific knowledge in regard to essence. "There are pure sciences of essential being such as pure logic, pure mathematics, pure time-theory, space-theory, theory of movement, etc."[18] Phenomenology is just such a science of essence.

15. Husserl, C.M., p. 11.
16. Husserl, Ideas, p. 47.
17. Ibid., p. 49.
18. Ibid., p. 55.

But which essences does phenomenology—that is, philosophical science—know? Each of the special sciences listed above attempts to gain knowledge concerning what is essential to this or that region or category of beings. Mathematics, for example, comes to have knowledge of what essential determinations belong to mathematical objects simply and solely *qua* mathematical objects, or insofar as they are mathematical objects. It knows this, according to Husserl, insofar as it comes to have knowledge of the *eidos* of the mathematical. But philosophy takes no particular category or region of being as its subject domain, so how is its object *qua* eidetic science to be delimited? The traditional answer to this question, insofar as philosophy is ultimately identified with its most far-reaching endeavor, metaphysics, is that philosophy is distinct from the positive sciences in that it studies being *qua* being, rather than any definite class of beings. This Aristotelian definition of metaphysics, which becomes a crucial spur to Heidegger's philosophizing, also exercises a claim on Husserl. But as we have already seen, for Husserl what it is to be, as such and in general, is involved with the fulfillment of meaning intentions. How, in Husserl, do we come to know this? What eidetic realm offers access to the determination of being *qua* being, which is the traditional subject domain of philosophy?

This question leads us to the second differentia of philosophy. Philosophy is just that eidetic science we have already been practicing in giving these various descriptions of intentionality and the meanings involved in it. That is, it is the eidetic science that intends the intentional, or the science of meanings insofar as they are the vehicles of intentionality or 'consciousness of' as such. The *eidos* that philosophy as phenomenology studies is what it is to be a consciousness of or a directedness toward . . . For Husserl, it is not only possible to intend what is ordinarily intended in natural consciousness, real objects, whether particular or essential; it is also possible to intend the intending of those objects. As the study of what it is to be conscious of . . . , phenomenology also studies what it is to be an object of such intentions, simply and solely insofar as the object is intended. And, insofar as the 'being' of some being can be intended or meant, it also can be investigated phenomenologically. As we have already noted, and as we will see more completely later on, Husserl begins the phenomenological investigation of being in his Sixth Logical Investigation. Heidegger seizes upon this investigation and makes it his own.

Philosophy is the science—that is, the knowing based on evidentiary grounds—of consciousness of or intentional directedness toward . . . Its problems include the making of essential distinctions among various kinds of intentional acts (perception, cognition, manipulation, imagination, and so on), the making of essential distinctions among kinds of intentional objects (the perceived as perceived, the willed as willed, and the like), the discovery of what meaning as such consists in, what evidence or meaning fulfillment consists in, and thus problems in regard to the meaning of truth or what it is to be true, the meaning of knowledge or what it is to know, and the meaning of being or what it is to be. For Husserl, all these issues fall within the scope of phenomenology *qua* scientific philosophy insofar as they concern questions of what it is to be conscious of or intend objects, in either an empty or a fulfilled fashion. These are 'transcendental' questions in almost exactly Kant's sense. "From its pure eidetic standpoint which 'suspends' the transcendent in every shape and form, phenomenology comes inevitably on its own ground of pure consciousness to this whole system of problems which are transcendental in the specific sense, and for this reason it merits the title of Transcendental Phenomenology. On its own ground it must come to the point, not of treating experiences as so much dead material, as 'systems of content', which simply are, but mean nothing, intend nothing, with their elements and ordered constructions, their classes and sub-classes, but rather of mastering its own intrinsically peculiar group of problems which present experience as *intentional,* and that purely through its eidetic essence as 'consciousness of'."[19]

Phenomenology is just the method that all science—as genuine grounded knowing—possesses, applied to the essences within the realm of phenomena, a realm established by the *eidos* 'consciousness of'. As with any other scientific knowing, we are entitled, in Husserl's view, to the claim of knowledge only when we can ground our judgments in regard to the intentional in pure intuited evidence or givenness of the essences of the various kinds of intentional acts, the essences of their noematic correlates, and of meaning as such. Further, for Husserl, that this is what knowledge consists in is itself discoverable and grounded as knowledge concerning knowledge, only within and for phenomenological investigation. It needs to be so discovered because knowing and truth themselves are certain characteristics of intentional performance itself. Therefore, Husserl thinks that philosophy as phenomenology has a priority over all the other sciences. It provides a ground for these sciences in that it makes explicit what can count as fully known by making explicit and coming to

19. Ibid., pp. 232–233.

have scientific knowledge of what it is for a judgment to be true and what it is for a judgment to be known as true.

Heidegger's Phenomenology

During the period of *Being and Time* Heidegger made two modifications in Husserl's phenomenology, one of which he explicitly emphasizes; the other is mostly tacit. The explicit modification, concerning the characterization of that which phenomenology investigates, really amounts to a change in emphasis. The second modification, concerning the nature of phenomenological evidence, is quite far-reaching in its implications.

In the introduction to *Being and Time* Heidegger describes that book's method as phenomenological. His preliminary account of that method quotes Husserl's maxim: "To the things themselves." In context, the point of this maxim is clear. For Heidegger, as for Husserl, no proposition will be considered as established unless it can be shown to be verified on the basis of a givenness that amounts to evidence of the truth of the proposition. Such evidence is just the evidentiary givenness of the thing itself that the proposition is about. So, for Heidegger as for Husserl, phenomenology is the method that looks to the things discussed themselves, as they are intuitively presented, in order to discover the truth concerning those things.

Heidegger's introduction goes on to investigate the Greek etymology of the components of the word 'phenomenology': *phainomenon* and *logos* (the term itself was first used by J. H. Lambert in the eighteenth century). After making a variety of distinctions among several senses of 'phenomenon', and distinguishing 'phenomenon' from 'appearance', Heidegger settles on "that which shows itself in itself, the manifest"[20] as the primary sense. He then circumscribes the phenomena that are the proper field for philosophical phenomenological investigation by suggesting that these are not the phenomena accessible by way of what Kant called the empirical intuition. Rather, he suggests in Kantian language, "that which already shows itself in the appearance as prior to the 'phenomenon' as ordinarily understood [the phenomena of empirical intuition] and as accompanying it in every case, can, even though it thus shows itself unthematically, be brought thematically to show itself; and what thus

---

20. *B.T.*, p. 51/28.

shows itself in itself (the 'forms of intuition') will be the 'phenomena' of phenomenology."[21]

There are two problematic elements in this specification. First, it is unclear how the formal identification of the phenomena of phenomenology as that which always unthematically accompanies all empirical intuition is to be correctly interpreted. Second, it is unclear how the allusion to the Kantian forms of intuition, space and time, is to be related to the formal specification and whether Heidegger really means that space and time are the sole phenomena studied in phenomenology. Such a limitation is at least suggested by this passage, since for Kant, the only intuitions that always unthematically accompany empirical intuition are the 'pure intuitions' of space and time.

These issues are quickly illuminated, however, at least to some degree. After a preliminary account of *logos,* which is in line with his early theory of assertion,[22] Heidegger goes on to assert categorically that being (as opposed to beings) is the phenomenon studied in phenomenology, and that time is important because it is the horizon in which there is an understanding of being. "Yet that which remains hidden in an egregious sense, or which relapses and gets covered up again, or which shows itself only 'in disguise', is not just this entity or that, but rather the being of entities. . . . This being can be covered up so extensively that it becomes forgotten and no question arises about it or about its meaning. Thus that which demands that it become a phenomenon, and which demands this in a distinctive sense and in terms of its ownmost content as a thing, is what phenomenology has taken into its grasp thematically as its object."[23] "Time needs to be explicated primordially as the horizon for the understanding of being."[24] In *Basic Problems* Heidegger is even more explicit: "Being is the proper and sole theme of philosophy"[25] and, as phenomenology "is the name for the method of scientific philosophy in general,"[26] phenomenology is just the method for the scientific study of

21. *B.T.,* pp. 54–55/31. The mention of Kant here is not idle. During this period, in *K.P.M.* and elsewhere, Heidegger associates his philosophical interest in being with an understanding of Kant as himself giving a general metaphysics. This interpretation is keyed to transcendental imagination as the source of the temporality that provides the horizon for any understanding of being.

22. Cf. the second and third sections of Chapter 3.

23. *B.T.,* p. 59/35.

24. *B.T.,* p. 39/17.

25. *B.P.,* p. 11/15.

26. *B.P.,* p. 3/3.

being. When we recast these various categorizations, we come to the conclusion that for Heidegger, phenomenology investigates being, which is a phenomenon that necessarily 'accompanies' all presentation of all other phenomena, a self-showing that 'unthematically' accompanies all self-showing. For the early Heidegger, the subject area of philosophy is identical with the subject area of Aristotle's first philosophy, metaphysics; phenomenology is merely the name of the proper method for approaching this field. Given this identification of his problem area with metaphysics, it is all the more remarkable that the late Heidegger comes to reject metaphysics as having reached an end, the culmination of its development toward natural science and technology.

But what does this phenomenological specification of being have to do with traditional notions of being, and how can we have an 'intuition' of being as opposed to anything that is? As we will see in detail in Chapter 6, Heidegger is here basing himself squarely on Husserl's Sixth Logical Investigation and on Husserl's doctrine of categorial intuition. We have noted that Husserl characterizes 'being' as the identity of the object at once meant and given in adequation: that is, as the identity of what is meant in an intention and what is given as fulfilled in an intention which is the fulfilling of that intention. As such, no content given in that fulfilling intention is the fulfillment of the meaning 'being'.

In a passage that Heidegger reproduces almost verbatim in *Basic Problems,* Husserl clarifies this point: "The form-giving flexion 'Being', whether in its attributive or predicative function, is not fulfilled, as we said, in any percept. We here remember Kant's dictum: Being is no real predicate. . . . I can see color, but not being-colored. I can feel smoothness, but not being-smooth. I can hear a sound, but not that something is sounding. Being is not in the object, no part of it, no moment tenanting it, no quality or intensity of it, no figure of it or no internal form whatsoever, no constitutive feature of it however conceived."[27] Rather, the source of the meaning 'being' is in the fulfillment of our intentions themselves, instead of in the intentions fulfilled. "Not in reflection upon judgments, nor even upon fulfillment of judgments, but in the fulfillments of judgments themselves lies the source of the concepts State of Affairs and Being."[28] The fulfillment of the meaning 'being' is in the fulfillment of any intention insofar as it is fulfilled. In that it is possible to

27. Husserl, *L.I.,* vol. 2, p. 780.
28. Ibid., p. 783.

intend 'being' and intend it as fulfilled—that is, intend something as really being—it must be possible, Husserl argues, to have an intuition, a direct evidential givenness of, fulfillment itself: that is, of the identification of that which is emptily intended and that which is intuitively given as it is given. While we are having a thematic evidential givenness of this white paper, for example, in sight, we are also unthematically aware of the fulfillment of the intention 'white paper', and this unthematic identification is the origin of the concepts 'Being' and 'State of Affairs'. Husserl uses this evidential givenness of being in an intuitive, unthematic awareness of meaning fulfillment as an example of the more general notion of categorial intuition, in which "the categorial forms of our meanings" (Husserl's examples include conjunction, disjunction, negation, and the logical constants in general) find fulfillment.

Heidegger's modification of Husserl in this area is to make the phenomenological investigation of being the sole object of phenomenology. For Heidegger in this period, the investigation is phenomenological in that there is a categorial, 'non-sensuous', intuition and self-giving of being as such, which manifests itself whenever there is a fulfillment of meaning. And being is understood whenever anything is intended with a meaning which we understand would be fulfilled under such and such conditions: that is, whenever we intend anything as anything (intend anything) at all. As we will see, a recognition of this development of Husserl is crucial to our comprehension of the many turns in Heidegger's long consideration of being and its meaning.

In the present context of trying to explicate the structure of Heidegger's arguments concerning understanding, however, Heidegger's second modification of Husserl's phenomenology is significantly more important. Heidegger hints at this change in the same passage we have been looking at in the introduction to *Being and Time:* "Our investigation itself will show that the meaning of phenomenological description as a method lies in interpretation."[29] That 'interpretation' is a word Husserl would never have used in this context is clear, especially in light of what we already know concerning Heidegger's theory of interpretation. Interpretation, for Heidegger, is always a taking-as, which always presupposes a context of practical activity on the part of Dasein. As such, each interpretation is relative to a fore-structure embodied in the context of purposive behavior that Dasein is engaged in while making the inter-

29. *B.T.*, p. 61/37.

pretation. For Heidegger, an interpretation without such a taken-for-granted background is no interpretation at all, hence neither 'correct' nor 'incorrect'. But for Husserl, phenomenological description is supposed to be the pure description of that which shows itself as it shows itself, and when one describes intentionality phenomenologically, one is supposed to eschew all interpretations that presuppose or embody any presuppositions whatsoever. For Husserl, this is accomplished in a pure evidential intuition of what is described—in the case of phenomenology, an intuition of meanings and intentions themselves. In short, Heidegger is hinting that the kind of pure, contextless, and thus presuppositionless intuition central to Husserl's method is impossible. "By showing how all sight is grounded primarily in understanding, we have deprived pure intuition of its priority, which corresponds noetically to the priority of the extant in traditional ontology. . . . Even the phenomenological 'intuition of essences' is grounded in existential understanding."[30]

We need to be careful here. Husserl is well aware that in general, objects are intended within horizons, both internal and external. That is, while I am seeing this piece of paper, I am seeing it as present within a spatial field and as such that if I were to look at it in slightly different light, it would appear in a somewhat different way. In order to intend this as a piece of paper at all, it is necessary that I intend it within such spatial and temporal contextual horizons. Indeed, this horizonal contextuality is one of Husserl's own phenomenological results, one that Heidegger fully shares. The differences here between Heidegger and Husserl rather concern the character of the primordial and basic horizon within which things are intended, especially the character of the evidence in and through which we come to have knowledge concerning such features of intentional givenness. Husserl conceives of the fundamental form of intentionality as cognitive; Heidegger conceives of it as practical. As a result, Husserl thinks of the horizons in which beings are presented on the model of sensuous fields in which objects are placed before us for our intuitive apprehension, whereas Heidegger thinks of these horizons as fields of activity.

In Husserl's case, even if it is an infinite task to explicate fully all the horizonal connections that implicitly define what it is to be some kind of thing (to be a piece of white paper is to appear such and such when seen in such and such a light and from such and such an angle) or what is

---

30. *B.T.*, p. 187/147. Translation modified.

implicitly contained in an intention that intends some thing as meant, the explication can in principle be carried out in such a way that we can arrive at apodictic knowledge concerning these matters, if not concerning whether there is this paper here. This is possible because what it is to be the paper can be intuited in a pure insight that needs merely to look at what is contained in this meaning and, in doing so, leaves unaffected that which it is viewing. As the ultimate horizon of intentions is likened to a sensuous field, my intending of the intending of the paper does place that intention within a further horizon, the horizon of theoretical cognition as such, but the latter is a horizon which itself just shows the intention as it is; it is, as it were, neutral in regard to what is intended. This means that the evidence in which the various ideas of phenomenology are given to us is conceived as a pure intuitive givenness of the ideas themselves, evidence is in no way relativized to the theoretical horizon in which it is given, because that horizon itself in no way affects that which is seen in terms of it.

Heidegger's key difference from Husserl concerns the character of the ultimate horizon of intentionality and thus the character of the horizon in which phenomenological evidence must be given and the character of that evidence itself. For Heidegger, all intentionality is essentially practical: to intend anything is to intend it in terms of a context of action; beings are intended as they appear within a world that is ultimately oriented on a for-the-sake-of. This applies equally to the intentions with which we philosophically intend what it is to intend and being itself. To have evidence, then, is primarily *not* to have a pure intuitive presentation of some quasi-sensuous content that fulfills some meaning; rather, it is primarily to experience some project as successful. To describe phenomenologically is to engage in interpretation, to take something as something for some end; and all interpretations, including phenomenological ones, are correct or incorrect depending upon whether they are instrumental to reaching that end. For Heidegger, it makes no sense to talk about phenomenological evidence that gives us meaning itself as it is in itself apart from our interpretive horizon, because all evidence is evidence only in light of some end, and what a thing (or meaning) is is what it is for some end. As we will see, this does not imply that interpretations, including theoretical ones, can't be objectively true or false, but it does imply that there is no objectivity and no evidence except as relativized to some purpose or other.

The situation, then, is roughly as follows. As a result of a phenomenological investigation of understanding, Heidegger comes to the conclusion that the methodological basis for phenomenology, the pure intuitive presentation of essences which gives us adequate and apodictic knowledge of essences as they are in themselves—including knowledge of the essences of intentionality and understanding—is impossible. But doesn't this result undercut itself? On what basis are we to accept this Heideggerian claim if not on the certain foundation supplied by Husserl's phenomenological method? On the basis of a pragmatically characterized evidence, of course—evidence that lacks both the foundational character of Husserl's evidence and its apodicticity. The whole notion of meaning, together with the coordinated notion of intentionality, is modified so that the primary sense of intending something becomes related to practical contexts of use. I intend something as having a certain determination precisely insofar as I take it as such and such: that is, in that I interpret it. Within such a structure there can still be confirming and disconfirming evidence, but such evidence has a determinate relationship with that for the sake of which the interpretation occurs.

In short, both Heidegger's doctrine of the coordination of meaning and interpretation and his actual philosophical practice imply the replacement of Husserl's 'intuitionist', 'theoretically' based account of truth and evidence with a pragmatic conception of truth and evidence, and this very pragmatic account must be applied self-referentially to Heidegger's own results. Heidegger's method remains fundamentally verificationist, but for early Heidegger, verification is always pragmatic.

Verificationism and the Structure of Heidegger's Argument

There is obviously a whole host of differences between the kind of verificationism practiced by Quine, or the positivists, and either Husserl's or Heidegger's phenomenology. Husserl's notion of evidence as the sort of self-evidence that can provide apodictic certainty for the truth of necessary judgments concerning essences, for example, is deeply at odds with the primary verificationist paradigm of evidence as empirical evidence supporting contingent propositions concerning matters of fact. Similarly, Husserl's doctrine of categorial intuition, which in some ways is central both to his work and to that of the early Heidegger, would seem bizarre to a standard positivist or to Quine. Quine's anti-realism concerning intentional mental states, which he considers an indirect consequence of the conjunction of verificationism and holism in regard to evidence, would clearly be anathema to Husserl and would seem to be so to Heidegger, as would Quine's extensional semantic views. Although Heidegger accepts that 'existence isn't a real predicate', for many it is odd and reprehensible that he has spilled so much meaningless metaphysical ink on the question, 'what is the meaning of being?' which is properly answered with a curt 'to be is to be a value of a bound variable' or 'existence is what the existential quantifier expresses'. Finally, from the positivist standpoint, Husserl's and Heidegger's reactionary insistence on thinking of things, in addition to states of affairs, as the objects of intentions leads them into some unfortunate positions.

Nevertheless, regardless of these substantial and important differences, there are significant points of similarity. In particular, there is the same relation among 'meaning', 'truth', and 'evidence' in Husserl and the classical verificationists, even though the relata are conceived somewhat differently. For Husserl, the meaning of x turns solely on what would count as evidence for x's truth. Consider an intentional mental act, which for Husserl could intend either an object or a state of affairs. (Similarly, linguistic speech acts have, for Husserl, a derivative intentionality and meaning and can intend either objects or states of affairs. In the first case we are dealing with the meaning of a certain class of words; in the second, with the meaning of judgments.) Insofar as it intends, the mental act has a meaning. This meaning is not, strictly speaking, the existing object itself that the intention is ultimately referring to. Rather, for Husserl, the meaning is the determinate manner in which the reference is accomplished. But what is the meaning of a mental act or linguistic expression itself? The meaning of an intentional act is just that content which would need to be given evidentially for that intentional act to be known to be true. This follows directly from the equation that truth is equivalent to the identification of intending meaning and fulfilling meaning in an experience of evidence. If for an intentional act to be true is for there to be evidence for its truth, and if for there to be evidence for its truth is for the specific meaning of the act to be fulfilled, then the specific meaning of an act is the evidence which, if given, would verify or confirm that act. For Husserl, the meaning of an act is the verification conditions for the act: what would be given were the act to be confirmed as true.

This is equally the case for Heidegger. The crucial passage in *Being and Time* in which he defines being-true as being-uncovering turns on the Husserlian idea that truth attaches to an intentional act insofar as a thing shows itself, in evidence, as the very same thing that is intended as meant in the act. Such acts uncover the thing as it is: that is, as it shows itself in confirming evidence. For Heidegger, the primary form of intentional comportment is practical understanding that becomes actual in practical interpretation. That is, the basic intentional act is an act of practical taking-as within a context of a purposive string of activities. Such an act is true if it reveals the real capacities of the thing intended. The basic meaning here is the meaning of the act as a taking-as or interpretation of some thing insofar as that act uses that thing, in a given situation, for a given purpose. The meaning of this act, for example, is that it is an act of hammering, or an act of taking this thing as a hammer. In a secondary sense the thing used—the thing taken as a hammer—is taken as having the meaning of being a hammer, insofar as it is used in an act that has the meaning of being an act of hammering.

In a further sense, which we will see is crucial to Heidegger's discussion of the meaning of being, the meaning attaches to the practical context in which the thing alone can reveal itself as it is understood to be, a context defined by that for the sake of which the act occurs. In this sense, the meaning of the hammering is that in which and for the sake of which it occurs: the functionality context of building so that there will be shelter. The meaning of the hammering is to bring about shelter. So, to be an act that has the meaning of hammering (or being an act of 'hammer interpretation') is just to be an act that attempts to use this thing as a hammer, which in turn is an act performed for some definite kind of end. This, however, is just an act that would be successful were it to be instrumental in reaching that end. To be successful, the act must bring about a state of affairs which the agent of the act recognizes as a successful result of that act. The reference to the acceptance of the result by the agent is necessary because it is only in light of the acceptance or rejection of results that an act counts as purposeful, and hence meaningful, at all; or as having the particular purpose, and thus meaning, that it does have. When an act is successful in that way, it is an act that uncovers the hammer in its capacity to be used as a hammer. That is, the act is true: it is a being-uncovering of the hammer. The specific meaning of an act of interpretation, then, is fixed by the conditions which that act is to bring about, and this in turn is the state of affairs which the agent of the act would take as evidence for the 'truth' of that act. For Heidegger, as for Husserl and the verificationists, the meaning of an intentional act is a function of what would count as evidence for the truth of that which possesses that meaning.

All the profound differences between Heidegger, Husserl, and the traditional verificationists stem from their radically different conceptions of what counts as evidence. These differences in turn are correlated with differences in what it is for something to be meaningful or true, and which sorts of entities can have a meaning or be true. For traditional verificationists, evidence is supplied primarily by what Kant would call empirical intuition: to be meaningful, an event or entity must be such as to have empirical content; it must be such that the truth of that propositional content would make a difference to the sum total of sensory evidence which, in principle, could be available.[31] For Husserlian phenomenology, evidence can be supplied by a pure, non-empirical intuition in regard to the essence of some individual, and Husserl's brand of Platonism follows from this fact. For Heidegger, the fundamental notion of evidence is tied to the way in which purposeful, practical activity must be recognizable as successful or unsuccessful if the activity is to count as purposeful at all. From this basic pragmatism follow his idiosyncratic notions of truth and meaning.

Heidegger's pragmatic conception of evidence is clearly a consequence of his analysis of intentionality and understanding in terms of practical 'understanding how'. So to use his particular variety of verificationism in order to argue for the priority of practical understanding would be viciously circular.[32] Instead, I suggest that his practice is such as to presuppose only the general verificationist principle he inherits from Husserl, and in a preliminary fashion he adopts it in a purely formal sense. He then uses this formal verificationist principle in an argument designed to show that because of what it means to understand something, evidence must be fundamentally pragmatic. Heidegger assumes, then, only the very general principle that the meaning of x turns on whatever evidence would count toward the truth of x. This easily converts into the principle that what it is to be an x, or to be as an x, is a function of what would count as evidence that would confirm that something was an x. These principles are the underlying presuppositions for the entirety of the early Heidegger's thought. They are, as he himself

---

31. Quine's holism makes the essential modification that evidence attaches to theories as a whole rather than to individual sentences, so the primary locus of meaning and truth is to be found in entire theories instead of in separate sentences within those theories. See W. V. O. Quine, "Two Dogmas of Empiricism," in *From a Logical Point of View* (Cambridge: Harvard University Press, 1953), pp. 20–46.

32. Such a circle should not to be confused with Heidegger's version of the famous hermeneutic circle; cf. appendix to Part I, below.

would put it, the 'unthought', the taken-for-granted ground for his thinking.

In particular, Heidegger applies these formulas, in a remarkably single-minded fashion, in his attempt to answer the question 'what is it for some thing to understand?' The form in which he raises this question is 'what is the meaning of the being of Dasein?' As he immediately takes a definite kind of understanding to be a necessary and sufficient condition for Dasein's being, however, to ask about the meaning of the being of Dasein *is* to ask about what a being must be insofar as it understands. But according to the principle given above, to be as an *x* (in this case, to be such as to understand) is a function of the evidence that would count as confirmation that some thing was an *x* (in this case, what would count as evidence that some thing possessed some understanding). It is this equation that generates Heidegger's conclusions concerning understanding, truth, meaning, and the being who understands, whose actions have meaning, and who is in the truth—Dasein.

In the following chapter we recast Heidegger's discussion of understanding so that its basic argument structure becomes clear. We do this by successively raising the questions 'what is it to understand *x*?' and 'what must some thing be if it is to understand *x*?' for various ranges of values for *x*, up to and including the understanding of *x* as another Dasein. In each case the answers we offer presuppose that what it is to understand *x* is determined by the conditions under which we would have evidence for the truth of a claim that something understood *x*. The conclusions of this argument coincide to a substantial degree with the interpretation of early Heidegger on understanding as put forth in Chapters 1–3. Heidegger accepts the premises of this argument and, as we shall see, follows basically this same procedure in his own philosophical practice.

5 The Argument for the Primacy of Purposive Action

Heidegger's Conclusions

As we have interpreted him, the early Heidegger holds six major theses concerning understanding.

(1) Understanding that something is such and such, or believing that some proposition is true, is impossible without understanding how to perform various actions or use various entities.

(2) To understand how to do something, the one who understands must be capable of acting in order to reach an end. To act in order to reach an end, conversely, the being must understand how to do a range of things.

(3) To act in order to reach an end is to act so as to reach some future possibility of oneself. To act in this way is what it means to have self-understanding. Therefore, self-understanding, acting purposively in order to realize ends, and understanding how to perform actions are always coextensive. No being can have any one of these determinations without having all of them.

(4) Understanding is always holistic. To understand any one entity practically or to perform any given action for an end, one must have understanding of a wide variety of entities and understand how to perform a wide variety of purposeful actions.

(5) Among humans, objects have standardized functions, and proper ways to use things develop among a group of beings who establish standard ends and communally shared ways of achieving those ends.

Such shared projects and practices involve a coordination of purposeful activity among members of the group. To be Dasein, one must be a member of some such group.

(6) Only a being who is Dasein can make assertions—which may be true or false—and only a being who can make assertions is capable of understanding (or believing) that extant entities have natural determinations. Assertions are tools for communicating interpretations, which are ways of taking a thing as something. Assertions can be true or false—that is, have semantic content—only insofar as they have roles within the purposive behavior of Dasein.

There is a sense in which (1) is the crucial Heideggerian claim concerning understanding. Much of Heidegger's work in the first division of *Being and Time* is devoted to an analysis of what it is to understand practically and of what is understood in practical understanding. It is only insofar as this claim for the logical priority of practical understanding over cognitive understanding can be supported, however, that the relevance of the 'existential analytic' of being-in-the-world to cognitive understanding, knowledge, language use, and intentions directed toward extant entities can be established. This priority of the practical in Heidegger shows up in a number of separate areas. The way in which the extant is understood as having properties is said to be the 'specialty' of assertion, and assertion itself is a 'derivative' mode of interpretation. Interpretation in turn is 'grounded on' practical understanding and is itself a type of overt practical performance. Knowledge is said to be a 'founded' mode of being-in, and being-in itself is interpreted in terms of practical understanding. Even that paradigm of theoretical cognition, Husserlian intuition of essences, is said to be 'grounded on' existential—that is, practical—understanding. The analysis of assertions as tools for interpreting and communicating and the early Heideggerian view of semantic meaning follow from this supposed priority. But Heidegger frequently fails to explicate the way in which the practical understanding is supposed to be necessary for the possibility of the cognitive. It is crucial that this dependence be articulated; theses (5) and (6) attempt the beginning of such an articulation and thus help both to provide an analysis of what it is to have a cognitive understanding and to show how such an understanding presupposes practical understanding.

Theses (2), (3), and (4) together constitute the heart of Heidegger's analysis of what is necessarily involved in any practical understanding and, as such, the heart of his existential analytic of Dasein. For Heidegger, the straight-forward observation that no being can understand how to do something unless it also acts in order to realize some purpose is of cardinal importance. Heidegger usually puts this in an ontological form akin to the one we just used: to be a being that can understand things as tools and understand how to do things, that being must understand things and activities as 'in-order-to' and 'for-the-sake-of'. Heidegger is equally convinced that unless a being has at least some practical understanding, it could not be such as to act in-order-to or for-the-sake-of at all. These claims sound less mysterious if we put them in a linguistic idiom. The logic of the words 'understand', 'in order to', 'purpose', and the like, are such that, first, it is never proper to say of some thing that it understands how to do anything, or how to use anything, unless it is also proper to say of it that it acts in order to realize ends and thus acts for some purpose; and, second, it is never proper to say of some being that it acts for a purpose unless it is also possible to say correctly of it that it understands how to do at least some things. That is, for Heidegger, it is a necessary condition for the proper ascription of practical understanding and the capability of using (and actually using) tools that it be correct to ascribe purposes to that being and ends for which its actions are performed. And it is a necessary condition for correctly ascribing purposes that we can also correctly ascribe some practical understanding.

Thesis (3) is a distinctive aspect of Heidegger's analysis of purposive action: his claim that to act in order to reach an end is to act so as to realize some possible future state of oneself. His way of putting this is to say that things understood as tools are understood as such in terms of the involvements they have—that is, what they can be used to bring about—but that every 'in-order-to' and 'toward-which' ultimately goes back to a 'for-the-sake-of', which is some possibility of Dasein and which has no further involvements. Translated out of Heidegger's ontological idiom, this is just the assertion that it is never appropriate to say a being is acting in order to realize an end or bring about a purpose unless it is also correct to ascribe self-regarding purposes to that being and self-regarding ends to its behavior, where a self-regarding purpose or end is one that intends a future state of the agent. There are many possible purposes that do not directly concern a possible future of the agent of the purposive behavior. I can act in order to build a house, for example. I can even act so as to build a house for someone else. Heidegger's point is that it is impossible that someone is acting in order to build a house unless he is doing so for a reason and that the logic of reasons is such that no one can act for a reason unless he is acting so as to bring himself into some future state. As this acting for the sake of some possible future of oneself is, for Heidegger, self-understanding (what I understand myself to be in detail is what I am acting in order to realize, my 'for-the-sake-of'), self-understanding is considered necessary for purposive action and practical understanding.

The holistic condition specified in (4) can be understood in two ways: from the side of what is understood, and from the side of purposive behavior. From the first standpoint: it is impossible for a being to have a practical understanding of any one thing or practical know-how in regard to any one activity unless it also has practical understanding of a network of other things and practical know-how of a background of other activities. From the second perspective: it is a necessary condition for a being acting in order to achieve any particular end that it also act so as to bring about a wide variety of other ends. If we consider these claims in a linguistic form, we get the assertions that it is a necessary condition for any correct ascription of a particular understanding-how that it is true to say that the being who understands knows how to do and to use many things; and, if it is correct to ascribe any one purpose to a being, then it must be possible to ascribe to that being a whole integrated system of purposes related in terms of means and ends.

Thesis (5) is a restatement of Heidegger's claim that the world in which Dasein dwells is a with-world. We can take this claim as definitive either of purposive behavior as such, or of a particular sort of being that is capable of engaging in a specific type of purposive behavior—Dasein. It is implausible, however, to take the presence of a 'shared world' as essential to all purposive behavior as such. Clearly, there are some beings of which we ordinarily say that they act in a purposive fashion but that are nevertheless for the most part solitary. It is hard to see how the world of a tiger, for example—the interlocking structure of instruments, purposes, and ways of accomplishing ends that is presupposed in and by all its teleological behavior—can be seen as a world it necessarily shares with others. The claim is plausible at all only when it is made of social beings, such as ourselves. But that which marks us as social is precisely the fact that our activity is such that there are standardized ends for our behavior in light of which it becomes proper to think of specific things as falling under instrumental types, in virtue of which they have standard functions. Standardized ends and instruments in turn rest for their possibility on a coordination of means and ends among a group of beings, beings that all act so as to establish conditions that others can use in order to realize their ends. Such a social coordination of purposive action would then be a necessary condition for the possibility of standardized ends and instrumentalities. The claim that the world of Dasein is necessarily a 'with-world' becomes plausible if it is interpreted in light of an understanding of Dasein as the special sort of purposively acting beings that are capable of understanding and using things as having standard uses for achieving standard or appropriate ends. In that case, the claim would be that the social integration of behavior is a necessary condition for there being Dasein. But why would anyone think that purposefully acting beings capable of such normative use of tools constitute an interesting kind, and why would anyone think that such an ability could serve as a differentia for humans?

It is a traditional differentia of humans that they are 'rational', the word originally used as a translation of the Greek for 'capable of using *logoi*': that is, capable of speech. It is central to thesis (6) that only a Dasein—a purposively acting being who acts in a coordinated social fashion—is capable of making assertions or of language use in general. Heidegger believes this because he holds that to make an assertion, to assert, is to use a certain kind of socially constituted tool in order to realize a particular kind of socially standardized end, and that an assertion itself is just a standard sort of tool. He holds *that* belief because he believes that assertions can be true or false, have semantic content, only insofar as they have standardized functional utilities within the projects of a group of Dasein. He sees such utilities as necessary because the conditions for the successful use of the assertion as a tool are necessary in order to fix the truth conditions for assertions. The ability to understand and use assertoric language is in turn a necessary condition for the ability to perceive and intend extant entities, where 'perception' is taken in the strong sense as an experiential intending of a being as continuing over time with natural properties. Thesis (6) thus includes a series of important subclaims: (a) Only a certain kind of purposively acting social being is capable of language; (b) that an assertion has semantic content, that it can be true or false, depends upon the assertion's appropriate use as a tool for communicating within some Daseinish community; (c) the truth conditions for any assertion are fixed by the social meaning$_h$ of that assertion—that is, by the role the assertion plays within the standardized projects of a group of Dasein—but those truth conditions themselves, the meaning$_i$ of the assertion, are the conditions in the world under which it is appropriate to use the assertion to communicate an interpretation; (d) only beings that are capable of language are capable of intending non-ready-to-hand beings.

The six theses fall naturally into two groups. Theses (2), (3), and (4) are all elements in a unified formal analysis of what it is to act purposively and to understand how to use instruments in order to achieve ends. Theses (1), (5), and (6) collectively present a formal analysis of what it is to understand that something is the case, an analysis asserting that no being can 'understand that' in anything other than a directly, functionally interpretive way unless it has language, and no being can have language without being a certain kind of purposively acting being. We will thus divide this argument into two parts: the first for Heidegger's analysis of purposive behavior, the second for Heidegger's analysis of cognitive understanding.

The Analysis of Purposive Action

When one attributes to some being an understanding of how to hunt something else, one is ascribing a certain kind of capacity to that being. If we say of some tiger, for example, that it knows how to hunt its prey, we are suggesting that under certain circumstances that tiger could actually hunt its prey. The relation this example illustrates, between understanding how to do x and doing x, is a quite general one. To understand how to do x is at least to have the ability to do x, and in some cases the best evidence that some being understands how to x is that it actually does x. Our only evidence that tigers understand how to hunt their prey is that they do hunt it; that a tiger does so is sufficient to warrant the claim that it understands how to do so.

But not all kinds of motions, doings, or behaviors are such that beings with the capacity to go through those motions count as understanding how to do them. This pen is fully capable, in certain circumstances, of falling off a table, but it is clearly wrong to say that the pen understands how to fall off the table. Similarly, even beings that are self-moving may perform some motion and yet fail to understand how to perform it. A baby, for example, may have the capacity (perhaps even the disposition) to leave a bed—which we know it has because we see it do so when it falls out of the bed—without understanding how to leave it. So, for all x, understanding how to x implies the ability to x, but it is not the case that for all x the ability to x implies an understanding of how to x.

Further, performing actions that are described in certain ways always counts as evidence for an understanding of how to perform that sort of action, while performing certain other behaviors never counts as such evidence, and performing actions described in other ways sometimes supplies such evidence and sometimes does not. If something hunts something, for example, this is always evidence that it understands how to hunt things; water has the capacity, the dispositional property, to dissolve salt, but this never counts as evidence that it understands how to dissolve salt; a weld performed by a person is evidence that she understands how to weld, but the same weld performed by a robot does not count as evidence for such an understanding.

The ability to x is a necessary condition for understanding how to x; actually doing x is always sufficient for ascribing the capacity to do x; but neither doing x nor being capable of doing x are sufficient for ascribing an understanding of how to x. As the informative case of welding suggests, one and the same sequence of behaviors can in some cases be evidence that the agent understands how to do something but fail to provide such evidence in others. This example suggests that at least one other condition is also necessary to understanding how to do x, which, jointly with the capacity to do x, is sufficient to warrant that there is such an understanding. In the instances where the ability to perform an action is sufficient to guarantee an understanding of how to do this action, the second condition is built into the description of the action. It is this complex further condition that Heidegger's analysis of purposive behavior is designed to illuminate.

The fact that the identical behaviors engaged in by a person and a welding machine can in the one case count as evidence of an understanding of how to weld and in the other case fail to do so indicates that the difference is a function of one or more of the relations of the doing rather than of any internal difference between behaviors that do betray the presence of understanding and those that don't. What relation to the act of welding does a person have that a welding machine does not? The simple answer to this question, of course, is that the person performs the weld 'on purpose', or 'intentionally', or in order to achieve some end; the machine does not. Just as the baby does not understand how to leave its crib (even though it does so) because it cannot act in order to leave the crib or with the purpose of leaving the crib, so the robot does not understand how to weld (even though it is capable of welding and actually does weld) because it does not act with the purpose of achieving a weld. But this answer merely moves the problem backward a single step. To count as understanding how to do something, a being must both be able to perform a certain action and be capable of doing so 'on purpose'. But under what conditions are we warranted in ascribing such purposes to an entity? Notice, it is not sufficient that the entity can successfully perform the action, or even that it invariably succeeds in performing the action. In fact, the robot is probably more reliable at welding than the person, but this is insufficient evidence that it understands how to weld because it is insufficient evidence that it welds 'on purpose'. Under what conditions must an act be performed to provide sufficient evidence that the act is performed on purpose?

Consider the case of a tiger hiding its prey. The act in question is embedded in a series of acts on the part of the tiger. First, the tiger crouches in the grass, downwind from a herd of antelope. It creeps closer to the herd in a way that keeps it out of the antelope's line of vision. At a certain point it springs up and runs toward the herd, apparently having singled out an individual member, which it then pursues, catches, kills, and begins to eat. After a certain length of time it stops eating, drags the carcass into a secluded hollow, and uses its paws to move loose brush in such a fashion as to cover the carcass. At a later point it returns to the same spot, removes the brush, and eats again. It repeats the procedure with the carcass and the brush several times over the course of three or four days. And then it repeats the *entire* procedure, in altered circumstances. If at any point the series is interrupted (the tiger fails to catch an antelope, say, or it returns to the hiding spot and finds the carcass missing or another tiger eating it), the tiger either goes back to the beginning of the full procedure or takes compensatory action (perhaps fighting with the other tiger until it wins or its survival is endangered).

Given such a sequence of actions, we are entitled to ascribe purposes to the tiger, in light of which we consider ourselves warranted in saying that the tiger hides the carcass 'on purpose'. The salient feature of the series is the mutual adjustment of each of the acts with the others in the series. Not only does each act cause effects (every event has effects, after all), but all the acts taken together seem 'designed' to bring about a favored effect, a chosen 'privileged' effect—in this case, the tiger eating. If at any point the causal sequence veers away from the likely outcome of the tiger eating, the tiger intervenes in that sequence in such a way as to increase the likelihood of the privileged effect. In addition, the tiger can and does influence the causal sequence, so as to increase its probability of eating, in a variety of initial conditions. The tiger not only 'hides' itself in the grass while hunting (it doesn't do so when not hunting); it also 'hides' its dead prey.

In general, it seems, we are entitled to ascribe purposes to beings that act on the causal process in this way. To intervene consistently in the causal process in a wide variety of circumstances, with the effect of bringing about a higher probability of a certain result, is to act purposively, and the purpose is the result whose probability the intervention causes to rise. Our evidence that some act is performed 'on purpose' is that it is part of such a pattern of intervention. When such a pattern is absent, as when water dissolves salt, we have no evidence that anything is done on purpose.[1]

It is crucial to recognize that there are several elements in the pattern we have been describing, the absence of any of which vitally disrupts the ability of the behavior to count as evidence of purposefulness. The baby moves in such a way as to increase the likelihood of its leaving the bed, and the event in fact occurs, but it doesn't act consistently to produce this effect; there is no repeated pattern of continual intervention in the causal series. The welding machine does repeatedly perform motions that bring about welds, but it acts to bring about this effect only in a very limited range of initial circumstances. Were the circumstances altered, it would either continue to enact the same physically defined set of motions— which in those circumstances would not increase the likelihood of there being a weld—or fail to move at all. The same could be said of 'lower' organisms, which do engage in behavior that seems 'adaptive' but that we are disinclined to call purposive. Their actions bring about a privileged result in too restricted a range of initial conditions to count as purposive, and we tend to see their behavior as 'mechanical'. Only when a consistent pattern of interaction and intervention in the causal series responds to a wide range of altered circumstances do we have reason to believe that the series is purposive or that a given act in the series is performed on purpose. And only when a being consistently engages in purposive behavior do we have reason to believe that the being acts intentionally, acts with understanding.

Typically, a being that acts 'on purpose' acts so as to bring about a

1. It is probably impossible to determine just how wide a range of interventive action is necessary for evidence of purposefulness to be present. We are probably dealing with a situation where a 'more or less' is required.

variety of distinct purposes. Tigers, for example, not only act in order to eat; they can also act so as to mate. So for an agent to count as acting in a purposive manner, it is not necessary that everything they do be capable of fitting into a single pattern of action oriented toward a single privileged end. All that is necessary is that much of what they do be such as to belong to one or another series of acts, each series tending to bring about some particular result.

Insofar as every act that is performed on purpose or in order to achieve an end can be recognized as such only if it is part of a sequence of such acts, we have evidence that any given act is performed on purpose only if we have equal evidence that a number of other acts were also performed in order to reach proximate as well as ultimate goals. The evidence for any single act being purposive presupposes the presence of evidence that other acts were also performed in order to reach ends, because its belonging to a series of such acts is what gives us grounds for believing that any act is purposive. When an entity on a given occasion performs only a single isolated act, not embedded in any proximate pattern, we are entitled to consider that it does so on purpose only if we have other evidence that this entity tends to act purposively.

It seems that at least in general, beings that act purposively act in order to bring about some state of themselves. The tiger kills and hides the antelope in order to have something to eat; that is, for the sake of a full stomach. For Heidegger, to have such a self-regarding end is a formal necessity for purposive beings. Many machines and some tools are designed to be instrumental for some end, but the ends they serve are extrinsic. They have a purpose, but it is not their own purpose. It is only those beings that we take as acting for their own sake that we take as acting intentionally or on purpose. In practice, the difference between those entities with intrinsic and those with extrinsic purposes seems to amount to a difference in the degree of flexibility and complexity with which the being is capable of acting so as to attain its end.

The case of Dasein is unique. Beings that are Dasein do not act only for the sake of some possibility of their own. As beings that belong to communities in virtue of engaging in standard patterns of action for the sake of socially standardized ends—and thus fitting into interpersonal patterns of purposive action that extend beyond the private ends of individuals—they choose a certain standardized place or role within such a social pattern by acting in certain definite ways. That is, Dasein act not only so as to bring themselves into some possible state of themselves but also so as to be some definite sort of being. In acting to attain some end, they are also acting to realize some socially possible pattern for their lives. And, for Heidegger, only beings that act in order to be something in this double sense, as both attaining some end and thereby becoming some sort of socially patterned being, count as Dasein.

We are still not quite in position to illuminate the structure of Heidegger's argument. We first need to articulate the way in which he analyzes the relations among practical understanding, purposive behavior, and the for-the-sake-of-which. Heidegger holds that for some being to understand how to do any one thing, that being must act in order to achieve ends, have a holistic understanding that involves understanding how to use a variety of things and/or do a variety of things so as to reach various ends, and act so as to achieve some possible future state of itself. 'Understanding how' is a capacity phrase. A being need not already have done something in order to understand how to do it. All that is required is the truth of a series of counterfactuals of the form 'If y were in conditions z, it would do x'. The most significant fact about the counterfactuals that define practical understanding, however, is that the conditions under which a being that understands how to do x would do x can only be characterized in terms that include references to purposes and intended ends. Built into what it is to understand how to do x is a capacity to act in a given way, given a variety of circumstances, if the agent intends to bring about some end. This fact, of course, is merely a definite instance of Franz Brentano's discovery that no intentionally determined state (desiring, believing, or whatever) can be reduced without remainder to the presence of a disposition to act in some physically defined way. For Heidegger, this fact applied to 'understanding how' guarantees that any being who understands how to do something must be capable of acting in order to achieve ends: that is, a being with practical understanding always is toward an end, or for the sake of some end. It is equally true for Heidegger, however, that no being can be capable of acting for the sake of an end unless it is capable of *practical* understanding. It is this priority of practical over theoretical understanding that we have been discussing.

Significantly, Heidegger uses a vocabulary to assert the interdependence of intentional descriptions different from the one that is common in the analytic literature, even though the analytic terminology closely parallels ordinary discourse. Analytic philosophy of mind speaks of the interdependence of ascriptions of beliefs and desires, and the impossibility of non-intentional definitions of either of the pair which dispense with all references to the other; Heidegger correlates the for-the-sake-of with practical understanding. His for-the-sake-of, however, differs from desires in a quite specific way. A desire is supposed to be a specific identifiable occurrence that causally interacts with other such occurrences (other desires) and with beliefs in such a way as to cause given bodily motions. But Heidegger's for-the-sake-of is not at all a specific event occurring at a particular time as the mental property or act of a person. Rather, it is that toward which the purposive behavior of a purposive being tends; it is the telos of that behavior pure and simple. The purposive action is not supposed to be caused by the for-the-sake-of-which. That there is a for-the-sake-of is part of what it is to act purposively; it is a formal constituent of purposive action. "The phenomenon of care in its totality is essentially something that cannot be torn asunder; so any attempts to trace it back to special acts or drives like willing and wishing or urge and addiction, or construct it out of these, will be unsuccessful. Willing and wishing are rooted with ontological necessity in Dasein as care; they are not just ontologically undifferentiated experiences occurring in a 'stream' which is completely indefinite in regard to the meaning of its being."[2] Thus the for-the-sake-of is thought of in such a way that it cannot be an element occurring in some sequence of mental and/or brain states that are causally efficacious in bringing about certain behaviors. It is just a formal property of behavior itself that is purposive and teleological.

While it is possible that there are desires for which we have no direct evidence in the behavior of an agent, it is *impossible* that there be a for-the-sake-of that is not evidenced by the actions of Dasein, because the for-the-sake-of is just the purpose of the directed behavior. Without a for-the-sake-of the agent wouldn't be purposive; but equally, without purposive behavior there would be no for-the-sake-of-which. For Heidegger, then, the appropriate way to fill in the form of the counterfactuals that define what it is to understand how to do x is not 'if in a given circumstance an agent desired to achieve a given end, y, and believed z, then it would do x' but rather 'if in given circumstances a Dasein were acting for the sake of y, it would do x'.

The cash value of the difference between these formulations arises from the fact that in the Heideggerian version, it is the overall structure of the series of actions (of which an act is a part having a particular telos),

2. *B.T.* p. 238/193–194.

together with initial conditions, which serves to provide the antecedent of the conditional that defines what it is to understand how. In the standard form, it is the presence of a desire, together with initial conditions, which is used to define what it is to understand how to do x. And for Heidegger, as we have seen, for a being to engage in purposive activity is for it to act so as to alter its circumstances so as to bring about an end, and to do so successfully is what it is to act with practical understanding. So the tiger understands how to hide its prey if, in the process of acting for the sake of eating, it is capable of keeping its prey from scavengers. But that it is acting in order to eat, or is acting purposefully at all, presupposes some practical skill in influencing its environment so as to bring about the eating. Every practical skill finally involves that the being exercising that skill is acting in order to achieve an end; but equally, acting in order to achieve an end—precisely because doing so is a characteristic of strings of actual acts of some being—presupposes some practical skills. If a being cannot successfully influence its environment at all, not only do we have no evidence that it is acting in order to achieve an end; for Heidegger, it would not be acting to achieve an end. Therefore, a being without practical skill cannot be acting for the sake of an end.

Now, finally, we are in position to understand the structure of Heidegger's argument. We ask twin questions: 'What is it to understand how to do x?' and 'What is it to act in order to realize end z?' It is a premise of the argument that what it is for something y to be x—or, equivalently, what the sentence 'y is an x' means—is determined solely by what could count as evidence for the fulfillment of the intention that y is an x (or the truth of the sentence 'y is an x'). But in the case of 'understanding how to do x', nothing can count as evidence for its fulfillment unless whatever is given is given as part of a sequence of acts that also supplies evidence fulfilling the intention that the agent is acting for the sake of some end. We have evidence for the truth of the judgment that the tiger understands how to hide its prey only if we also have evidence that it is acting on purpose in moving the brush, and we have evidence that it is acting on purpose only if we have evidence that it is acting in order to reach some end. Equally, and conversely, nothing can count as evidence that some being is acting in order to achieve some end unless we also have evidence that the being has some understanding of how to perform some tasks. We are entitled to the judgment that the tiger is acting for the sake of obtaining food only because it is usually, or at least often, successful in obtaining it.

As we have already emphasized, global failure entails the absence of any purpose at all.[3] But because actual success in doing something is always evidence for the presence of the capacity to do it and, *ex hypothesi,* we have reason to think that the being is acting on purpose, then whenever we have evidence that some being is acting in order to achieve some end, we also have evidence that it understands how to do some things. Given our verificationist premise, then, something can be such as to act for the sake of an end if and only if it is such as to know how to do some things: that is, if it possesses some practical understanding. In fact, given the holistic character of the evidence required to fulfill the intention that x is acting for the sake of y, x must understand how to do quite a variety of things and how to use quite a variety of equipment if it is to count as acting in order to do or as understanding how to do any one thing. As Heidegger puts these points, there is no such thing as an equipment, and all practical understanding is an understanding of the world.

In addition, for Heidegger, all practical understanding is oriented toward a merely possible end: that which would be were the purposeful action successful but which is not at present. We can now see why Heidegger characterizes this possible end state as a state of the purposive being itself. To be a purposive being is just to be a being with a purpose, a for-the-sake-of, to its behavior. What it is, a being with an end, is what it does: that is, what it acts so as to bring about. This end is thus always its end not because it is some property that the organism comes to possess but rather because it is the characteristic end of its behavior, and its purposive behavior *is what it is* qua *teleological agent.* The end is a feature of the teleological action, and the characteristic action is the principle of identity for this being *qua* purposive being. To act with practical self-understanding is just to act so as to bring about the ends that define and determine the individual purposive being as the individual it is. Hence, whenever a being acts with practical understanding and for the sake of an end, it is also acting with practical self-understanding. To be Dasein is to be a definite sort of purposive being. Dasein is a social being whose teleological behavior fits with that of others in such a way as to form an integrated web of purposeful acts; specific acts, objects, and ends fit into standard types in virtue of that web. So the possible ends that define what an individual Dasein is are determinate ends within a particular historical and social field of means and ends. Dasein's practical understanding

3. Cf. Chapter 3.

always includes a self-understanding (it acts for the sake of a possible future, and to act for that future is to be the being that so acts and to have practical self-understanding), and that self-understanding is always in terms of possibilities predelineated by the 'they'.

These results complete our description of Heidegger's arguments concerning the structure of practical understanding. But why does Heidegger believe that practical understanding is necessary for cognitive understanding but not the reverse? Why does the early Heidegger give priority of place to practical understanding and thus to practical goal-oriented action among all intentional performances?

The Priority of Practical Understanding

What sort of evidence can we have that some person believes some proposition? For Heidegger, to believe that some propositional content obtains is to understand some thing as having some determination. As the history of philosophy makes clear, there are a number of different ways to classify the sort of determinations that entities can have. In the period of *Being and Time* Heidegger focuses on three ontologically distinct kinds of being, each with a corresponding characteristic type of determination. If a being is *ready-to-hand,* then it is such that what that entity is is determined by its instrumental capacities, and the determinations of ready-to-hand equipment *qua* the ready-to-hand are all instrumental determinations. If a being is *extant* then it is such that what it is is determined by its causal powers, the evidence for which ultimately depends upon the causal powers of some extant beings to affect us. If a being is *Dasein,* then it is such that what it is is determined by the socially possible telos of its being, and its determinations are structural moments involved in the movement toward that end.

When we ask what it is to believe or understand that something is the case, we are asking about one particular type of Dasein determination, the kind that finds expression in predications of the type 'p understands x as y'. The general verificationist premise is that what it means for some entity x to be y turns solely on the potential evidence that bears on the fulfillment of the intention that x is y; or, equivalently, the meaning of the sentence 'x is y' turns solely on what would count as evidence for its truth. In the present case, we are trying to grasp what it means for p, some Dasein, to understand that x is y, or what understanding x as y is or amounts to. Following the general procedure, we should approach this question by examining what would count as evidence for the truth of the claim 'p understands that x is y'. As there are various ways in which x can be y, however, it is at least possible (though obviously not certain) that what it is to understand that x is y varies as a function of what ontological sort x is and thus of what sort of properties x is understood as having. For this reason, concerning the possible evidence for the fulfillment of the meaning that 'p understands that x is y', we ask for separate answers where x ranges over equipment, where it ranges over extant beings, and where it ranges over Dasein.

Before we can begin to follow this procedure, however, we must make note of one additional complication. As is immediately apparent when we are dealing with humans, the overwhelming bulk of the evidence available for confirming any of these cognitive ascriptions is supplied by the linguistic reports of the person to whom the understanding is ascribed. In fact, the early Heidegger often suggests that the relation between the use of language—which is of crucial importance in human dealings—and cognitive understanding accounts for the traditional priority given to cognitive understanding. The role of language use in providing evidence complicates the issue, however, in that what a person says counts as evidence for what he believes only if he understands that what he is saying means what it means in general use. That is, using the schema we have been developing, p's utterance with the phonetic form 'x is y' counts as evidence that p understands x as y (or that p understands or believes that x is y) only if p understands (or believes) that this phonetically characterized utterance means 'x is y'. But what is it for p to understand that some utterance a has meaning b? It seems that the understanding of the meanings of assertions is a potential fourth kind of understanding-that, in addition to the cognitive understanding of tools, physical things, and purposive beings. And it is central to the investigation into what it is to 'understand that', because much of our evidence concerning 'understanding that' appears to presuppose cognitive understanding of language utterances as meaningful by the beings to whom we ascribe cognitive understanding of other things.

We are thus faced with a choice between two possible strategies. First, we can make our investigation of the nature of cognitive understanding wait upon an analysis of language and what it is to understand language, and then analyze all other instances of cognitive understanding in light of our understanding of the understanding of language. (Early Heidegger thinks that this is the strategy covertly or overtly followed by traditional philosophy, and he thinks that it usually leads to the doctrine that believing that x is y is analyzable as some sort of mental entertaining of the truth of some kind of mental analogue of a linguistic utterance. He also thinks that to follow this strategy is to illicitly divorce language from its role as something that is the product of Dasein: that is, teleologically directed beings.) Alternatively, we can start with the apparently deviant cases in which we ascribe specific cognitive understanding and beliefs to beings regardless of language use on their part or even in the face of their direct avowals to the contrary. There are numerous such cases: animals, infants, people whose language we don't understand, mutes, people who say they think the Yankees will win the pennant while betting on the Tigers, and so on. The advantage of this strategy is that it highlights the fact that whatever linguistic evidence we have for the beliefs of others presupposes that our informants understand the language they use as we understand it, and that our evidence for this must ultimately be based upon the pattern of their behavior. It is obvious that Heidegger follows this second strategy and that he comes to the investigation of linguistic understanding only after he has already considered what it is to understand tools, physical things, and people.

Heidegger begins with an investigation into what it is to be a tool, an examination of the being of the ready-to-hand. This analysis is closely coordinated with a parallel investigation of what it is to understand a tool as a tool. His conclusion is that to be a piece of equipment is to be serviceable within an equipmental context, and that equipment can be understood as equipment only if it is revealed against the background of a world that is oriented toward and by a for-the-sake-of-which. According to the early Heidegger, it is impossible to understand some object as capable of being useful in some instrumental fashion unless the being that understands is a being that acts toward ends. This would seem plausible in regard to the practical understanding involved in knowing how to do something. But why can't some being be capable of understanding that some object could be used for some purpose, even though that being itself never acts purposefully? The picture here is something like a computer, a being capable of recognizing the equipmental potentialities in things even though it lacks any ends of its own.

If we recognize Heidegger's verificationism, we can comprehend his strategy for dealing with this issue. How could one know that such a being understood that some x could be used for purposes of type y? It could, of course, tell us that it believed that x could be used in that way.

But we have already agreed to abstain from that sort of evidence for the moment. Failing this, the only possible evidence we could have that some p understands that x could be used as a tool of type y is p's behavior, and that behavior can supply relevant evidence only if it is purposive. Consider our tiger once again. On the basis of its behavior we may want to ascribe to it the belief that loose brush can be used to camouflage things. After all, it both hides its dead prey in brush and itself hides behind brush during hunting. But unless what the tiger did was part of a pattern of purposive action oriented toward the end of eating to stay alive, what it did in particular wouldn't be 'hiding' and thus would provide no evidence for the claim that the tiger understands that brush can be used for camouflage. Similarly, if a tiger were to 'work on' the brush so as to improve it as a tool for hiding, then we would have evidence that it understands the brush as such a tool. But once again, nothing can count as evidence that any x is 'working on' any thing so as to improve it unless this 'work' is part of a pattern of purposive action. That is, what the tiger does counts as evidence that it has a given belief or understanding-that in regard to tools only if it acts purposively, with practical understanding, as a teleological being. But then, given the verificationist premise, what it is to understand that x is y, where x is a tool, is such that only beings that act for purposes can have beliefs of this sort.[4] In the absence of language, only beings that act for ends and thereby count as having a global understanding of how to do things are capable of understanding that beings have instrumental capacities.

But can beings without purposes and without language understand that some thing has some natural or extant property? Once again we start with the verificationist premise. In the absence of linguistic communication, what could count as evidence in favor of such an understanding? At the very least it seems that a being with such understanding must respond differently to the presence of different natural properties. But this condition is too weak to be of much help here; a large number of entities respond differentially to the presence of variable natural objects. I suppose we first think of mechanisms such as record changers in this regard, but the class of such differentially responding beings is hardly so limited. There is even a sense in which chemistry, for example, is a science that

4. Notice, the being need not actually use some thing as a tool of a given sort to warrant our ascribing to it a belief that the thing could be so used. We could infer that belief from other parts of its purposive behavior. A pattern of action toward an end can be detailed enough so that we can, as it were, fill in the missing steps.

details the laws governing certain differential responses. But in neither case are we tempted to ascribe beliefs to the responding beings.

Rather, we ascribe understanding-that only when we have reason to believe that the being is responding in order to achieve some end. It is easy enough to construct a machine that responds by emitting a signal if and only if red light is present, but that it does so is far from sufficient to support a claim that when it emits the signal, it believes that there is red light present. A rat that has been trained to press a red lever in order to get food is a better candidate for the belief that a lever is or is not red. The pressing of the lever counts as evidence for such a belief, however, only insofar as it is performed in order to reach an end, and this occurs only when the various conditions for purposive action are met. But even when those conditions are met, what we have evidence for is not that the rat has beliefs concerning the extant property of redness belonging to the lever. Rather, we have evidence that the rat understands how to get food by pressing the lever. That is, we have evidence only that the rat understands the lever as a certain sort of tool with a certain kind of ready-to-hand character.

So, absent language, we have no evidence for belief without patterns of overt practical activity, and such activity does not give us evidence that a being understands that some extant being has some natural determination. Given the basic verificationist axiom, it follows that being capable of purposive behavior—which formally must include possession of a stock of know-how, an understanding of how to get things done—is a necessary condition for a nonlinguistic being's believing anything at all, and that without language, beings are incapable of beliefs or understanding regarding extant entities.

Under what conditions would we be warranted in claiming that some being has an understanding of some other being as a purposive being, a being that acts in order to achieve ends? Once again, our tiger can serve as a paradigm case. Both in hunting and after finishing its meal, the tiger hides things, first itself and then its food. Such hiding behavior is evidence that the tiger is treating the antelope it hunts and other carnivores in the vicinity as themselves engaged in purposive action. The tiger behaves quite differently toward the live antelope than it does toward the carnivores, and it acts differently in relation to both than it does toward its dead prey or toward, say, water. It doesn't hide itself from the dead antelope or from other tigers; it hides only from living antelope, which indicates that the tiger is 'taking into account' that the antelope is such that it will act so as to keep itself from being eaten. Hiding the dead antelope (or standing guard over it in other circumstances) counts as evidence that it understands other carnivores as purposive beings that will act to obtain meat as food. Once again, however, this behavior is evidence for such understanding only insofar as it is itself part of a pattern of purposive behavior engaged in by the tiger. And, given the verificationist premise, it follows that, absent language, only those beings that engage in purposeful action are capable of understanding other beings as engaged in purposeful action.

The striking thing about these various results is that they are so easy to obtain. Absent speech, there is no difference between the evidence that an entity believes or understands that something is the case and the evidence that it understands how to use various other entities and how to perform various activities so as to achieve an end. Given verificationism, a tiger believes that brush can be used as camouflage only in the case that it understands how to use it as camouflage; it believes that the wind is blowing in a direction only in the case that it knows how to use this information in, among other things, avoiding detection by antelope on a particular occasion; it understands antelope as acting so as to avoid being eaten only in the case that it understands how to respond to the antelope in such a way as to overcome or use the antelope's projects in the accomplishment of its own ends. As there is no understanding-that without some practical understanding, the conditions for practical understanding also apply to understanding-that. In particular, one can't believe that a thing can be used as a tool, or that some being has some natural property or is acting for some purpose, even falsely, unless one is capable of an extended series of mostly successful behaviors: that is, unless one is a being that acts purposefully. Absent language and given his premises, Heidegger's thesis (1) above, that there is no understanding-that without understanding-how, is trivial, because the only possible evidence for beliefs must be given in the context of skillful, purposeful action on the part of the being to whom the beliefs are ascribed. Further, the last clause in thesis (6), that only linguistic beings are capable of understanding extant entities, is a consequence of the fact that, absent language, we can have no evidence that a purposive being understands any entity as extant.

The presence of language use among humans greatly multiplies the evidential resources available for judgments concerning beliefs. In addition, it allows for the possibility of evidence in regard to a wide range of beliefs for which there is otherwise no evidence. What evidence could count in favor of an entirely nonlinguistic being's believing that Kant died in 1804 or that electrons form a natural kind? Language allows for such evidence, however, only insofar as we have evidence that the speaker understands what she says on given occasions as having particular meanings. To understand the meaning of a sentence or phrase would seem to be a paradigmatically cognitive activity, but as Heidegger analyzes it, it too must be understood in practical, action-oriented terms. Applied to this case, the verificationist principle states that what it is to understand some sentence as having some meaning turns solely on the evidence that could count in favor of such understanding. When do we have such evidence?

The strategic argument situation here might seem to be that outlined by Quine as radical translation or (perhaps better, since we are countenancing beliefs) Davidson's radical interpretation. We can easily take the question to be as follows: How can we assign meanings in a speaker's language in the absence of any already presupposed semantic information concerning that language? The question here, however, is oriented a bit differently: Under what conditions would we be justified in asserting that the actions of some entity count as having semantic content at all for that entity: that is, when are we warranted in the belief that some other entity is making assertions at all? Ultimately, our concern is with the evidential basis on which we assign understanding—in particular, understanding-that, or belief—to entities. Where that evidence is supplied by language use, this concern has two sides. First, we must have evidence that what this being does, the 'signal' it emits or the behavior it engages in, is understood by it as expressing an assertion or interpretation or as having any semantic content at all. It is only if this condition is met that the specific meaning of the signal becomes relevant to the ascription of beliefs to the entity that emits it.

It might seem that this is a distinction without a difference: if we have evidence that some signal has a particular semantic meaning, then it follows immediately that we also have evidence that it has the same meaning for the being that is the source of the behavior with that meaning, and thus that it has some meaning for that entity. This inference, however, is invalid. My personal computer is quite capable of emitting strings of symbols which, grouped together, count as having definite meaning within a community of Dasein. It is even capable of manipulating those symbols so as to perform correct inferences among semantic groups. For all of that, no one would dream of ascribing mathematical beliefs to it on the basis of its being able to perform what seem to us to be mathematical operations (whatever the status of its more powerful cousins). Something else is required in addition to the emission of semantically evaluable behavior, or even the syntactically correct manipulation of the symbols used in that behavior, if we are to have reason to believe that some being understands that behavior as having a meaning$_i$. It is one thing to examine the meaning of a sentence or an assertion for a language user when we presuppose that that behavior has some intentional content for that entity; it is quite another thing to determine that some behavior has a semantic meaning for the one engaged in the behavior.

The situation is analogous to a case we have already considered. In one sense my small computer is a far more complex version of the machine that emits a particular signal when irradiated with red light. The computer responds differentially to a wide range of inputs by emitting a wide range of outputs. But we feel warranted in ascribing beliefs to such beings on the basis of their differentiated outputs only if some other conditions are met. The question we have been raising here is what those further conditions are. That is, we are asking for the necessary conditions for the ascription of beliefs to some being on the basis of its linguistic behavior, and thereby for necessary conditions for ascriptions of their understanding of their own behavior as having some semantic meaning. This problem should not be confused with the difficult problem of determining a theory of meaning for a language once we have allowed that it has semantic content, or with the related question of determining what such semantic content consists in.[5]

When, then, do we have evidence that the behavior of some entity counts as having semantic meaning for that entity? Although Heidegger never confronts this issue in anything like this form, we can tease out several conditions from what he does say. In order for us to have evidence that some entity is asserting—that is, is making assertions that it understands as having a semantic content—the entity must (1) be a purposively acting being that (2) belongs to a community of such beings (a community that establishes standard ways of using tools); and the be-

---

5. If I am not mistaken, this is the problem that John Searle's Chinese Room example turns on. See John Searle, "Minds, Brains and Programs," *Behavioral and Brain Sciences* 3 (1980), 417–424.

havior interpreted as having semantic content must (3) be consistently useful within that community for standard functions of communication and inference (that is, the 'assertions' themselves must have a standard meaning$_h$ within a community) and (4) be used by the being in accordance with this standard function. That is, the being must utter the 'assertion' mostly when it is appropriate to do so, given the initial conditions that obtain and the end it is attempting to reach.

The microcomputer's behavior meets condition (3) and even, in a sense, condition (4), but we do not consider that the computer itself meets conditions (1) and (2). The signals the computer emits do indeed have a standard communicative and inferential function within a community of purposive beings. It is even the case that the pattern of emission is such that the syntactically correct inferential patterns of use are preserved. But because these inferential chains of assertions are not anchored semantically in the way appropriate to genuine language use, it is improper to ascribe semantic beliefs to the computer and thus improper to ascribe to it beliefs concerning the entities referred to in its 'assertions'. In genuine language use, assertions are useful as tools for achieving the ends of beings with purposes—in particular, the social purposes of communication and inference—and these purposes themselves have a point within the overall behavior of a community of purposeful beings; it is these facts that supply the nonlinguistic initial conditions of appropriate use that allow for the assignment of semantic content to the whole series of inferentially connected assertions. But we do not consider the behavior of the computer sufficiently flexible, wide-ranging, and adaptive enough to count as being performed for the sake of reaching any end, let alone the end of communicating interpretations; we thus refuse to ascribe to the machine any understanding-that or beliefs concerning the meaning$_i$ of its 'assertions'. The computer does not itself use the assertions in an overall pattern of social activity; although it is used as a tool in such patterns, it lacks its own ends.

Only to beings which themselves use assertions for purposes do we assign an understanding of the semantic content of those assertions, and only to beings to which we ascribe such understanding is it proper to ascribe substantive beliefs on the basis of their linguistic behavior. It is only insofar as an entity acts purposefully that we ascribe beliefs to it, and this is just as true for beliefs concerning semantic content as it is for beliefs concerning states of affairs in the world. And since an entity's possession of beliefs about semantic content is a necessary condition for using what that being 'says' as evidence of its beliefs concerning what is asserted, we lack evidence that the computer believes what it 'asserts'.[6]

We refuse to assign semantic content to what the tiger does for a different reason. We find sufficient evidence that it acts purposefully, that it has know-how concerning how to survive and achieve its ends, and thus, trivially, that it has beliefs concerning beings in the world. But we lack evidence that what it does signifies and is capable of communicating interpretations or the taking-as of any thing as any thing. For that to be possible, the behavior of an entity must be such as to have a function or purpose within a group of interacting purposive beings. In particular, the behavior must be in order to communicate some way of taking things as being determinate in some definite fashion. And, ultimately, our evidence that some action has such a function derives from the way in which what entities say or do functions so as to bring about a coordination of a group's activities toward some end. Just as road signs fail to signify apart from their utility within some community for directing purposive action so as to be mutually supporting, so assertions fail to have semantic content unless they also function so as to communicate interpretations, and our evidence that some sign is being used to impart an interpretation finally goes back to how it is used to guide and regulate what entities do within communities.

To ground these claims adequately, one would need to develop these lines of argument far more fully than I have done here or, indeed, than Heidegger does. The strategy, however, is clear. One starts with the verificationist premise that what it is for x to be y turns solely on the possible evidence that x is y. We apply that principle to the question of what it is for p to understand that some of its behavior expresses some meaning, or that behavior a expresses some interpretation, x as y. It is

6. We need to be careful here. As with any other machine and even some simple tools, it is in one sense true to say that microcomputers act so as to achieve ends. After all, they are *designed* to add, alphabetize, and so forth. But since we don't think the machine acts for its own sake, we don't think it acts out of its purpose. A calculator has a purpose or function but not its own purpose; it acts as it does in order to realize our end or as an instrument used to reach our goals. It is designed to fulfill some end, as a hammer is; but it is not, as Kant and Heidegger would put it, an end in itself. And only beings that are ends in themselves can have purposes in the pregnant sense and thus have beliefs. The distinction here (which we will need to reexamine in Part II, in light of our discussion of being) is roughly comparable to the distinction Daniel Dennett draws between the design stance and the intentional stance, although the early Heidegger means the distinction to carry an ontological import that Dennett denies to his distinction. See Daniel Dennett, *Brainstorms* (Montgomery, Vt.: Bradford Books, 1978), esp. chap. 1, "Intentional Systems," pp. 3–22.

important to raise this issue because what a being 'says' can count as evidence for its beliefs only if we have evidence that it takes what it says as having some meaning, and so the ascription of beliefs on the basis of linguistic behavior presupposes such understanding. And given the verificationist presupposition, to have beliefs that are mediated by language (in general, beliefs about extant or non-equipmental beings) involves being capable of understanding language as having semantic content. Any necessary conditions for the latter are also necessary conditions for the former. From a reconstruction of Heidegger's discussion we can identify four elements that must be present if we are to be warranted in ascribing linguistic understanding to an entity. That being must (1) act in a purposeful fashion (2) and do so as a member of some community of purposeful beings whose behavior is integrated so as to reach mutually supporting ends; (3) the 'assertions' that such entities make must have standardized functions for communicating and inferring within that community and (4) must be mostly used appropriately according to those functions. In other words, were we to assign semantic beliefs to a computer, we would willy-nilly be ascribing purposes to it, among which would necessarily be the purposes involved in using its outputs to communicate with other purposive beings. This is not because, according to the early Heidegger, these conditions cause its behavior; it is because these conditions are part of what it is for something to have semantic beliefs and thus to understand—beyond simple know-how—that something is the case. But to be a being that fulfills these conditions is just to be Dasein; hence only Dasein is capable of understanding, whether 'understanding how' or 'understanding that'.

This argument strategy could be attacked at several points. Verificationism is a premise rather than a conclusion of the argument. It is only because what it is to have an understanding is identified with the possible evidence for having an understanding that Heidegger can show purposive behavior to be necessary for—rather than a mere indication of—intentional states. Further, as Heidegger never fleshes out his hints concerning assertion and interpretation, it has been necessary for us imaginatively to fill in considerable chunks of absent argument in relation to the philosophy of language; the result is at best an argument sketch.

We will not halt over these potential problems, however, because our ultimate end is not the complete analysis of understanding. Like the early Heidegger himself, we have not undertaken the analysis of understanding for its own sake. Rather, just as the early Heidegger performs fundamental ontology (the analysis of Dasein's being) for the sake of the study of being itself (ontology), we have been interested in Heidegger's analysis of the crucial character of Dasein (that it understands) for the sake of illuminating his consideration of being. And just as Heidegger discovered that the implications of his existential analytic of Dasein for ontology did not conform to the strategic plan he had adopted at the outset, we will discover that the ontological implications of the analysis of understanding require a reexamination of the metaphysical terms in which we and Heidegger have carried out that analysis. The analysis of Dasein in general and understanding in particular, which starts out as a radical new foundation for ontology and metaphysics, ultimately becomes, in Heidegger's thought, a radical undercutting of the entire metaphysical enterprise and suggests a new, nonmetaphysical question for thinking.

Appendix to Part I
The Hermeneutic Circle

In the introduction to *Being and Time* Heidegger tells us that the meaning of phenomenological description as a method lies in interpretation, and that "the *logos* of the phenomenology of Dasein has the character of a *hermeneusis*."[1] He further tells us that the 'philosophically primary' sense of 'hermeneutic' is the sense in which the analytic of the 'existentiality of existence' is hermeneutic. In Division 1, Chapter 5, Heidegger concludes the section on understanding and interpretation with a discussion of the 'hermeneutic circle' in which he tells us that "the 'circle' in understanding belongs to the structure of meaning, and the latter phenomenon is rooted in the existential constitution of Dasein— that is, in the understanding which interprets."[2] In this passage, the hermeneutic circle is associated with the fore-structure of Dasein, which is worked out in interpretation. In Division 2, Chapter 3—just before the section in which Heidegger sets out the meaning of the being of Dasein as temporality—he returns to the hermeneutic circle, this time in connection with the structure of the procedure he has used to uncover the being of Dasein. To claim that this procedure is viciously circular and illicit, he tells us, is fundamentally to misunderstand what it is to understand. "When one talks of the 'circle' in understanding one expresses a failure to recognize two things: (1) that understanding as such makes up a basic kind of Dasein's being, and (2) that this being is constituted as

1. *B.T.*, pp. 61–62/37.
2. *B.T.*, p. 195/153.

care. To deny the circle, to make a secret of it, or even to want to overcome it, means finally to reinforce this failure."³

The hermeneutic circle is thus a theme that runs through the published portion of *Being and Time,* a topic that Heidegger clearly associated with the acts of understanding and interpretation in general and, in particular, with the act in which we philosophically understand and interpret Dasein's being. We end our interpretation of the early Heidegger on understanding with this appendix interpreting Heidegger's treatment of the hermeneutic circle for two reasons. First, this strain in Heidegger's thought has frequently been used as a premise in an argument designed to show that there is some necessary and essential difference between the scientific methods that can successfully be used to study extant beings and the procedures through which we can successfully come to understand human beings. Interpreted in this way, Heidegger's version of the hermeneutic circle is taken to be a variation on a common theme of the *Verstehen* tradition of humanistic investigation and program for social studies.⁴ Such an interpretation, however, misses the truly interesting and important features of Heidegger's version of the hermeneutic circle, features that make impossible the use of this doctrine in an argument for some necessary difference of method between natural and social science.⁵ To take Heidegger's discussion as suggesting such a difference is fundamentally to misunderstand what Heidegger has to say about understanding and interpretation and their relation to meaning and truth.

The second reason for examining Heidegger's consideration of the hermeneutic circle is related to the first and is equally important from the perspective of this book. As we have seen, Heidegger particularly associates the question regarding the circularity of understanding with a possible objection to the way in which he carries out the analytic investigation of Dasein's mode of being, existence. As he himself states this objection, it accuses Heidegger of question begging. Doesn't the analysis presuppose the idea of existence, and then merely unpack what is contained in that initial assumption? "Where does this interpretation [of authentic

---

3. *B.T.,* p. 363/315.

4. Among others, Hubert Dreyfus and Charles Taylor interpret Heidegger in this way. Cf. Hubert Dreyfus, "Holism and Hermeneutics," *Review of Metaphysics* 34 (1980), 3–23. Charles Taylor, "Self Interpreting Animals," in *Human Agency and Language* (Cambridge: Cambridge University Press, 1985) pp. 45–76.

5. Cf. my "Hermeneutics, Transcendental Philosophy, and Social Science," *Inquiry* 27 (1984), 23–49.

Dasein] get its clue, if not from an idea of existence in general which has been 'presupposed'? How have the steps in the analysis of inauthentic everydayness been regulated, if not by the concept of existence which we have posited? And if we say that Dasein 'falls', and that therefore the authenticity of its potentiality-for-being must be wrested from Dasein in spite of this tendency of its being, from what point of view is this spoken? Is not everything already illumined by the light of the 'presupposed' idea of existence, even if rather dimly? Where does this idea get its justification? Has our initial projection, in which we called attention to it, led us nowhere?"[6]

It is in response to this objection that Heidegger recurs to the hermeneutic circle. Dasein's being is such that it always has an understanding of its own being. To be Dasein is to understand oneself as Dasein, but as we have seen, to understand oneself as a Dasein is to intend oneself as an end to be realized, a 'for-the-sake-of' of the world. It is only in light of such a projection that anything can be understood at all. So any understanding of anything as anything rests upon the projection of a future to be realized. In particular, the philosophical investigation of our being as existence must rest upon such a disclosing projection. But that something is understood as something does not guarantee that it is that thing; for that, the thing understood must show itself to be as it is understood. "In positing the idea of existence, do we also posit some proposition from which we deduce further propositions about the being of Dasein, in accordance with formal rules of consistency? Or does this pre-supposing have the character of an understanding projection, in such a manner indeed that the interpretation by which such understanding gets developed, will let that which is to be interpreted put itself into words for the very first time, so that it may decide of its own accord whether, as the entity which it is, it has that state of being for which it has been disclosed in the projection with regard to its formal aspects? . . . We cannot ever 'avoid' a circular proof in the existential analytic, because such an analytic does not do any proving at all by the rules of the 'logic of consistency'."[7]

So, according to Heidegger, the fact that understanding has the peculiar structure it has—the structure detailed in his version of the hermeneutic circle—is what indicates to us the conditions that must be satisfied if any particular ontological interpretation is to be justified: that is, given

6. *B.T.*, p. 361/313.
7. *B.T.*, pp. 362–363/314–315.

160 Heidegger's Pragmatism

his verificationism, what it is for such an interpretation to be true and what it means for some entity to have the sort of being outlined in the interpretation. And, conversely, we know that understanding has the structure it has only insofar as our ontological interpretation is justified. No wonder Heidegger says that in regard to ontological investigations, circularity can't be avoided!

Part II of this book amounts to an investigation of the relations among being, the understanding of being, and the truth of being in Heidegger's thought (a complex of relations which displays a continuous development from the period of *Being and Time* to Heidegger's death) and of the implications of this complex for significant problems in contemporary philosophy. In *Being and Time* Heidegger himself connects the procedure for answering the question of the meaning of the being of Dasein, and by extension the meaning of being as such, with what he there calls Dasein's understanding of being. And, he suggests, to comprehend Dasein's understanding of being, one must recognize that understanding always has the structure identified in the hermeneutic circle. The hermeneutic circle thus supplies a bridge between our discussion of understanding and our discussion of being. This is the second reason for taking up the hermeneutic circle here.

The interpretation of this strain in Heidegger's thought has frequently been colored by the fact that the phrase 'hermeneutic circle' has its origin in exegetical and philological studies and attained prominence in the nineteenth century beginning with Friedrich Schleiermacher. In those contexts it refers to a structure that is supposed to be unique to investigation in the 'human sciences'. In order to understand a whole text, or the life-world or structure of meaning of an entire society, one must understand the parts of which it is composed, whether sentences or particular types of action. What a text, for example, means as a whole is clearly a function of its component parts, and an interpretation of the text as a whole requires justification in terms of evidence supplied by the meaning of those parts. To this extent, investigation in these fields seems to parallel the presumed atomistic character of investigation and knowledge in the natural sciences. In the case of the human sciences, however, it is claimed that in order to understand the individual components of which such wholes are constituted it is necessary to understand the contexts—that is, the wholes—in which they are embedded. One can't understand a passage in the Bible until one understands that it is a passage in the Bible: that is, that the passage performs a role in a 'work' devoted to spreading the gospel of fall and (in its Christian versions) redemption. Similarly, it is suggested that one can't understand or correctly interpret an action within an alien society unless one understands the context in which it is performed: that is, the role of actions of that sort within the set of practices governing action within that culture. This investigative procedure is clearly going to involve its practitioners in a circle of justification. Our knowledge claims in regard to the meaning of a whole text or of the meaning structure of some society will be supported by evidence supplied by our knowledge of the meaning of particular sentences or acts. On the other hand, our knowledge claims in regard to the meanings of those individual elements will be supported by and justified in terms of our knowledge of the meaning of the entire structure. Our justifications will thus have a circular structure. This is the classical form of the hermeneutic circle as developed in the nineteenth century.

It has been suggested that for knowledge in regard to this sort of human meaning to be possible, there must be an additional ability to be sensitive to the meaning of an entire text, to intuit its significance or at least 'dialectically' go backward and forward between whole and part so as to reduce the circle of justification—an ability that is not necessary for understanding and interpreting nonhuman natural phenomena. This is the origin of the claim that a different sort of 'understanding' (*Verstehen*) is exercised in the human sciences than in the natural sciences, and that the methods of the natural sciences are necessarily inadequate when applied to the study of human beings. Because Heidegger uses the phrase 'hermeneutic circle' prominently in *Being and Time,* this position is often attributed to him.

Further, this characterization of the hermeneutic circle is often associated with a definite doctrine in regard to the truth of interpretations of human actions or cultured productions. As the object that is interpreted, the sentence, text, action, or artifact is itself what it is only within the context or horizon of a human understanding. Because its meaning is established only within such a holistic human system, it is claimed that to interpret the meaning of such an entity correctly must be to understand the entity as it is understood by the community that constituted it as it is. On this view, it is only by adopting the standpoint of the other—by understanding as the ones who constituted the object understood—that one can see what the object is. And since to understand is to have a set of projects and practices, it is only by coming to inhabit, imaginatively, the cultural world of the alien group that we can come to a correct appreciation of what they say, create, and do. For such an interpretation to be true, therefore, is for the horizon of our interpretation to coincide with the horizon of understanding of those whose products and doings we are trying to understand. To share their horizon of understanding is to understand their understanding, and in order to do this we must correctly interpret the cultural whole in which a human element subsists. The hermeneutic circle as it is often understood seems to prescribe a particular, definite view of what it is to understand human beings and a strong conception of what it is for an interpretation of human beings to be true.

This position, however, is certainly not Heidegger's. His account differs in three important respects, all of which are related to the fore-structure of interpretation. First, for Heidegger, the hermeneutic circle is an absolutely general phenomenon; it applies to all interpretation and understanding, regardless of the ontological character of the entity interpreted. The interpretation of a mark on a screen as the path of an electron, or the interpretation of a liquid as water, or the interpretation of a rock as a potential hammer are just as 'circular' as the interpretation of the Bible.

Second, while the characteristic holism of Heidegger's position on understanding certainly commits him to the view that to understand any one thing requires understanding many, and that to interpret any single element in a system requires understanding the whole of which it is a part and vice versa, he does not much emphasize this kind of circularity; when he discusses the hermeneutic circle, this is not precisely what he has in mind. Rather, for Heidegger, as we have seen in connection with the existential analytic, the primary circle in interpretation and understanding is that between the assumption of the interpreter and the result of the interpretation. I, as an interpreter, appear to assume something in regard to what I am interpreting, and then, after painstaking investigation on the basis of that assumption, I discover that I was right all along. Heidegger's whole discussion of the hermeneutic circle is designed to show that while there is a sense in which this description is always accurate of the interpretive situation, the sort of 'assumption' involved here in no way generates a vicious circularity in argument. Once we see that it is this very general feature of all interpretation which is at issue, we can see that the familiar part-whole hermeneutic circle is at most a derivative, second-order case of the overall hermeneutic phenomenon.

Third, standard interpretations of the hermeneutic circle tend to emphasize that for an interpretation of a human phenomenon to be correct, it must coincide with the interpretation of that phenomenon within the society that generates it; thus, the interpreter must, as a methodological principle, make it her aim to understand the understanding of the human with which she is dealing. In other words, an interpretation is right, on this view, if it articulates the meaning that some thing, action, or product has for those we are interpreting. Given the holistic nature of human understanding, every correct interpretation thus involves the sympathetic articulation of the world of the other, as it is for the other. The early Heidegger's discussion of the hermeneutic circle, by contrast, emphasizes precisely the same pragmatic conception of truth that he always employs. For an interpretation to be true is for it to uncover the thing it is interpreting as it is: that is, as it is capable of being dealt with. The context of understanding that is presupposed by an interpretation, even a correct one, is the understanding of the one who interprets. The truth of the interpretation is not a matter of correspondence between the meaning a thing has for me and the meaning it has for the producer or agent. Rather, the truth of an interpretation rests on the success of that interpretation for the ends for which it is carried out, whatever those should happen to be. That is, the significant whole that must be understood if anything is to be interpreted, that is necessary for any meaning and is invoked in any justification, is always the significant whole of the interpreter's own community. This is so even in the cases where what is interpreted is the language, the directed activity, or the artifacts of a member of an alien group of Dasein, so that that which is interpreted is interpreted as itself belonging to a community of purposive agents and thus being in the world.[8]

We will deal in turn with these three differences from the familiar version of the hermeneutic circle, and their relations with the Heideggerian fore-structure of interpretation.

Aside from everything else that tells against identifying Heidegger's

---

8. In this respect Heidegger is closer to the holistic position of Quine and Davidson—who tend to think of interpretation in terms of the translation of foreign speech behavior into our own idiom using our own conceptual resources—than he is to more standard hermeneutic theorists, who tend to take the case of interpretation of literary texts as paradigmatic and to think that correct interpretation involves understanding what is interpreted in its own terms and its own context. See W. V. O. Quine, *Word and Object*, chap. 2, pp. 26–79. Donald Davidson, "Radical Interpretation," in *Inquiries into Truth and Interpretation* (Oxford: Oxford University Press, 1984), pp. 125–139.

version of the hermeneutic circle with the standard sort of *Verstehen* position, Heidegger clearly says that the hermeneutic circle in his sense applies to all interpretation and understanding, not just to the understanding of intelligent human action and production. "Any interpretation which is to contribute understanding, must already have understood what is to be interpreted. This is a fact that has always been remarked, even if only in the area of derivative ways of understanding and interpretation, such as philological interpretation."[9] He even goes so far as to say that there is no question in this area of distinguishing 'understanding' from scientific knowledge, because natural scientific knowledge itself is merely a species of understanding and interpretation and, as such, involves the same circle. "The assimilation of understanding and interpretation to a definite ideal of knowledge is not the issue here. Such an ideal is itself only a subspecies of understanding—a subspecies which has strayed into the legitimate task of grasping the extant."[10] Heidegger does not think there is any essential difference in the kind of understanding involved in understanding humans and nonhumans, even if to understand humans as humans is to understand a sort of being ontologically different from entities that are extant. (Ready-to-hand entities, although they are not Dasein, could not be without Dasein and are thus in some sense intermediate between the other two.) For him the understanding and interpretation of extant beings has precisely the same circular structure as the understanding of humans.

Heidegger associates his version of the hermeneutic circle with the 'fore-structure' of Dasein. "This circle of understanding is not an orbit in which any random kind of knowledge may move; it is the expression of the existential fore-structure of Dasein itself."[11] The circle is the result of the structure of meaning and arises out of the nature of all interpretive understanding. "The 'circle' in understanding belongs to the structure of meaning, and the latter phenomenon is rooted in the existential constitution of Dasein—that is, in the understanding which interprets."[12] For Heidegger, to interpret is to take something as something. What the being is taken as in an interpretation is the meaning assigned to it by the interpretation; when I take a rock as a hammer, I am understanding it as having the meaning of being a hammer. There are two ways in which this

---

9. *B.T.*, p. 194/152.
10. *B.T.*, p. 194/153. Translation modified.
11. *B.T.*, p. 195/153.
12. *B.T.*, p. 195/153.

can be done: either directly as part of a practical, purpose-oriented sequence of actions, or indirectly by making an assertion. Even in this second case, every interpretation occurs only as an element within a system of practically oriented activity. But to have the capacity to engage in such activity is to have a practical understanding, the particular kind of understanding corresponding in each case with the particular character of the potential activity, and actually to engage in such purposeful activity (which is necessary for every interpretation), one must at least have the capacity to do so. So every definite interpretation, regardless of the ontological character of what is being interpreted, presupposes some prior understanding on the part of the interpreter. In order to interpret some rock as a hammer, I must know how to use things in order to hammer and how to hammer in order to build; perhaps most important, I must have some definite end to be realized in and through the hammering and building, for the sake of which I act. In order to assert that a rock is capable of being used as a hammer, I must both understand how and for what hammers are used and understand how and for what to use the socially standardized tool that is the assertion 'this is a hammer'. An act can be an act of hammer interpretation only if it is part of an organized pattern of actions, and these other conditions are merely statements of what it is to be so involved.

This intertwining of interpretation and understanding is the fore-structure of interpretation. Every interpretation, whether true (uncovering) or false, is grounded in a fore-having (that is, to interpret any entity, one must understand many others), a fore-sight (we approach the rock 'under the guidance of a point of view': can it be used for hammering?), and a fore-conception (in terms of some definite network of concepts, especially in the case of linguistic interpretations, or assertions), because nothing can count as an interpretation without such a fore-structure embedded in patterned practical activity. Even to interpret a trace on a screen as the path of an electron by asserting that it is necessarily involves a whole host of practical abilities with language, which amount to a prior understanding of many extant entities.

So every interpretation, every assigning of meaning, every taking-as, regardless of the ontological character of what is interpreted, operates under a 'presupposition'. Stated in a purely formal way, this presupposition is that it is possible to interpret something only in accordance with the interpreter's own understanding. Every interpretation interprets an entity from the standpoint generated by the interpreter's own way of being-in-the-world: that is, by the pattern of purposeful activity in which he is engaged or which he is capable of engaging in. "Any interpretation which is to contribute understanding, must already have understood what is to be interpreted."[13] "If, when one is engaged in a particular concrete kind of interpretation, in the sense of exact textual interpretation, one likes to appeal to what 'stands there', then one finds that what 'stands there' in the first instance is nothing other than the obvious undiscussed assumption of the person who does the interpreting. In an interpretive approach there lies such an assumption, as that which has been 'taken for granted' with the interpretation as such—that is to say, as that which has been presented in our fore-having, fore-sight, and our fore-conception."[14]

This conception of interpretation, however, seems to lead to a vicious circle in regard to all our knowledge. If to know is to know some thing as it is, with the meaning it has 'in itself'; and if to count as knowledge an interpretation must be fully justified by the evidence; and if every interpretation one can ever engage in and every proposition we can ever assert presupposes some prior, ungrounded understanding of things on our part, then isn't it the case that all our supposed knowledge rests upon an ungrounded assumption and thus doesn't count as knowledge? An examination of the texts indicates that whenever Heidegger discusses the hermeneutic circle in *Being and Time,* he is concerned with this problem as it relates to the structure and foundation of his own argument, rather than to any supposed structure of the relation of part and whole that is unique to interpretation in the human sciences.

How, then, does Heidegger propose to deal with this issue, and does it amount to a *reductio ad absurdum* of his views? It is first necessary to become clear on exactly what this 'presupposition' or 'assumption' of understanding and interpretation is supposed to be in Heidegger. In order to interpret something as a hammer, I must have a practical understanding of hammering and thus of the equipmental context of building. If I am to assert that some thing is a hammer, I must also understand how to use assertions—in particular, the assertion 'this is a hammer'—in order to communicate and draw inferences. In order to interpret something as an electron, I must have a practical understanding of how to use the vocabulary of modern physics appropriately, and thus have a grasp on

13. *B.T.,* p. 194/152.
14. *B.T.,* p. 192/150.

the causal roles that electrons are supposed to play in our ultimate perceptions, and thus have a cognitive understanding of what it is to be an electron. In order to interpret some behavior of a tiger as an act performed in order to reach some end, I must have a practical understanding of that for the sake of which the tiger is acting, and this amounts to a practical way of dealing with the tiger through taking its ends into account in pursuing my own ends, just as the tiger in crouching during the hunt is interpreting the antelope as trying to stay alive.

In all these cases the understanding presupposed by the interpretation is not primarily a cognitive holding-to-be-true of a proposition, even if we can assign such beliefs on the basis of understanding. Rather, what is 'presupposed' is an end to be realized and a (mostly) successful capacity to achieve that end. Nothing can be interpreted as a hammer apart from the practical understanding of hammering, and this understanding is contained in an overall ability to achieve the ends for which hammers are serviceable. The practical context of activity 'grounds' and supplies the conditions that must be met if a being is to be a definite sort of thing. A hammer is a thing that can successfully be used in hammering, and what it is to be a hammer and what a thing must be in order to be a hammer are fixed only within that practical context of activity in which hammers function. Even an incorrect interpretation of something as a hammer requires a general ability to perform the acts in which hammers are used and a capacity to act so as to achieve the ends of hammering, because without these it is impossible to do anything that is an interpretation of a thing as a hammer. But—and this is the crucial point—my practical understanding in no way determines whether the thing *is* a hammer, or even whether I eventually come to believe that it is. To be a hammer, this thing must be capable of being used as hammers are used, and whether this is possible is determined solely by what the hammer is. For us to know that this is a hammer is for us to have evidence that it is, and this evidence is provided only by what happens when we use it as a hammer. If we can successfully use it as a hammer, then we have evidence that it is one, and, given enough such evidence, so it is.

There is a similar structure to the way understanding is 'presupposed' by the interpretation of every ontological sort of entity, whether extant, ready-to-hand, or Dasein. What the presupposed understanding does, and what it is necessary for, is to fix the evidential conditions that must be met if a thing is to be a being of a given kind. The end toward which a practical series of actions is directed can serve to supply conditions under which it is appropriate to use a kind of thing, or assertion, and under which an interpretation counts as successful. Just as the use of a thing as a hammer is successful if the thing shows itself in the use as serviceable in hammering, so every interpretation operates within a predelineated horizon of purposes for which the interpretation is carried out, and which serves to determine the conditions under which that act of interpretation is true. Without such a horizon specified by a for-the-sake-of, nothing could show itself as anything, because there can never be any *as such:* that is, any conditions an entity would need to fulfill in order to be some type of thing. That there is the determination that a thing is interpreted as having depends upon there being a practical understanding in and for which there is such a determination. But, for Heidegger, whether an entity has any determination in particular depends only upon what it reveals itself to be when it is interpreted as having that determination. Applied to assertions, this means that it is a condition for an assertion having a meaning$_i$ that it fix conditions under which it would be true if those conditions were fulfilled, that those conditions be fixed by the assertion's having a meaning$_h$ within a practical horizon of activity in which the assertion itself is used. An assertion can be true or false, can have some semantic content, only within a 'presupposed' practical understanding. But that it is true or that it is false depends upon some thing meeting the conditions laid down in the assertion, and that depends on the stuff within the world.

There is thus no real problem of vicious circularity involved in Heidegger's analysis of interpretation. The 'circle' in which interpretation depends upon understanding, and is unsupported by evidence, is real enough but should in no way be taken as calling into question the results of the interpretation or making them 'merely subjective'. The 'dependence' of interpretation on understanding merely fixes the kinds of properties or characteristics a thing can be interpreted as having; it does not determine which properties from among some set of possible ones the thing actually has.

What makes this situation appear viciously circular is only the traditional notion that to know some thing, to interpret it as it truly is, is to discover what it is by and in itself, to discover the properties and character it has in itself. And, it is asked, how are we to justify that the determinations allowed for by our practices and purposes, the terms in which we interpret things, are the right ones, the determinations that uncover the thing itself? Isn't the assumption that they are the right ones an illicit, unjustified assumption? To ask these questions is one way of raising the metaphysical question of the being of beings and of considering the relation between being and Dasein's understanding of being, which we consider in Part II.

First, however, we will consider the supposed implications of this version of the hermeneutic circle for the human sciences. For Heidegger, given what it is to be a Dasein or even a purposive being, to interpret x as a Dasein must necessarily involve a global interpretation (1) of the behavior of x as oriented toward a goal, (2) of x as having a practical understanding of things other than itself, (3) of x as engaging in interpretations, and (4) of x as belonging to a community of interacting purposive beings that are taken as sharing a world. That is, to interpret x as a Dasein is to interpret x as having a rather definite understanding of itself and its world, on its own account. But what it means for such an interpretation to be true is fixed by the purposes for which the interpretation itself is designed, and those purposes are the interpreter's own, not the purpose ascribed to the interpreted, even when we interpret those beings as having a self-understanding. Further, the very terms we use in correctly characterizing such beings need not be their terms. They are the categories and *existentialia* relevant to the realization of the interpreter's—not the interpreted's—ends, either 'in themselves' or 'for us'.

It is certainly possible, for some reason, to be interested in an interpretation of another Dasein which would be true if and only if it corresponded with that Dasein's own self-interpretation. But there are many situations where that self-interpretation is simply irrelevant to the issues addressed in and through our own interpretations of that Dasein, and thus irrelevant to the truth of those interpretations. For example, we might interpret a slave with whom his master converses as a Dasein, as human, and as a member of a community together with his master—and be right to do so, even though neither master nor slave have available to them any concept that encompasses both of them but excludes, for example, earthworms or rocks. For the interpretation of a human entity (an entity interpreted by us—who else?—as Dasein) or of its cultural productions to be true, it need not in any way correspond to the self-interpretation of the interpreted. As with any other interpretation for Heidegger, it must merely successfully uncover the entity interpreted. And to do this is to reveal an entity as it is revealed to be when it is interpreted in terms established by the purposes, practices, and concerns that are operative in the interpreter's own world.

It follows from these considerations that no argument in this area shows that it is impossible to interpret as extant a being that is also interpretable as a Dasein. To say that a being, x, is correctly interpretable as extant is just to say that for some for-the-sake-of of the interpreter, y_1, such an interpretation is successful and useful. To say that it is correctly interpretable as Dasein is to say that for some other for-the-sake-of of an interpreter, y_2, an interpretation of x as a Dasein is suitable and successful.

But isn't a Dasein correctly, and uniquely, interpretable as a Dasein in virtue of its *being* a Dasein, in virtue of its being as Dasein? Doesn't the being of Dasein constrain how—according to what ontological catego-ries—we can correctly understand an entity that is a Dasein? With these questions we have passed over from the region of transcendental seman-tics to the region of metaphysics.

PART II
Being

Introduction

To this point we have been concerned with what might be called the early Heidegger's transcendental semantics. Our primary interest has centered on the issue of the conditions under which it is possible for an overt act, a mental intention, or a linguistic assertion to be about or directed toward something. To this extent we have been concerned with the foundations of semantics. The conditions for intentionality we have focused upon have been necessary conditions rather than causal or sufficient conditions. In addition, they have been 'transcategorial' in the sense that they are conditions under which there could be ways of understanding what it means for there to be the various kinds of things that are and hence any understanding of particular things. To this extent these conditions make possible an understanding of things and are thus properly seen as transcendental. Finally, Heidegger's argument in regard to these conditions has a classical transcendental form. He starts with a fact of intentionality, in his case the fact that we intend things that are. He then goes on to determine the formal structures that make such an intentional performance possible.

It is immediately apparent from the texts we have been considering, however, that in the period of *Being and Time* Heidegger's primary interest was not in transcendental semantics. Rather, the project of what I am calling transcendental semantics was a part of and a stage in a much larger program, the program of constructing a new metaphysics. At that time Heidegger, influenced by Husserl, still thought of himself as providing a truly scientific basis for philosophy. And the science of philosophy, for the early Heidegger, is just the science of being. "Philosophy is the

173

science of being. . . . Philosophy is the theoretical conceptual interpretation of being, of being's structure and its possibilities."[1] Early Heidegger
tends to call this science 'ontology' ("philosophy is not a science of beings
but of being or, as the Greek expression goes, ontology"),[2] but he is well
aware that the traditional name for it is 'metaphysics' ("metaphysics
means ontology").[3] For Heidegger at this time every genuine philosophical enterprise was at bottom part of the science of metaphysics, and
insofar as he saw his own work as philosophical, he understood it as
metaphysical. Interestingly, even after he gave up the notion that his
work was a kind of metaphysics, he maintained the position that philosophy was essentially metaphysical. In 1964 he wrote in "The End of
Philosophy and the Task of Thinking" that "philosophy is metaphysics"[4]
and drew the obvious conclusion, that his own work no longer counted
as philosophy.

Heidegger never completed the metaphysics he intended to construct
on the basis of the published portion of *Being and Time*. It is well known
that instead he not only abandoned the project of *Being and Time* but also
abandoned all attempts to do metaphysics and came to the conclusion
that metaphysics itself had come to an end. In many of the places in which
the late Heidegger speaks about the end of philosophy—that is, the end
of metaphysics—he does so in terms of the completion of metaphysics in
the rough-and-ready pragmatism that he takes to be central in modern
science and technology. "Philosophy is ending in the present age. It has
found its place in the scientific attitude of socially active humanity. . . .
The sciences will interpret everything in their structure that is still reminiscent of the origin from philosophy in accordance with the rules of
science, that is, technologically. Every science understands the categories
upon which it remains dependent for the articulation and delineation of
its area of investigation as working hypotheses. Their truth is measured
not only by the effect which their application brings about within the
progress of research. Scientific truth is equated with the efficiency of
these effects."[5]

Such passages are often interpreted as laments for the unfortunate end
of philosophy, and there is no doubt that they frequently adopt a nostal-
gic tone. It is nevertheless the case that the late Heidegger is unam-

1. *B.P.*, p. 11/15.
2. *B.P.*, p. 11/15.
3. *B.P.*, p. 137/195.
4. *E.O.P.*, p. 55/61.
5. *E.O.P.*, p. 58/64.

biguous in his assertion that metaphysics is *properly* completed by the pragmatism of modern science and technology. He does not see the modern world as incorrect in thinking that metaphysical philosophy has always tended toward a pragmatically understood science or in thinking that it is completed by such a science. He does hold, however, that there is still a possibility for a nonmetaphysical, nonphilosophical, non-pragmatically evaluated thinking concerned with what he variously calls '*aletheia*', 'opening', 'lighting', or the '*aletheia* of being'. "But is the end of philosophy in the sense of its development to the sciences also already the complete realization of all the possibilities in which the thinking of philosophy was posited? Or is there a first possibility for thinking apart from the last possibility which we characterized (the dissolution of philosophy in the technologized sciences), a possibility from which the thinking of philosophy would have to start out, but which as philosophy it could nevertheless not experience and adopt?"[6]

Part II of this book asserts three theses. (1) Both the abandonment of the metaphysics of *Being and Time* and Heidegger's later attack on the possibility of metaphysics as such are grounded on the results concerning the possibility of understanding and intentionality that we have extracted from the early Heidegger. (2) Heidegger was right in thinking that his conclusions concerning transcendental semantics could be used as premises from which to argue that anything other than a generalized pragmatism concerning metaphysics is impossible. (3) The topic of the other nonmetaphysical 'thinking' that Heidegger holds to be still possible is to be identified with the subject matter we have been examining under the heading of the transcendental conditions for understanding.

We work toward these theses in three stages. Chapter 6 offers an interpretation of the metaphysics that the early Heidegger thought could be derived from the transcendental semantics of *Being and Time*. Our major evidence for this interpretation comes from *The Basic Problems of Phenomenology,* although many of Heidegger's works from this period relate to this metaphysical project. Chapter 7 discusses the later Heidegger's attempt to 'overcome' metaphysics. It offers an interpretation of 'the truth of being' and of how this crucial notion functions in Heidegger's critique of metaphysics. Chapter 8 attempts to reconstruct the argument structure of the late Heidegger and places Heidegger himself in a larger philosophical context by considering the question of whether the position we have ascribed to him is relativistic.

6. E.O.P., p. 59/65.

6 The Early Heidegger's Metaphysical Strategy

Being Is Said in Many Ways

It is well known that Heidegger was interested in the 'question of being'. Indeed, he frequently proclaims that this is the central question of philosophy. What is not immediately apparent, however, is just which question is *the* question of being, for several questions concerned with 'being' have been raised, or could have been raised, in the philosophical tradition. Heidegger, both early and late, was not only aware of this multiplicity of questions; he insisted upon it.

In 1929 in *Kant and the Problem of Metaphysics,* for example, Heidegger distinguishes three levels of questioning in regard to being. In increasingly fundamental order there questions are: (1) 'what is that which is?'; (2) 'what do we understand by the word "being"?' (or alternatively, 'what is being as such?'); and (3) 'how is it possible to have any understanding of being?'

Heidegger says the answer to Aristotle's classic question of metaphysics, *'Ti to on?'*—'What is that which is?'—asked of beings that are, rests upon an answer to a preceding question—and that answer upon the answer to a still more fundamental question. In order even to understand Aristotle's question, one must understand 'being as such and in general': "Thus, the question *Ti to on* (what is the essent) implies a more original question: What is the significance of being which is precomprehended in this question?"[1] Heidegger specifically says that this second (prior) question should be read as 'What is the meaning of being?' and this is the

1. *K.P.M.,* p. 230/201.

official form of the 'question of being' in *Being and Time*. But in the structure of that text, in *Kant and the Problem of Metaphysics,* and other places, Heidegger makes explicit the third question and its relation to the 'question of being'. "So the question of 'first philosophy', namely, 'What is that which is as such?' must force us back beyond the question 'What is being as such?' to the still more fundamental question: 'Whence are we to comprehend a notion such as that of being, with the many articulations and relations it includes?'"[2] And this question is specifically clarified as "the question of the possibility of the understanding of being in general".[3]

Similarly, during a radio interview in 1969, Heidegger distinguished between two 'questions of being', roughly comparable to the second and third questions formulated in *Kant and the Problem of Metaphysics*. "Here the phrase the 'question of being' is ambiguous. Here 'the question of being' on the one hand, means the question concerning being as being. And we determine what being is in this question. The answer to this question gives us the definition of being. The question of being, on the other hand, can also be understood in the following sense: Wherein is each answer to the question of being based, i.e., wherein, after all, is the unconcealment of being grounded?"[4]

In the passage at the end of *Kant and the Problem of Metaphysics* to which we have already alluded, Heidegger suggests that the being of beings, what it is for any entity to be, has traditionally been interpreted in a threefold way. First, every being is *what* it is. Insofar as something is, it is something definite. It has not only determinate characteristics, however, but also some defining characteristic that makes it the being it is and makes it possible for it to be the particular being it is. This is being as 'what-being' [*Was-sein*], *essentia,* or essence, and every entity, insofar as it is, has its essence. Heidegger tells us that the essence, or what a thing is if it is, supplies the 'intrinsic possibility' of the thing: the cowness of the cow is what makes it possible for it to be a cow. Included in the essence are the identity conditions, the individuation conditions, and the conditions of unity of the thing. The essence supplies the conditions under which a being is a single unified thing (as opposed to a mere collection), identical with itself across time and through changes, and distinct from

2. *K.P.M.,* p. 232/203.
3. *K.P.M.,* p. 233/204. Translation modified.
4. *M.H.C.,* pp. 44–45.

everything else that is. Insofar as it includes these, the essence also specifies what sort of thing a thing is.

Second, the being of beings has been interpreted in terms of the answer to the question of whether a being is or is not. Even granted an understanding of the essence of a thing, it is an open issue as to whether the conditions specified by the essence actually obtain. That they obtain is involved in what Heidegger calls the 'that-being' [*Dass-sein*] of a thing, which has traditionally been called '*existentia*' or 'existence'. It is at least initially unclear, however, whether we conceptually and explicitly understand 'existence', or what it is for it to be the case that something is.

Third, Heidegger tells us that both these aspects of our traditional understanding of 'being', as well as the distinction between them, are 'intertwined' with a final notion of being, 'being-true' [*Wahr-sein*].[5] It is clear that this notion is proximally derived from the discussion of being and truth in Husserl's Sixth Logical Investigation. Ultimately, however, Heidegger sees all these determinations as derived from the discussion in the *Metaphysics* in which Aristotle says that being is said in many ways. Of these various ways, Heidegger here emphasizes the way it is said in terms of actuality and potentiality and the way it is said in terms of truth. What remains obscure, however, is whether there is a central sense of 'being' standing behind all of these—and if so, what it is. This is just the second level of Heidegger's questioning concerning being which we distinguished above: 'What does 'being', as such and in general, mean?' But if the traditional metaphysical determinations of 'being' merely led to this problem, how did the early Heidegger propose to deal with it?

The answer is supplied in the intended structure of *The Basic Problems of Phenomenology*, which was designed as a working-out in class lecture form of the metaphysical continuation of *Being and Time*.[6] *Basic Problems* was to include three parts. The third, never begun, was to discuss phenomenological method and thus doesn't concern us here. The first part, which was completed, involves a "phenomenological-critical discussion of several traditional theses about being."[7] The point of this extended critical inquiry into the history of metaphysics is to show in detail that it is impossible to understand what is involved in this history unless we first understand the meaning of being as such. The second part of the course,

5. Cf. *K.P.M.*, pp. 230–231/201–202.
6. *B.P.*, p. 1/1, carries the designation "A new elaboration of division 3 of part 1 of *Being and Time*."
7. *B.P.*, p. 23/32.

which is incomplete, was meant to answer the question of the meaning of being as such through a determination of temporality as the horizon for every understanding of being. "Attention to what is denoted in these theses leads to the insight that they cannot be brought up adequately— not even as problems—as long as the fundamental question of the whole science of being has not been put and answered: the question of the meaning of being in general. The second part of our course will deal with this question."[8] We look at Part 2 of *Basic Problems,* and Heidegger's strategy for answering the fundamental question of being, in the second and third sections of this chapter. In this section we examine the first part of *Basic Problems* to see why and how the early Heidegger thought the traditional answers to the question '*Ti to on?*'—answers that constitute the many ways in which 'being' is said—depend for their intelligibility on a prior, inexplicit understanding of being in general.

Whereas *Kant and the Problem of Metaphysics* speaks of three ontological determinations, *essentia, existentia,* and being-true, *Basic Problems* considers four theses: (1) Kant's thesis that 'being' is not a real predicate; (2) the medieval thesis that every being involves both *essentia* and *existentia;* (3) the Cartesian thesis that there are two basic ways of being, *res extensa* and *res cogitans;* and (4) the 'logical' thesis that every being can be talked about by means of the 'is' of the copula.

Heidegger's discussion of the second thesis is clearly meant to address the issue of the relation between essence and existence, and treats those two ontological determinations by going back to 'being' in the sense of *energeia* and *dynamos* in antiquity. The discussion of the fourth thesis is explicitly meant to deal with being-true. The consideration of the first thesis directly treats the issue of existence in the modern sense. Finally, the third thesis concerns the distinction between beings that are intentional, or have intentional determinations, and those that do not. Does a being that has intentional characteristics have a different 'way' of being from one that does not? As we have seen, Heidegger thinks the distinction between intentional and non-intentional being is misunderstood when it is interpreted in terms of different essential properties of substances. Rather, intentional beings are not substances at all; they are Dasein, agents of the sort we discussed above, who have a different way of having characteristics than do substances. Thus, oddly enough, it is the discussion of the third thesis that treats the most famous of Aristotle's

8. *B.P.,* pp. 15–16/20–21.

determinations of being, the categories that are divided between substantial being and predicative being. Taken together, the treatment of these four theses discusses all the ways in which Aristotle says that 'being' is said, with the exception of accidental being.

As we have emphasized, the ultimate point of Heidegger's discussions in *Basic Problems* of existence, actuality and potentiality, being-true, and the way of being of intentional beings is to show that we cannot understand these terms or the problems they are meant to address unless we already implicitly understand the meaning of being in general. We clearly lack such an understanding at the explicit conceptual level, but we are supposed to have access to the meaning of being in general in some preconceptual way. Indeed, Heidegger holds that without such an understanding of being, it would be impossible for us to understand any entity at all.

Heidegger tries to start to show this, as well as to begin to articulate the content of this preconceptual understanding of being, by pointing out an essential unclarity in Kant's positive understanding of 'being'. One way to see what is involved is to say that Kant attempts to determine the conditions for application of the existential quantifier. Kant's thesis, that 'being' isn't a real predicate, is the conceptual ancestor of the many modern views which hold that the 'is' of existence should not be treated as a predicate qualifying some subject but rather in terms of the existential quantifier. Heidegger endorses Kant's statement of this view, for example, when it leads Kant to suggest that " 'God exists' would mean, more precisely expressed, 'Something existing is God'."[9] In other words Heidegger, as well as Kant, rejects the assertion that existence is an ordinary, if high-level, property.

But merely to say that 'existence' isn't a predicate is to say nothing positive concerning existence. Something existing is *F;* can anything further be said than this? Heidegger feels that in addition to his negative thesis, Kant also advances a positive thesis concerning existence. One formulation of it immediately follows the most famous statement of the negative thesis in Kant's First Critique: " 'Being' is obviously not a real predicate; that is, it is not a concept of something which could be added to the concept of a thing. It is merely the positing of a thing, or of certain determinations, as existing in themselves."[10] But Kant's clearest state-

9. *B.P.,* pp. 41–42/55–56.
10. Kant, *C.P.R.* p. 504, A598, B626.

ment of the positive thesis is given in the postulate chapter of the section on the analytic of principles. Although Heidegger does not note the fact, it is expressed in two distinct ways. According to the first formulation, perception (together with its causal extension) is the only evidence that can be used to guarantee the existence of a being: "The perception which supplies the content of the concept is the sole mark of actuality. . . . Our knowledge of the existence of things reaches, then, only so far as perception and its advance according to empirical laws can extend."[11] The other formulation, that actuality amounts to some relation to perception, is implied in Kant's initial statement in the explanation of the modal categories ("The categories of modality have the peculiarity that, in determining an object, they do not in the least enlarge the concept to which they are attached as predicates. They only express the relation of the concept to the faculty of knowledge")[12] and is expressly asserted in a footnote: "But while possibility is merely a positing of the thing in relation to the understanding . . . actuality is at the same time a connection of it with perception."[13] These two formulations are equivalent only under the verificationist assumption that the meaning$_i$ of an expression is determined solely by the evidence that could count in favor of the truth or satisfaction of the expression.

What is the basis for Kant's claim that 'existence' isn't a real predicate? According to *Basic Problems,* the assertion is a consequence of the different logical status that Kant ascribes to the categories of existence and reality. All categories express the form of some type of relation in a judgment. The categories of quality, of which reality is one, express relations between concepts in a judgment. If concept A is connected with concept B in a positive judgment 'A is B', this expresses that what A is is partially determined by the concept B. The modal categories express no relation between concepts but rather a connection between a concept and an object. "The relation that is posited is that of the entire conceptual content, the full reality of the concept, to the object of the concept."[14]

'Existence', then, posits a relation between a concept and an object. It says that there is something existing, an object, which is identical with the character expressed by the concept. According to Kant's interpretation of the modal categories, however, to say that there is something, or is

11. Ibid., p. 243, A225–226, B273.
12. Ibid., p. 239, A219, B266.
13. Ibid., p. 252, A239, B287.
14. *B.P.,* p. 41/54.

possibly something, or is necessarily something is itself to express a relation between the object so determined as identical with our concept and our own cognitive faculties, although that relation does not go into determining *what* that object is. When it is specifically said that something is, it is said that the object, which answers to our concept, is related to our perception. "It is perception which intrinsically bears within itself the reach to the actuality, the existence, or, in our terminology, the extantness, of things. Thus the specific character of absolute position [existence], as Kant defines it, reveals itself as perception."[15]

Of course, the last claim, as stated, is wildly false. This gives Heidegger the opportunity to point out what he takes to be the unclarity in Kant's understanding of existence. Given the character of 'perception' as an intentional term, the claim that 'existence equals perception' is ambiguous among the claims that existence equals (a) the perceiving, (b) the perceived, (c) the being perceived of that which is perceived, or (d) the perceivability of the perceived. But surely the first three options are false. Of these the third, that 'existence' means the fact that the object is perceived, or the being perceived of the object, is most in accord with Kant's texts and the most plausible. But surely that *x* is perceived is possible only *because x* exists. That it is perceived is not identical with its existence; it is perceived in virtue of being perceivable. But we have already seen that for Heidegger, that which exists—or, in his terminology, is extant—is that which is perceivable, in the extended sense that includes causal efficacy for theoretical entities.

Does this mean that existence is simply to be identified with perceivability? At this time Heidegger thinks not. He asserts that we ordinarily take even the perceivability of a thing to be in some sense a *consequence* of its existence, not identical with it. "Are existence, actuality, and perceivedness one and the same? The window, however, surely does not receive existence from my perceiving it, but just the reverse: I can perceive it only if it exists and because it exists. In every case, perceivedness presupposes perceivability, and perceivability on its part already requires the existence of the perceivable or the perceived being."[16] As we will see in detail later on, the distinction Heidegger draws here is crucial in his interpretation of the metaphysical tradition, and the denial of this distinction is crucial in his own ultimate criticism of that tradition.

15. *B.P.*, p. 46/62.
16. *B.P.*, p. 49/66.

At this point the early Heidegger claims that the fact that a thing is perceived, its being perceived, involves us in an understanding that the thing exists, and that it does so necessarily includes an understanding of what it is for it to exist. 'Existence' is not an aspect of the actual perception; rather it is a special kind of intentional *object* that is in some way associated with the perceptual act.

In that I perceive an object, I am directed toward that object: that is, I intend it. But, Heidegger reminds us (for all the usual reasons having to do with intending unreals and the difference between sense and reference), to intend an object can't involve a real relation between two real objects. Neither should intentionality be analyzed as a relation between a mind and a purely mental content. He points out that when I see a window, what I am intending is the window itself, as extant, and not an idea or a sensation. But this is just to say that to perceive a thing is to perceive it precisely as extant, as existing: it is the mark and character of perception as a species of intentionality to be directed toward existing things, and just insofar as x is perceived, it is perceived as existing. I can be in error about the existence of the object of a perceptual illusion only because to perceive that object is already to take it as existing. "In conformity with its sense of direction, perception is directed toward a being that is extant. It intends this precisely as extant."[17] So the existence of a thing perceived is no real element in the perceptual relation; it is not the perceiving, nor the thing perceived, nor the being perceived of the thing. Rather it is an aspect of what is understood when something is perceived. It is, in some sense, an intentional object cointended along with the direct object of the perceiving intention, even though it is no part of the object that is perceived. "In accord with its directional sense, perceiving intends the extant in its extantness. The extant in its extantness belongs to the directional sense—that is to say, the *intentio* is directed toward uncovering the extant in its extantness."[18]

Given that insofar as I perceive x, I perceive it as existing—I understand it to exist—I must have some understanding of what it means for it to exist. "The *intentio* [of perception] itself includes an understanding of extantness, even if it is only pre-conceptual. . . . Not only do *intentio* and *intentum* belong to the intentionality of perception but so also does the understanding of the mode of being of what is intended in the *intentum*."[19] So, Heidegger concludes, even to begin to comprehend the

17. *B.P.,* p. 63/88.
18. *B.P.,* p. 71/100.
19. *B.P.,* pp. 71/100–101.

metaphysical term 'existence', one must understand the way in which the being of the thing perceived is understood in the perceptual act itself. Existence is a mode of being, where being is the intentional correlate of an intentional act in which the being of the thing perceived is intended and understood every time a thing is perceived. To analyze 'existence', we must understand 'being' as a certain sort of intentional object, which can be articulated in the case of existence through an intentional analysis of the intention in which we understand being as existing whenever we perceive. The being of the extant object, its existence, is cointended along with the object itself in the act in which the object is perceived, and that it can be perceived is always correctly correlated with the fact that it can be correctly understood as existing. But the evidence, the fulfillment of sense involved in the understanding of existence, is distinct from, although always accompanying, the perceptual evidence in which the thing perceived is given to us.

Heidegger's discussion of the other ways in which 'being' is said has a similar structure. In each case the articulations of being can be comprehended only insofar as we see being in general as a peculiar sort of intentional object and realize that being can be conceptually grasped only through an intentional analysis of our preconceptual, understanding intention of being. The different ways in which 'being' is said involve either different aspects of the intentional character of the understanding of being or different specific types of intention directed toward beings.

The second (medieval) thesis concerns the relation between the traditional determinations of *essentia* and *existentia*. As Heidegger has already discussed 'existence', it would seem that all that is left to do is to discuss 'essence' and its relation to 'existence'. But Heidegger maintains that the sense of *existentia* that is relevant in its relation with *essentia* in antiquity and the Middle Ages is quite distinct from the modern sense of 'existence' as perception, even if it turns out that the modern sense arises out of the ancient one. "In no case are we now permitted to inject into the discussion the Kantian concept of existence as tantamount to absolute position. In our characterization of the concept *existentia*, whether in Scholasticism or in antiquity, we must lay the Kantian interpretation wholly aside. It will appear later that the Kantian interpretation is not as far from the ancient one as might seem to be the case at first sight."[20]

We soon see what the ancient interpretation involves when we remember that it goes back to the Aristotelian *energeia*; it is 'effectedness',

20. *B.P.,* p. 87/122.

'enactedness'. "Something exists if it is *actu*, ergo, on the basis of an *agere*, a *Wirken*, a working, operating, or effecting (*energein*). Existence (*existere*) in this broadest sense . . . means *Gewirktheit*, enactedness, effectedness, or again, the *Wirklichkeit*, actuality, that lies in enactedness (*actualitas, energeia, entelecheia*). . . . The phenomenon of *actualitas* . . . is the Greek *energeia*."[21] By contrast, *essentia* concerns the 'what' of a thing and involves the possibility of the thing as the thing which it is. Heidegger says that the *essentia*, or reality of the thing in the traditional predicative sense, is itself said in many ways: *quidditas* (whatness), *quod quid erat esse* (*Wesen*, essence), *definitio* (circumscription, definition), *forma* (shape, figure, aspect, look), *natura* (origin).[22] All these determinations ultimately go back to the attempt to answer the question '*ti estin?*'—'What is it?'—which Heidegger thinks is answered in terms of what the thing must already have been so that it could be actualized. This claim will seem somewhat less bizarre if one remembers that behind these determinations stand the Aristotelian concepts of actuality and potentiality. "Aristotle formulates more exactly this what, which defines the *ti estin*, as *to ti en einai*. Scholasticism translates this as *quod quid erat esse*, that which each thing already was in its thingness, before it became actual. Any thing—a window, a table—was already what it is before it is actual, and it must already have been in order to become actual. It must have been with regard to its thingness, for it could become actualized only so far as it is thinkable as something possible to be actualized."[23]

Once we understand Heidegger's interpretation of *essentia* and *existentia*, his strategy becomes transparent in the light of his overall project. In just the same way that the modern concept of existence is thought to have a fundamental relation with the intentional comportment of perception, *essentia* and *existentia* have a basic relation to the intentional comportment of production, Dasein's productive behavior.[24] Roughly, the various "characteristics of *essentia* developed in reference to what is produced in producing or else to what belongs to producing as producing."[25] The *essentia* is the mode of being of the thing that is intended to be produced solely insofar as it is intended. It is related to the *eidos* or look the thing has insofar as one imagines it in the course of intending to make

21. *B.P.*, p. 87/122–123.
22. *B.P.*, pp. 85–86/119–121.
23. *B.P.*, pp. 85/119–120.
24. Cf. *B.P.*, pp. 100–112/141–58.
25. *B.P.*, p. 109/153.

it. "The *eidos* as the look, anticipated in imagination, of what is to be formed gives the thing with regard to what this thing already was and is before all actualization. Therefore the anticipated look, the *eidos*, is also called *to ti en einai*, that which a being already was."[26] *Existentia*, or *actualitas*, is interpreted in relation to the act of production as the mode of being of the end which is to be enacted in the productive act. The end enacted is intended to stand in itself, apart from the act that produces it, as available either for perception or for another productive act. "But to pro-duce, to place-here, *Her-stellen*, means at the same time to bring into the narrower or wider circuit of the accessible, here, to this place, to the *Da*, so that the produced being stands for itself on its own account and remains able to be found there and to lie-before there as something established stably for itself."[27] So there are two main varieties of actuality, of the mode of being of that which is to be produced: standing available for further use in production, to be ready-to-hand, *zuhanden*, as tools are; and standing available for perception, at hand, *vorhanden*, extant.

Just as 'existence' can't be identified with 'being perceived', '*existentia*' can't be identified with the fact of having been produced, or produced-ness. It is possible that in an extended sense of 'production' everything that exists is enacted, produced. After all, nothing comes from nothing. But what it is to be actual is not to have been produced; the causal principle is not analytic. Rather, the existence of the thing produced—its standing on its own, available for use and perception—is what is aimed at in the act of production along with the thing itself, and it is understood in that act as the cointended intentional object of the productive act of comportment. I understand actuality through producing, but actuality is no real element in the act of production. For a thing to be actual is for it to satisfy the intention toward being that I have in the act of production, whether or not the thing has in fact been enacted. "In productive comportment toward something, the being of that toward which I act in a productive manner is understood in a specific way in the sense of the productive intention. Indeed, it is understood in such a way that the productive activity, corresponding to its own peculiar sense, absolves what is to be produced from its relation to its producer. . . . The being

26. *B.P.*, pp. 107/150–151.
27. *B.P.*, p. 108/152.

that is understood in productive comportment is exactly the being in itself of the product."[28]

So, finally, to comprehend the metaphysical determinations *existentia* and *essentia,* we must recognize that being in general is such as to be intended along with the intentions directed toward things that are, and these intentions directed toward being specify their own criteria of fulfillment, which are not reducible to the criteria of fulfillment of the intentions directed toward objects. And, once again, we must have a preconceptual understanding of both the specific metaphysical determinations and the meaning of being in general insofar as we do intend in purposive, productive action.

The third (Cartesian) thesis deals with the relation and difference between non-intentional beings (and their being) and intentional beings (and their being). Is Dasein, insofar as it is capable of intentionality, merely a special sort of being at hand, or tool, or does it have a different way of being? Given that we have already seen that, for Heidegger, being in general is some kind of intentional object, which is correlated with different varieties of intentions directed toward entities, this question relates both to the sort of intention that intends being-Dasein and what is thereby intended.

The answer to this question is just a consequence of the examination carried out in detail in the first part of this book; indeed, in *Basic Problems* the discussion of the third thesis repeats much of the existential analytic of the first division of *Being and Time*. I intend myself in that I intend the for-the-sake-of of my projects, and in doing this I intend myself as 'existence' (in Heidegger's sense) or being-in-the-world: that is, purposive action of a certain social type. Here it is the context of purposive action rather than that which shows up in that context which is ontologically at issue. But once again, there is no hope of comprehending the traditional metaphysical determination of *res cogitans,* or intentional being, unless one already grasps being in general in terms of intentional correlates, as something that is understood along with intentions directed toward objects. In this case, Dasein is the being that understands its own being in that it intends beings other than itself as well as understanding their being; it intends itself as the context of purposive action whenever it intends what it is acting on, with, or toward.

The discussion of the first thesis from the history of metaphysics

28. *B.P.,* pp. 113/159–160.

concerns the sense of the existential quantifier; the discussion of the second concerns the status of conditions of individuation, identity, and unity and their relation with existence; and the consideration of the third examines the difference and similarity between intentional and non-intentional being. The discussion of the fourth ('logical') thesis officially has to do with the 'being of the copula'. This would lead one to expect a discussion of predication, or of what is involved in x being F in the sense of x having the property F. And, to some degree, this is what we get, as Heidegger looks at a series of historical determinations of the 'is' of predication. It eventually becomes apparent, however, that he is interested in using this discussion to focus on Aristotle's odd use of 'being' in the sense of 'truth', or 'being-true', a sense that Brentano discusses and that Husserl resurrects in the Sixth Logical Investigation. The two topics are connected for Heidegger in that it is the 'is' of predication, either actually present or implied, that has been traditionally taken to be the mark of assertion, and it is assertions that have been predominantly taken to be capable of being true or false.

When we remember that early Heidegger follows Husserl in thinking of truth in terms of the identification of an object of an empty intention with the object given in a full giving, the connection becomes even stronger. To see this, however, we must briefly recall what an assertion is for Heidegger and what its truth consists in. Every asserting is an intentional act directed toward entities within the world. In particular, asserting is a 'communicative-determinative exhibition'; it communicates a determinate way in which a thing may be. It is true, for Heidegger, if and only if it successfully exhibits the entity it is directed toward. And just as perceiving a thing intends a thing as extant and, insofar as it does so, involves an understanding of existence; and just as productive behavior intends the thing to be enacted and, insofar as it does so, understands enactedness, so asserting behavior—using assertions—intends the thing as true (in just the way we assert it to be) and hence involves an implicit understanding of 'being-true'.

This dark saying seems entirely opaque until we remember that for Heidegger as well as for Husserl, truth is basically the identification of an object of an empty intention with an object given in a fulfillment and, as such, the uncovering or unveiling, the manifesting of an entity. It is for this reason that they both think nonpredicative acts can be true or false. So the being-true of an *entity* is the being-unveiled of the entity: that is, its being given in such a way as to fulfill an intention of it. "The extant entity itself is in a certain way true, not as intrinsically extant, but as uncovered in the assertion."[29] The intentional sense of any assertion, insofar as it is an assertion, aims for an uncovering of or to uncover some entity; and in order to intend in the mode of asserting, one must understand what it is to be in the sense of being unveiled, in the sense of 'being-true'. That is, one must understand what it would be for this assertion, or any assertion, to be fulfilled by the presentation of the entity that it is about—that is, to be true. For Heidegger, no matter what else the 'is' of predication signifies, it marks an assertion as an assertion: that is, an intention to exhibit an entity, something intended as true. In this way an 'is' is both the characteristic trait of assertion and the sign that embodies an understanding of being as being-true. "In addition, 'is' signifies being-true. Assertion as unveiling intends the extant entity in its unveiled, its true being-such. . . . So far as the 'is' in assertion is understood and spoken, it already signifies intrinsically the being of a being which is asserted about as unveiled. In the uttering of the assertion, that is to say, in the uttering of exhibition, this exhibition, as intentionally unveiling comportment, expresses itself about that to which it refers. By its essential nature, that which is referred to is unveiled. So far as this unveiling comportment expresses itself about the entity it refers to and determines this being in its being, the unveiledness of that which is spoken of is *eo ipso* co-intended. The moment of unveiledness is implied in the concept of the being of the entity which is meant in the assertion."[30]

As the 'is' of predication refers precisely to the intended fulfilling of the intention expressed in the assertion, it is indifferent to the differences among the kinds of entities spoken of in the assertion. Regardless of the differences in the types of evidence that would fulfill the intentions expressed in assertions concerning, for example, Dasein and tools, since it is fulfilling as such that is meant in the copula, the same copula can be used in both types of assertion.[31]

So, once again, a traditional metaphysical determination is analyzed in such a way that it is claimed to be incomprehensible without an under-

---

29. *B.P.*, p. 219/312.

30. *B.P.*, pp. 218–219/311–312.

31. It will be remembered from Part I that I have reservations concerning the claim that true assertions are fulfilled assertions; at best, it seems that they might be fulfillable assertions. Also, early Heidegger does discuss the 'is' of predication, not in *B.P.* but in *H.C.T.* and *M.F.L.;* as far as I can tell, these interpretations are quite similar to Husserl's views in *L.I.*

standing of a central notion of 'being' as such and in general. But to this point we have not been told concretely what that signification of 'being' is which we must use in order to understand metaphysical determinations. At best we have been told that (1) being in general is a co-intended intentional correlate that is intended along with every entity insofar as that entity is intended at all; (2) insofar as any entity is intended, the one intending it must have an implicit understanding of being; and (3) being and the fulfillment of intentions in general are intimately related. To advance beyond this point, the early Heidegger thinks, one must understand the being of Dasein and grasp the transcendental conditions under which it is possible to intend anything at all, which are also the conditions under which it is possible to intend or understand being. That is, Heidegger held that to advance beyond this point metaphysically, he must write *Being and Time*.

Temporality: The Meaning of Dasein's Being and the Horizon for Understanding Being

In the introduction to *Being and Time* Heidegger makes two highly characteristic and important claims. (1) "We shall point to temporality [*Zeitlichkeit*] as the meaning of the being of that entity which we call 'Dasein'."[32] (2) "Time must be brought to light—and genuinely conceived—as the horizon for all understanding of being and for any way of interpreting it."[33] In *Basic Problems* Heidegger tells us that as the horizon for any understanding of being, time will be called 'Temporality' [*Temporalität*]. At the beginning of the second part of *Basic Problems* Heidegger repeats assertions (1) and (2) with two slight additions. The 'time' that is the horizon for the understanding of being, not to be identified with 'ordinary time', is the condition for the possibility of the understanding of being—"The ontological condition of the possibility of the understanding of being is temporality [*Zeitlichkeit*] itself"[34]—and, as this statement suggests, the temporality that is the meaning of the being of Dasein is to be identified with the Temporality that is both the horizon for understanding being and the necessary condition for any understanding of being. (3) "It [*Temporalität*] means temporality [*Zeitlichkeit*] inso-

32. *B.T.*, p. 38/17.
33. *B.T.*, p. 39/17.
34. *B.P.*, p. 228/323.

far as temporality itself is made into a theme as the condition of the possibility of the understanding of being and of ontology as such. The term 'Temporality' is intended to indicate that temporality, in existential analytic, represents the horizon from which we understand being."[35]

In order to understand the role that temporality (in both its guises) was to play in the early Heidegger's metaphysics, we must comprehend the first two propositions as well as the third, which gives the relation between them. Each represents a different problem for interpretation. Proposition (1) asserts that the meaning of Dasein's being is temporality and is, in fact, the major thesis of Division 2 of the published portion of *Being and Time*. But our interpretation of *Being and Time* has rested primarily upon Division 1 and has analyzed the meaning of Dasein's being in accordance with the care structure uncovered in that division, as a certain species of purposive agency. Thus, we have not yet investigated what Heidegger means by 'temporality', discussed how temporality is supposed to be related to purposive action, or explained how both purposive action and temporality can be the meaning of the being of Dasein. Indeed, we have not even explicitly addressed the issue of which, if any, of the various senses of 'meaning' we have distinguished in Heidegger is operative in the phrase 'the meaning of Dasein's being'. Proposition 2, together with its gloss from *Basic Problems,* asserts that Temporality is the 'horizon' for any understanding of being and that as such it is the necessary condition for any understanding of being. This proposition is one of the two major theses to be demonstrated in Part 2 of *Basic Problems*. (We treat the second, that presence is the significance of 'being' in general, in the next section.) Here the problems for interpretation turn crucially on the question of what is meant by the term 'horizon' and on why the horizon for understanding being should be a necessary condition for understanding being. Proposition (3) asserts that the meaning of Dasein's being is identical with the horizon for understanding being and that the being of Dasein is necessary for the possibility of any understanding of being. Here the problems turn on the grounds for making this identification. This section deals with each of these issues in turn. At its conclusion it should be possible to explain why the early Heidegger thought that the examination of the meaning of Dasein's being was relevant to and necessary for the scientific investigation of the meaning of being in general, and thus crucial for metaphysics.

35. *B.P.*, p. 228/324.

In *Basic Problems* Heidegger gives the following definition of 'temporality': "The original unity of the future, past, and present which we have portrayed is the phenomenon of original time, which we call temporality."[36] At first this sounds as if Heidegger is identifying temporality with J. M. E. McTaggart's A series—that is, the plurality of instants organized into a series according to the determinations 'present', 'past', 'more past', 'future', 'more future'[37]—but Heidegger is quick to disabuse us of this notion. "What alone is important here is to see more or less that we are talking about future, past, and present in a more original (existential) sense and are employing these three determinations in a signification which lies in advance of common time."[38]

We soon discover how Heidegger is using these words. 'Future' refers to the act in which Dasein expects, anticipates, or intends a possible future being for itself. Heidegger takes this future to be more 'original' then the ordinary future because it is a necessary condition for the possibility both of being aware of a possible future state of any being other than Dasein and of intending the moment at which that state is intended as being. That is, only because Dasein projects a possible future for itself, as the for-the-sake-of of its action, is it capable of intending what a being other than itself is capable of, or when it is to realize that possibility. Here is the crucial passage:

> When we are expecting any particular happening, we comport our Dasein always in some particular way toward our own most peculiar ability to be. Even if what we are expecting may be some event, some occurrence, still our own Dasein is always conjointly expected in the expecting of the occurrence itself. The Dasein understands itself by way of its own most peculiar capacity to be, of which it is expectant. In this comporting itself toward its own most peculiar capacity to be, it is ahead of itself. Expecting a possibility, I come from this possibility toward that which I myself am. The Dasein, expecting its ability to be, comes toward itself. In this coming-toward-itself, expectant of a possibility, the Dasein is futural in an original sense. This coming-toward-oneself from one's most peculiar possibility, a coming-toward which is implicit in the Dasein's existence and of which all expecting is a specific mode, is the primary concept of the future. This existential concept of

36. *B.P.*, p. 266/376.
37. See J. M. E. McTaggart, *The Nature of Existence*, vol. 2 (Cambridge: Cambridge University Press, 1927), Book V, chap. 33.
38. *B.P.*, p. 266/376.

the future is the presupposition for the common concept of the future in the sense of the not-yet-now.[39]

Similarly, when Heidegger uses the term 'past', or 'having been' in his definition of 'temporality', he is referring to the way in which any project of Dasein's is an ongoing enterprise that presupposes a set of initial conditions and activities already carried out: something is done for the sake of x only if it is a stage in a process that has determined Dasein as having done, and thus been, such and such. Any act is the act it is, and is done for the sake of some determinate end, only insofar as it is a stage in a process of purposive activity that has already been underway when the act is performed. Thus Dasein's 'having been' necessarily belongs to the original concept of the future. In addition, in retaining what it has been through acting for the sake of a possible future for itself, Dasein equally opens up the possibility of intending what things other than itself have been, and the times when they were. As my own having-been is properly described as, and can only be intended as, 'then, when I was doing x', and doing x necessarily involves actions on and with things, my having-been involves the possibility of my remembering, or forgetting, what I was doing with or to what, as well as the time when this doing occurred. Again, here is the crucial passage:

> Retaining or forgetting something, the Dasein always comports itself somehow toward what it itself already has been. It is only—as it always factically is—in such a way that it has in each instance already been the being that it is. . . . In retaining and forgetting, the Dasein is itself concomitantly retained. It concomitantly retains its own self in what it already has been. That which the Dasein has already been in each instance, its [past as] having-been-ness, belongs concomitantly to its future. This having-been-ness, understood primarily, precisely does not mean that the Dasein no longer in fact is; just the contrary, the Dasein is precisely in fact what it was. . . . The Dasein, in being, necessarily always has been. It can be as having been only as long as it exists. . . . This entails that having-been-ness belongs to the Dasein's existence. From the viewpoint of the moment of the future, as previously characterized, this means that since Dasein always comports itself more or less explicitly towards a specific capacity-to-be of its own self, since the Dasein always comes-toward-itself from out of a possibility of itself, it therewith also always comes-back-to what it has been.[40]

39. *B.P.*, pp. 265/374–375.
40. *B.P.*, pp. 265–266/375–376.

Finally, the present is just a particular aspect of the act in which Dasein acts toward a possible future for itself: namely, that to act for-the-sake-of is also in the same act to make present that with which one is at present working as that which is worked with and on. To count as acting toward a particular possibility of itself, a Dasein must also count as understanding that with which and on which it is working as having some definite determination. It must 'make present' those things as such and such if it is to exist: that is, it must be a being that acts purposively toward a future. Thus the present in Heidegger's 'original' sense, is the making-present of what is present, just as the future is the act of coming toward one's own future, and the past is the way in which any project always involves continuing projects already underway. "The present in the existential sense is not the same as presence or as extantness. The Dasein, in existing, is always dwelling with extant beings, beings that are at hand. It has such beings in its present. Only as enpresenting [making present] is the Dasein futural and past in the particular sense. As expecting a possibility the Dasein is always in such a way that it comports itself enpresentingly toward something at hand and keeps this extant entity as something present in its, the Dasein's, own present."[41]

In short, temporality as 'the unity of past, present, and future' is nothing other than the structure of Dasein's purposive social activity insofar as that activity is both a necessary and sufficient condition for Dasein's counting as intending any past entity or event as past, any present entity or event as present, and any possible future as future. Further, it is only insofar as Dasein acts in such a manner that it can be aware of the time series in the ordinary sense at all. In his doctrine of temporality, then, Heidegger is asserting that the purposive social behavior of Dasein is in itself not only an organization of a being's activity in that it is a going toward a future, but that as such it must be seen as involving the revelation of itself as acting toward that goal and thus an intention of the future, present, and past through which that action occurs. To be Dasein *is* to act toward a social end, but to act toward such an end is to count as being aware of that end as to be accomplished—that is, as a possible future for oneself—and to count as being aware of what one is at present working on and with, and to count as being aware of continuing the process of acting toward that goal. Acting toward an end, being Dasein, *is* temporality, if temporality is defined as a making-present

41. *B.P.,* p. 266/376.

by coming-toward-oneself out of a future in coming back to what one has been.

We are now in position to interpret 'meaning' in the claim that temporality is the meaning of the being of Dasein. According to the results arrived at in the first part of this book, Dasein is a being that understands its own being, and to be such a being is to act purposively within a community so as to achieve an end. But according to the results of Division 2 of *Being and Time* and Section 19 of *Basic Problems,* some x can be correctly interpreted as acting toward such an end just in case x intends a possible future for itself in light of an awareness of what it has been doing, which involves a making-present of that with which x is dealing; and all of this is the case only if x's behavior has a certain organized unity through time in which each act is tied to those that precede and those that follow it. The structured activity that is Dasein's being *itself* has a temporal structure, and a being has intentions directed toward temporally determined entities and events and those temporal determinations themselves (which are seen to be necessary for the possibility of intending any entity) if and only if its activity has such a structure. Hence, that activity can be seen both as necessarily organized temporally and as making possible the awareness of time in the ordinary sense. That is, x is Dasein if and only if x is temporal in Heidegger's unique sense. The satisfaction conditions for x's being Dasein are identical with the conditions under which x is temporal.

But then, one is warranted in asserting that x is Dasein just in case one is warranted in asserting that x is a being with the kind of organization that Heidegger calls 'temporal', together with all that that entails in regard to intentionality directed toward temporally determined entities and the time series itself. That is, temporality is the meaning$_i$ of the being of Dasein, or the condition under which it would be true to say that 'there is an x' in the sense of the existential quantifier that is appropriate to Dasein. (Remember, Heidegger holds both that 'being' isn't a predicate and that there are different ways of being in the sense that there are different sorts of conditions under which it is appropriate to say 'There is something existing which is F.) The question of the meaning of Dasein's being is just the traditional metaphysical question of what it is to be a person, even if both Heidegger's formulation of and answer to this question departs from the tradition in certain important respects.

So temporality is the meaning of the being of Dasein. But in what sense is it also the 'horizon' for any understanding of being? What is a 'horizon' anyway, and why is this one the necessary condition for any understanding of being? 'Horizon' is a Husserlian term. In *Ideas* it is used in a rather vague and nontechnical way to refer to the aspect of an apprehension which, while not focused upon or explicitly intended, forms the background or context in which the explicitly apprehended object appears. "What is actually perceived, and what is more or less clearly co-present and determinate . . . is partly pervaded, partly girt about with a dimly apprehended depth or fringe of indeterminate reality."[42] Husserl calls this fringe a 'misty horizon'. The most obvious horizons are the spatial and temporal horizons of the objects of ordinary sensuous perception, but Husserl also suggests that every experiencing is given within the horizon of internal time consciousness.[43] That is, every experience is itself experienced as happening now, in the present, and for it to be experienced as now is for it to be experienced as occurring after experiences that preceded it and before those that are expected. It is the case, however, that what I am focused on, what I am explicitly intending, is what is actually given to me now; those experiences that are 'retained' and 'protended', together with their intentional content, form a horizon around the actually occurring present experiencing.

In Husserl's *Cartesian Meditations*[44] this notion has been expanded. First, every actual intending has a specific predelineated horizon of retentions and protentions that belong to it as the intention with the intentional content it has: "Every actuality involves its potentialities, which are not empty possibilities, but rather possibilities intentionally predelineated in respect of content—namely, in the actual subjective process itself—and in addition, having the character of possibilities actualizable by the Ego. With that another fundamental trait of intentionality is indicated. Every subjective process has a process horizon. . . . For example, there belongs to every external perception its reference from the

42. Husserl, *Ideas*, p. 92.
43. Cf. ibid., section 82.
44. *Cartesian Meditations* was written in 1929; its composition thus follows that of both *Being and Time* and *Basic Problems*. This might lead one to believe that the doctrines of horizonality and the temporal horizon as expressed in Husserl, *C.M.*, could have been borrowed from Heidegger, but this is highly unlikely: Husserl's doctrine of horizonality was worked out earlier in the 1920s, and his basic views on time emerged as early as the 1905 lecture course "Internal Time Consciousness," which Heidegger edited. Further, it is clear that Heidegger's views on temporality as the horizon of all understanding of being are his own; what he takes from Husserl is merely the general notion of a horizon and the suggestion that time is an important horizon.

'genuinely perceived' sides of the object of perception to the sides 'also meant'—not yet perceived, but only anticipated . . . a continuous pro-tention. . . . to every perception there always belongs a horizon of the past, as a potentiality of awakenable recollections. . . . The horizons are 'predelineated potentialities'. . . . The predelineation itself, to be sure, is at all times imperfect; yet with its indeterminateness, it has a determinate structure."[45]

Second, the objective sense of any actual *intentio,* what it intends or means, what is meant over and beyond what is presented in the actual present *intentio,* is *constituted* by the temporal horizon of that *intentio.* This temporal horizon thus makes possible an intention directed toward, for example, a physical object intended as having a being that transcends what is actually given in the particular *intentio.* "By explicating their [subjective processes'] correlative horizons, it [intentional analysis] brings the highly diverse anonymous processes into the field comprising those that function 'constitutively' in relation to the objective sense of the cogitation in question—that is to say: not only the actual but also the potential subjective processes, which, as such, are 'implicit' and 'pre-delineated' in the sense-producing intentionality of the actual ones and which, when discovered, have the evident character of processes that explicate the implicit sense."[46] In the next sentence Husserl suggests that one can understand how it is possible to intend 'fixed and abiding objective unities' only if one engages in such horizonal analysis, from which it immediately follows that it is possible to intend such unities (which include everything that is) only in terms of such temporal inten-tional horizons. He even goes on to suggest that the being of the various kinds of transcendent intentional objects, what it means for each type to be, can be determined by investigating the various types of temporally structured horizons implicit in any intention directed toward these ob-jects.[47]

Heidegger and the Husserl of the same period, then, agree in the suggestions that temporality is the horizon for the understanding of the meaning of being and that as such it is the necessary condition for any understanding of either being or things that are. Following Husserl, we can comprehend how the various technical terms in these assertions are

45. Husserl, *C.M.,* pp. 44–45.
46. Ibid., p. 48.
47. Cf. ibid., section 21.

being used and thus understand the sense of these claims. A horizon is a predelineated and structured context in terms of which any actual experiencing, or what is actually presented in it, is said to occur. While the horizon of both the experiencing and the presented is said by Husserl to be experienced in the actual experience, it is given only 'implicitly' or nonthetically. Concretely, the fact that any actual experience is lived as the present one implies that it is given within the context of preceding and potentially following apprehensions, so *the* horizon par excellence of all experiences is the consciousness of internal time, or the horizonal consciousness implicit in any experience of any thing whatsoever. I am ordinarily conscious of this only horizonally—as the ultimate horizon of all my actual intentional acts—and not explicitly, but every actual *intentio* is placed, and must be placed, within this horizon.

This analysis has two ontological implications or corollaries. First, it is possible to intend something as something that is transcendent only if it is intended within the temporal horizon. To intend an objective being— that is, to intend at all—is just to intend what is actually presented within a specifically structured horizon of what is retained of past givings of whatever in the experience is taken to be the thing presented and of what is expected in the experience to be available of the object in the future. But such a concretely delimited horizon, which is necessary if we are to understand anything that is as something that is, is possible only if we implicitly grasp what it is for an experiencing, and the content of an experiencing, to be future or past as such; and this is just what is implicit in the horizonal structure of internal temporality itself. That is, the understanding or intending of any being presupposes the intentional horizon that is temporality itself, which is thus the necessary condition for the understanding of any being.

Second, for both Heidegger and Husserl, the horizon of temporality isn't merely the horizon for the understanding of every thing that is and thus the necessary condition for such understanding; it is also the necessary condition for any understanding of *being,* or what it is for any extant being to be. When I intend that rock, for example, as an objective, transcendent being, I intend it as actual: that is, as something that would be there to be perceived in some determinate way if I were to look at it at some determinate future time. Each different type of transcendent intentional object, whether physical object, idea, value, or whatever, has its own mode of being, its own way in which it is at present intended as to be available to be presented in the future. For us to have evidence that any such entity in fact is, this structure of predelineated possibilities would need to be 'filled in', fulfilled in and through *presentations,* which are identified with that which had been protended in the original intention. But these modes of being are just the particular determinate predelineated structures of the horizons of the actual intentions in which these ontological sorts of things are intended. Every being of the same categorial type is given within a temporal horizon of the same structural type, but two beings of different ontological sorts are always presented within differently structured temporal horizons. To understand the being of some being is just to intend it in accordance with the horizonal, temporal structure appropriate to that kind of being and thus to understand what would need to be presented for it to be.

Husserl and the early Heidegger agree on much concerning the analysis of temporality and the temporal horizon. But as is to be expected, Heidegger also disagrees with Husserl in crucial ways. These differences make comprehensible Heidegger's identification of the temporal horizon, which is the necessary condition for the understanding of both beings and being, with the temporality that constitutes the meaning of the being of Dasein. He differs most obviously from Husserl in his view of the character of the temporal horizon and the model of intentionality associated with it. The paradigm mode of intentionality for Husserl is theoretical or speculative, in the sense that perception and its abstract genus, intuition, are considered to be the primary forms of intentionality; as a result, he tends to describe the horizonal structure of temporality as analogous to a perceptual field, a field that is dim, misty, marginal, and merely implicitly seen, though *seen* nonetheless. For Heidegger, the fundamental form of intentionality is practical action, and all other types are analyzed in terms of it; hence, the temporal field or horizon is conceived in terms of the structure of action. To act for an end is always to intend what one is working on or with as functional, either serviceable or detrimental to an end. We practically understand some entity, which is the basic mode of intending it for Heidegger, insofar as we intend it in terms of its functionality: that is, in terms of what it would be for it to perform successfully a function conducive to arriving at an end. To understand a hammer practically primarily involves picking it up and hammering with it—an act in which we understand the hammer as capable of functioning toward an end: that is, in terms of its functionality. In intending the hammer in this way we also implicitly understand what it would be for it really to be a hammer: that is, in fact capable of being used successfully as we are trying to use it. Indeed, to intend or understand it as a hammer is just to 'protend' this possible use while at present dealing with, or making present, the thing—a protention that is built into the fact of our intentionally *using* the thing at all.

In just the same way that, for Husserl, a present intuition always involves its placement in a field of retentions and protentions—a placement that constitutes and makes possible our intending a being as objective and transcendent—for Heidegger, to intend a tool as a tool is to intend it within a field of protentions and retentions that constitute and make possible our intention of it as an objective and transcendent being. But in Heidegger's case, these protentions and retentions are identified with the temporal links that any *action,* as purposive, has with preceding and expected actions and results. As we have just seen, these retentions and protentions constitute the temporal structure of practical action itself, and to say that an act is purposive is to say the same thing as that it is performed within a practical temporal horizon of what has already been and what is to come. And just as, for Husserl, the determinate being of any being intended is correlated with the particular structural type of the system of retentions and protentions in which it is intended, so for Heidegger the being of any intended being (extantness or readiness-to-hand) is correlated with the particular structure of the purposive action in terms of which we deal with it. The special case of Dasein is handled by noting the fact that every purposive act, regardless of type, also amounts to 'dealing with' and understanding Dasein itself. As every act is done for the sake of some possibility of Dasein, every act implicitly involves an understanding that to be Dasein is to be such a structure of acting toward possibilities. In acting in the temporal horizon of action, one also intends that horizon and thus both treats and intends oneself as Dasein.

It should be noted that this modification in the Husserlian notion of a horizon accounts for some of the most characteristic moves and terminological innovations in the early Heidegger. For example, he uses the phrases 'projected upon' (*entwurf auf*) and the 'upon which' (*Woraufhin*) of a projection in speaking of the horizonal character of our understanding, especially our understanding of being: "We understand a being only as we project it upon being. In the process, being itself must be understood in a certain way; being must in its turn be projected upon something."[48] This 'something', of course, is time: "The series . . . under-

48. *B.P.,* p. 280/396.

standing of beings, projection upon being, understanding of being, projection upon time . . . has its end at the horizon of the ecstatic unity of temporality."[49]

The relation 'projected upon' is always predicated of an act of understanding and the horizon in terms of which that act is carried out; it asserts of the act that it is carried out within that context. What is distinctive about this relation is that it involves the projection that Heidegger takes to be characteristic of all practical understanding, a projection that is a throwing-off or throwing-ahead into or toward the future. That 'upon which' such a projection takes place is the 'place' or structure of places that that which is thrown off is 'thrown off to'. For example, when I understand this entity as a hammer, I do so in terms of a schema supplied by the structure of functionality relations that constitutes its being—in understanding the hammer I 'project it upon' its being. In turn, I understand this structure of functionality relations only in terms of a way of acting for Dasein: that is, in terms of Dasein's temporality—I 'project it upon' time. To call this relation 'projection' emphasizes the purposeful, future-oriented character that Heidegger wishes to give all intentionality. To understand is to place within a context of purposeful action, to 'project' what is understood upon some possible future for Dasein. As there is even a sense in which the early Heidegger identifies 'meaning' with the 'upon which' of a projective understanding ("meaning is the 'upon which' of a projection in terms of which something becomes intelligible as something"),[50] there is a sense in which temporality, as the horizon for any understanding of being, is itself the meaning of being. Needless to say, this use of 'meaning' is not identical with the sense of meaning$_i$, which tends to be dominant when the early Heidegger considers the meaning of being. It does, however, provide a bridge to the later Heidegger's talk about the truth of being; when he looks back on his early metaphysics, he tends to highlight this use.[51]

Similarly, early Heidegger always speaks of Dasein's transcendence, rather than the transcendence of beings over the intentions directed toward them.[52] If to be Dasein is to engage in purposive action, and purposive action is essentially objective (in the sense that it must work on and with beings other than Dasein), then there is simply no room for an

49. *B.P.*, p. 308/437.
50. *B.T.*, p. 193/151.
51. Cf., e.g., the 1949 note to O.E.T., p. 140/201, and A.W.P.
52. See any of the early Heidegger's works but esp. *The Essence of Reasons*.

intentional space of 'appearances' or merely intentional entities. There is thus no special epistemological problem involving the necessity of relating such appearances with transcendent entities. Rather, insofar as Dasein is at all, it intends entities that must be worked on and with and that are intended as other than dependent on Dasein's intention of them. So transcendence belongs to Dasein; Dasein 'steps over to' things other than itself in that it is Dasein and insofar as it intends them as being: that is, as available to be encountered in a fulfillment. Early Heidegger's way of putting this is to say that Dasein transcends beings toward their being. The only real question in this area is how Dasein does this. Heidegger's answer, of course, is the transcendental analysis we reconstructed in Chapters 1–5.

Our results in regard to the temporality of practical action as the horizon for the understanding of being, used together with the results of the published portion of *Being and Time,* imply the first major thesis of Part 2 of *Basic Problems:* that "the ontological condition of the possibility of the understanding of being is temporality itself"[53]. Temporality is this condition insofar as it is "the horizon from which we understand being," and, as such, 'temporality' is identified with the meaning of Dasein's being, or what it is to be Dasein. It also follows that temporality, so understood, is the necessary condition for understanding, or intending, anything that is. The argument advances in two stages. First, from Husserl, it is possible to intend something that is only if what is actually at present apprehended of the thing is experienced within a temporal horizon of retention and protention. Such placement amounts to, and constitutes, the objective sense of the present intention, or what is meant in the intention, over and above what is actually apprehended at a moment; and it is in intending an objective sense that we intend a transcendent object, a being that is taken to transcend any consciousness of it. Any being that is so intended is intended as having a particular definite being, or what it is for it to be. The being of any being is constituted through and projected upon the particular formal structure of the temporal horizon in and through which it is intended, so any being that is intended is intended as having some being. But second, from *Being and Time,* the fundamental form of intentionality is practical action; that is, nothing can be intended as being unless it is intended by a being who engages in practical activity, and the necessary condition of any intention

---

53. *B.P.,* p. 228/323.

whatsoever is the being of the one who acts purposively. Regardless of the details of the particular determinate sort of activity, which correlate with the specific being of the beings intended, all such action has the overall temporal horizonal structure that Heidegger labels 'temporality', or action for the sake of some possibility of the one acting. According to Division 2 of *Being and Time,* this temporality is also what it means to be Dasein, or the meaning of the being of Dasein. So temporality (as the meaning of the being of Dasein) is also (as horizon for all intentionality) the necessary condition for the possibility of any understanding of beings, or being, whatsoever.

In form, this argument is classically transcendental. One starts from a given fact concerning intentionality (or some type of intentionality—knowledge, or consciousness, or language): in this case, that we intend things that are, or transcendent beings. We then argue to the necessary conditions for this intentional performance: in this case, 'temporality' as both the meaning of the being of Dasein and the horizon for any understanding of being. Only two elements formally distinguish this Heideggerian argument from its Kantian (and other) forebears. First, there is the fact that the initial step of the argument has in this case a metaphysical rather than epistemological ring to it: we can intend things as things that are—beings. To what degree this really is a metaphysical starting point remains to be seen. Second, the conclusion explicitly involves a positive statement of positive fact, concerning not only what it is to be Dasein but also asserting that there is a being with Dasein's kind of being. It is only insofar as there are Dasein that being, or beings, can be understood. Again, to what extent this fact distinguishes Heidegger's argument from other transcendental arguments remains to be examined.

How does any of this help us with metaphysics? Both in *Kant and the Problem of Metaphysics* and in the first half of *Basic Problems,* Heidegger makes a point of stressing that we can deal with the traditional issues of metaphysics, which he consistently associates with questions concerning what it is for beings to be, only if we make progress in determining the meaning of being in general. Indeed, the entire investigation of *Being and Time,* which results in the argument we have just rehearsed, is designed to shed light on this issue. But how does knowing that temporality, in Heidegger's sense, is both necessary for the understanding of being and the horizon for such understanding help Heidegger in determining the meaning of being?

The Signification of 'Being'

The entire program of *Being and Time* is designed to explicate the meaning$_i$, or signification, of 'being'. To this point we know several things about what Heidegger takes to be the signification of 'being', even if we have yet to determine it concretely. From his examination of the traditional metaphysical determinations and problems, we know that being is an intentional correlate that is co-intended insofar as any entity is intended, that it is always pre-thematically understood by the one intending any entity, and that it has some connection with the fulfillment of intentions. From Heidegger's development of the meaning of the being of Dasein, the one who understands being, we know that he regards temporality, in the sense of the temporal structure of social purposive action, as the horizon 'upon which' all understanding of being is projected. But how does all of this help to determine concretely the meaning$_i$ of 'being', and what, after all, does the early Heidegger think that the meaning$_i$ of 'being' is?

We can begin to get a grip on these questions if we look at Heidegger's extended commentary on Chapter 6 of Husserl's Sixth Logical Investigation, which appears in the lengthy introduction to Heidegger's lecture course of 1925 (published as *History of the Concept of Time*). For there is a sense in which everything the early Heidegger has to say about being presupposes the truth of two sentences (which he quotes in full)[54] from this chapter of Husserl's, along with the formal distinctions Husserl invokes there. We have already looked at the sentences in another context: "Not in reflection upon judgments, nor even upon fulfillments of judgments, but in the fulfillments of judgments themselves lies the true source of the concepts State of Affairs and Being. Not in these acts as objects, but in the objects of these acts, do we have the abstractive basis which enables us to realize the concepts in question."[55]

Heidegger begins his discussion in a straightforwardly Husserlian fashion by distinguishing between intentional 'presuming' (or merely intending in an empty manner) and intentional fulfillment. When I merely think about *x*, *x* isn't given to me in such a way as to give me reason to believe that there is an *x*; I do intend *x*, but I do so in an 'empty' way. When I intuit *x* (intuition is a mode of intending), I simply ap-

54. *H.C.T.*, p. 59/79.
55. Husserl, *L.I.*, pp. 783–784.

prehend the given as it shows itself, and x is given to me bodily. This is the meaning of 'intuition': "simple apprehension of what is itself bodily found just as it shows itself."[56] It is important, however, that it is the very same x that is intended emptily and that is given in intuition, and that in the intuition x is given as *identical* with what I previously intended merely in thought. As we have had several occasions to mention, when I intuit or perceive, what I perceive is not a sense datum but a thing; what is given to me bodily in intuition is the thing I have an intuition of, a thing that can be identical with the thing I intend emptily. "I can in an empty way now think of my desk at home simply in order to talk about it. I can fulfill this empty intention . . . by going home and seeing it itself in an authentic and final experience. In such a demonstrative fulfillment the emptily intended and the originally intuited come into coincidence. This bringing-into-coincidence—the intended being experienced in the intuited as itself and selfsame—is an act of identification. The intended identifies itself in the intuited; selfsameness is *experienced*."[57]

In other words, there is an act (a "lived experience which has the character of intentionality"),[58] an intentional relation, directed toward the being-identical of empty intuition and its fulfillment. The act is the act of identifying presumed with intuited; what is intended in that act is the being-identical of the two. "The demonstration of the presumed in the intuited is identification, an act which is phenomenologically specified in terms of intentionality, directing-itself-toward. This means that every act has its intentional correlate, perception the perceived, and identification the identified, here the being-identical of presumed and intuited as the intentional correlate of the act of identification."[59]

Significantly, I experience the being identical of the emptily intended and the intuited only obliquely, as it were. I see the desk, not the being-identical of what I see and what I have been thinking; nevertheless, I see what I see as the desk as being identical with what I previously thought about. I am focused only on the desk, but in experiencing the desk I also experience the being-identical of what I see with what I thought. "In the coming into coincidence of the presumed with the intuited, I am solely and primarily directed toward the subject matter itself, and yet—this is the peculiarity of this structural correlation—evidence is experienced in

56. *H.C.T.*, p. 47/64.
57. *H.C.T.*, p. 49/66.
58. *H.C.T.*, p. 36/47.
59. *H.C.T.*, p. 51/69.

this apprehension of the intuited matter itself. The correlation is peculiar in that something is experienced but not apprehended."⁶⁰ Further, as the act of identification is an intentional act, it must be possible to intend the correlate of this act, the being-identical of intended and given, in a purely empty way. The act of identification is fulfilled when the thing intended is bodily given, even though its being given as intended is a specifically different intentional object from the thing that is given itself. But when the object itself is merely intended, the being-identical itself is merely intended.

These various determinations of the intentional act of identification give us three (in Husserl, four) determinations of the meaning of 'truth'. First, 'truth', or what it is to be true, is simply the being-identical of intended and intuited, which is just the intentional correlate of the act of identification. "The first concept of truth is this being-identical of presumed and intuited. Being-true is then equivalent to this being-identical, the subsistence of this identity."⁶¹ This is truth as a relationship between a state of affairs (given in intuition) and a 'subject matter' (an entity intended in some way), or truth as adequation. Second, truth can be determined as a relation between two acts, the act of merely intending emptily and the act of intuiting. It is my knowing that is true in this sense. Finally, truth can be determined in terms of the intended entity—the being-unveiled of what gets identified in the act of identification. As all of these determinations of the meaning of 'truth' go back to the fundamental fulfilling of the act of identification in a being-identical—a being-identical that is given along with the intuiting of an entity, which is thereby open for view—we can see the origin of the classic Heideggerian position that truth is fundamentally 'being-unveiling'. To be true, an intention must uncover an entity, must be such as to intend the identical thing that is given in intuition.⁶²

Similarly, the analysis of the act of identification and of being-identical gives us the first of the various ways in which 'being' is said. 'Being' has

---

60. *H.C.T.*, pp. 52/69–70.
61. *H.C.T.*, p. 51/69.
62. It is significant that just as the later Heidegger turns away from the question 'What does "being" mean?' to focus exclusively on the question 'How is an understanding of being possible?' he also turns away from the question 'What does "truth" mean?' to focus on the question 'How is an understanding of truth possible?' This question amounts to the question of how there can be an intention directed toward the being-identical of intended and intuited. A great deal of confusion could have been avoided had Heidegger distinguished these two questions clearly (see Chapter 7); eventually, in 1964, he did.

the sense of 'being-true' in the first sense. Heidegger takes the intentional act of asserting 'the chair is yellow' as his example. "What is asserted as such, the asserted content of this assertion, is the being-yellow of the chair. . . . I can stress the being in the *being*-yellow, and so mean that the chair is really and truly yellow. . . . Underscoring being means that the truth-relation just discussed subsists, an identity between presumed and intuited subsists. 'Being' here means something like the subsistence of truth, of the truth-relation, subsistence of identity."[63] Here a thing is if it is given as being identical with some empty intention of it, and there is thus a fulfilled act of identification intending the being-identical, which accompanies the act in which the thing is intuitively presented. It is intended as being insofar as along with the intention that intends the entity emptily there is an empty act of identification that intends it as if presentable. The being of a thing is intended in the empty act of identi-fication that accompanies every act intending the thing; and 'being', in the sense of 'being-true', is the being-identical that is intended in the act of identification.

This way in which 'being' is said is not the only way, however. It is helpful to our understanding of the others to note that the act of identi-fication is, for Husserl and Heidegger, only one among a whole class of similar acts, the categorial acts. Two features characterize acts that are categorial. First, as in the act of identification, what is intended in any categorial act is intended along with what is straightforwardly intended but typically in a merely tacit, nonfocal way. Second, again as in the act of identification, the fulfillment of the act is given not in a *sensuous* intuition but rather in a categorial intuition. For example, the being-identical of what I am seeing with what I have intended is itself not seen; instead I intuit—it is given to me in a nonsensuous way—that they are identical, even though I never *perceive* this identity. I see the desk, but I do not *see* the being-identical of the desk with my intention of it. Similarly, I see yellow, but I do not see the being-yellow of the chair—I cannot see the 'being-the-property-of'. Nevertheless, when I see the yellow chair, I also have the fulfillment of the intention that the chair is yellow, that yellow is a property of the chair. But this intention can't be a sensuous intention, because it is not fulfilled in a sensuous intuition. The intention that is directed toward, that thinks of, 'y is a property of x'—the intention that intends 'being' in the sense of the copula—is not identical with the

63. *H.C.T.*, pp. 53–54/71–72.

perceiving or thinking of *x* or *y*, but it is fulfilled when we see *x* insofar as to see *x* is also to experience, though not apprehend, that *x* is *y*.[64] Categorial intentions are categorial in that, among other things, such intentions intend being in the sense of the various categories, and there is categorial intuition insofar as we intuit in a nonsensuous way that something is something. (Husserl and the very early Heidegger also speak of categorial intuitions directed toward universals as such; we discussed these in passing in Chapter 4, but they are irrelevant here.)

Given this background we can also understand how Heidegger's handling, in *Basic Problems*, of some of the other ways in which 'being' is said goes back to the Husserlian notion of categorial intuition. *Essentia* and *existentia* go back originally to the intentional comportment of production. If, in producing, there is an intention directed toward what is to be produced, there must be another, categorial intention directed toward the being-identical of what is to be produced—what is purposively intended—and its potential fulfillment. But in production, for Heidegger, the being-identical of the intended and the intuited is structured functionally, not perceptually, as it is in Husserl and in the modern notion of 'existence'. For the intended in production to be identical with its intuitive fulfillment is for the thing to be serviceable in the way functionally characterized in the production itself. Correspondingly, the *essentia* of an *x* is just the sense that is fulfilled when *x* is used successfully, a sense that presents emptily in an act of production a thing that is experienced in use as being identical with what is so presented. "The specific thisness of a piece of equipment, its individuation, if we take the word in a completely formal sense, is not determined primarily by space and time in the sense that it appears in a determinate space and time position. Instead, what determines a piece of equipment as an individual is its equipmental character and equipmental contexture. . . . Equipmental character is constituted by what we call functionality. The being of something we use, for instance, a hammer or a door, is characterized by a specific way of being put to use, of functioning . . . what and how it is as this entity, its whatness and howness (*essentia, existentia*) is constituted by this in-order-to as such, by its functionality."[65]

---

64. If the question of the meaning of existence and *existentia* concerns the conditions under which an existential quantifier can be invoked (conditions often taken to be self-evident in the analytic tradition), what is at issue here is the relation between function and argument: what is it for some value of *x* to satisfy some function?

65. *B.P.*, pp. 292–293/414–415.

But this way of characterizing *essentia* and *existentia* points up the basic question of being. Heidegger says in this passage that the 'howness', the *existentia* or *actualitas* of a tool, is constituted by its functionality. This can be true only in the sense that what we are asserting when we say that some tool exists is determined by its functionality, by its being in-order-to. That *x* is intended as in-order-to, however, is not the same as its existing as a tool, as its *existentia*. What it is to exist in the sense in which a tool exists might, as Heidegger says here, be constituted in and through functionality, but this by itself is insufficient to tell us what, exactly, is meant by *existentia* when we speak of the existence of some tool.

Similarly, we may know that the existence, in the modern sense of 'extantness' of some entity—what it is for it to exist in the modern sense—may be prescribed within a perceptual context without knowing definitely and concretely what is being said when it is said that it exists. We have already seen that 'existence' cannot be equivalent to 'being perceived' and *existentia* can't be equivalent to 'being produced', even though they can show up only within the intentional context of perception and production respectively. In light of the discussion of categorial intuition, we can see why this must be so. For example, the perceptual fulfillment of my intention of the desk over there, the being perceived of the desk, can't be the existence of the desk. Whatever 'existence' is for Heidegger, it is intended in a categorial intuition that accompanies the intention of the desk as such but is not fulfilled in the perceptual intuition itself, even though it is fulfilled whenever the perceptual one is.

But then, what is the sense intended in the categorial intention intending 'existence', an intention that is fulfilled insofar as it is truly asserted that something existing is *F*? In fact, of course, for Heidegger there are at least three questions here, differentiated by the character of *F* as an extant, functional, or Daseinish characteristic. This differentiation, together with the relation between all of these senses of 'exist', on the one hand, and on the other the senses of 'being' we have already considered—'being-true', being a property, and *essentia*—leads us back, finally, to the Heideggerian question of the meaning of 'being' as such and in general, the question of the unity of the various senses of 'being'.

Heidegger's long detour into the meaning of the being of Dasein is for the sake of answers to these questions. Having gone through that process, we know that the ultimate horizon for the understanding of being is temporality. That is, we must investigate 'being' and its central meaning, which includes the various meanings of 'existence' (extantness, *existentia,* and Dasein's existence), from the perspective of temporality. What does this really mean? Temporality, for Heidegger, is the temporal structure of purposeful action; as such, it involves retentions, protentions, and presentations of a definite sort—the sort that goes along with the action itself. As we saw in the last section, to act as Dasein acts is to expect, retain, and make present things and events as functionally determined. It is also to count as intending the temporal determinations when what is expected, retained, and made present occurs, and thus to understand the temporality of Dasein itself. I can't act as Dasein acts or be as Dasein is unless my action organizes a practical temporal series. "Original familiarity with beings lies in dealing with them appropriately. This commerce constitutes itself with respect to its temporality in a retentive-expectant-enpresenting of the equipmental contexture as such."[66] Within this temporal horizon of activity, and only within it, am I capable of encountering—making present—things, with their own already displayed tendencies, capacities, and so on. It is also within this horizontal structure that I can recognize that something is missing or unavailable, as I notice the absence of the pen when I am intending to write. To notice such an absence need not imply that the pen isn't; indeed, noticing the unavailability of a tool is one way of making it present, and making it present precisely in its functional character as a pen.

What is the character of the intention directed toward the *existentia* of a tool, and what are the conditions under which it would be fulfilled? What makes it proper to say that there is x in the sense of 'is' appropriate for tools? What I aim for in the production of a tool, the way of being of the tool that I aim for in the production, is the meaning of 'existence' in this case. But what is so aimed for is that the tool will be there to be used when I am able to use it. Of course, the tool would be missing, or—for some contingent reason having to do with the situation—currently unavailable, but insofar as it could be made present in a use, it is as a tool. The use makes present the fact that the thing is there to be used; it is an 'intuition' of the tool's being there to be used, of its present availability for use. In appropriate dealings with things, in using a thing successfully, the presence of the thing for use—its being there to be used—gets demonstrated along with the thing itself. The categorial intuition directed toward the being of the tool gets fulfilled, but what is so demonstrated is the present serviceability of the tool, or the fact that at present it

66. *B.P.*, p. 304/432.

is there to be used. My categorial intention directed toward the *existentia* of the tool is directed toward the presence for use; the intention is fulfilled in the use, but it is not reducible to the intention directed toward the what, the thing, that is shown to be present for use. Presence, being, is distinguishable from what is present, the thing that is. For Heidegger, what gets demonstrated in use, the *existentia* of the thing as a tool, is the presence of the tool, a presence that is made present to the Dasein in use. "The readiness-to-hand of the ready-to-hand, the being of this kind of being, is understood as praesens, a praesens which, as non-conceptually understandable, is already unveiled in the self-projection of temporality, by means of whose temporalizing anything like existent commerce with entities ready-to-hand and extant becomes possible. Handiness formally implies praesens, presence [*Anwesenheit*], but a praesens of a particular sort."[67]

The making-present of a tool in this way is never an instantaneous occurrence; something can't be being used at an instant. It is used, and thus made present as available for use, in the present in light of what has already been and for the sake of a possible future. Something can be made present in use, can show itself as something that is and is at present a tool, only if it plays a role in a continuing project. And, as Heidegger's statement above makes clear, the horizon for the understanding of the *existentia* of the tool itself, its presence as there to be used, is temporality as the structure of purposeful action. The tool's presence, its being there to be used, is itself unintelligible except within the structure of purposeful action. Finally, whether or not there is a tool of the appropriate sort, whether or not it exists, is an entirely objective matter. The fact that I need a certain tool or believe there to be that tool doesn't imply in any way that there is such a tool.

There are other ways in which beings make themselves present, or show their presence, aside from use. Corresponding to these different ways of making-present—in perception, for example—there are dif-

---

67. *B.P.*, pp. 309/438–439. Translation modified. Heidegger uses 'praesens' in *B.P.* to refer to "the whither of the 'beyond itself,'" toward which or upon which making-present projects itself. He calls it "the horizonal schema" of the present. The basic idea seems to be that every making-present, every disclosure as such, occurs toward a background that is pre-understood, so praesens supplies the 'place' for the entity encountered, out, away from, over there. I have intentionally ignored much of Heidegger's talk concerning the 'ecstases' of temporality and their 'horizonal schemata', because I take such talk to be a picture-thinking ultimately derived from Husserl's emphasis on intuition and consciousness and thus, finally, out of place in Heidegger.

ferent ways of being that disclose themselves. Thus, perception demonstrates the present availability of the thing for perception, or the extantness of the thing. But regardless of the fact that the way of being, the meaning of 'existence' in 'something existing is *F*', is different, it is still a variety of presence. "When Kant says, therefore, that existence—that is, for us, extantness, being on or at hand—is perception, this thesis is extremely rough and misleading; all the same it points to the correct direction of the problem. On our interpretation, 'being is perception' now means: being is an intentional comportment of a peculiar sort, namely, enpresenting; . . . 'Being equals perception', when interpreted in original phenomenological terms, means: being equals presence [*Anwesenheit*], praesens."[68] All the various determinations of being in the generalized sense of 'existence', all the various senses of the existential quantifier, go back to modifications of the central sense 'presence'. This presence is made present, 'intuited', in acts that accompany the acts in which we deal with things, acts that fulfill senses that are understandable only insofar as they are prestructured in terms of the organized structure of Dasein's activity. All the other ways in which 'being' is said—for example, in the sense of being-true, or *essentia*—become comprehensible as various ways of articulating the basic intentional situation in which being is intended, emptily and fully, or as elements articulated in such an intentional analysis. 'Being', as such and in general, means presence.

With this conclusion the central program of *Being and Time* is also concluded. The transcendental argument, beginning with the fact that we intend beings that are and progressing through a statement of the necessary conditions for the possibility of such intentions, is completed—as Kant's argument is—with a metaphysical conclusion. But whereas Kant finishes with a metaphysics of the things of nature and experience (the necessary conditions for experience are also the necessary conditions for the objects of experience), Heidegger's primary conclusion is neither restricted to a metaphysics of the objects of experience nor directly related to beings at all. Heidegger claims that we have come to understand what 'being' as such and in general means. Only after this has been determined does he intend to use the determination to solve the classical problems of metaphysics having to do with the identity and essence of things. Further, because 'being' is the intentional object of a categorial intuition, rather than some element in an intention, what is

---

68. *B.P.*, 315/448.

understood when we understand the meaning of 'being' is supposed to transcend the subjective realm—or the conditions of experiencing—that makes it possible for us to understand this meaning.

There is, however, a deep problem in this metaphysics of *Being and Time*, a problem serious enough to be termed an *aporia*. I will argue that this *aporia* motivates the transition to the late Heidegger and, ultimately, his critique of metaphysics.

It is clear that the distinction between the object of the intention that intends being and the acts in which that intention is carried out is meant to preserve the independence and ideality of what is understood—being. But the exact character of what is understood in the understanding of being, being as presence, is itself ambiguous. Consider three passages from *Basic Problems* and *Being and Time*. The first, in discussing Kant, distinguishes between an extant entity's being-perceived and its existence. In the course of the passage, however, Heidegger also distinguishes the perceivability of the entity from its existence, understood as the ground or reason for that perceivability. "Are existence, actuality, and perceivedness one and the same? The window, however, surely does not receive existence from my perceiving it, but just the reverse: I can perceive it only if it exists and because it exists. In every case, perceivedness presupposes perceivability, and perceivability on its part already requires the existence of the perceivable or the perceived being."[69] Existence can never be equated with the being-perceived of an entity, because for the entity to exist implies that it is there, that it exists, whether or not it is at present being perceived. That the thing is perceived implies that it is perceivable, and the ground, reason, explanation, or cause of this perceivability is the existence of the thing. The existence of the thing, that it exists, is independent of my actually perceiving it, though it is revealed in that perception.

But what makes itself present to us in and through the perception, the mode of being of the entity that is revealed to us, is not, strictly speaking, the *ground* of the perceivability of the thing, which Heidegger equates with existence here; it is just that perceivability itself. I do experience an entity as there to be perceived, insofar as I perceive it, as existing independently of my actual perception, but that objectivity and independence is already captured by the perceivability of the entity. To say that x is perceivable is already to say that were any Dasein to intend it in the

69. *B.P.*, p. 49/66.

intentional mode of perception, it would reveal itself. Perceivability is a kind of capacity, and capacity involves counterfactual conditionals, and these conditionals already capture the ideal independence and objectivity of the thing vis-à-vis our perception of it: if any *y* were to intend *x* in mode *z*, *x* would be made present. At best we infer that there is a continuous presence of the thing that accounts for its perceivability, but the presence we understand in the perception itself, insofar as the entity perceived is intended as existing, is just the presence of the perceivability or ability to be perceived of the entity itself.

Why, then, does Heidegger attempt to distinguish existence from perceivability? We get the answer to this question in the second passage. "The mode of uncovering and the mode of uncoveredness of the extant obviously must be determined by the entity to be uncovered by them and by its way of being. I cannot perceive geometrical relations in the sense of natural sense perception. But how is the mode of uncovering to be, as it were, regulated and prescribed by the entity to be uncovered and its mode of being, unless the entity is itself uncovered beforehand so that the mode of apprehension can direct itself toward it? On the other hand, this uncovering in its turn is supposed to adapt itself to the entity that is to be uncovered. The mode of the possible uncoveredness of the extant in perception must already be prescribed in the perceiving itself; that is, the perceptual uncovering of the extant must already understand beforehand something like extantness."[70]

The way in which a being's being is to be uncovered—which always means the appropriate manner of intending it, which in turn involves the character of the horizon in which the entity is to be revealed—must be, Heidegger tells us, prescribed by the entity and its being itself. That *x* is understood as extant means that it is intended as extant—that is, perceived within the intentional horizon that involves linguistic assertion—and it is appropriate thus to intend it only if *x* is in fact extant, not Dasein or ready-to-hand. Yet I can know that *x* is extant only by intending it within the horizon of perception and actually perceiving it. Now, if the being of the being that is perceived were merely understood as perceivability, not as the ground of perceivability, then what I would understand when I perceive the thing would be that it is *capable* of being understood as extant, not that it *must* be understood in that way. This very same thing might also be capable of being used and/or dealt with as a

70. *B.P.,* p. 70/99.

Dasein. In that case the mode of uncoveredness that correlates with the being of the entity would not be 'prescribed' or 'regulated' by the entity. In a certain sense the objectivity of the being of the entity would be preserved; not every possible being, or even every being with being, can be perceived and successfully intended as extant. As Heidegger points out, geometrical relations are not perceivable. And whether any particular being has any definite sort of being—that is, is capable of being given in a fulfilled intention in any particular mode—is entirely independent of the way in which it is actually intended.

Moreover, one and the same being could be uncovered as having a variety of different ontological characters, and which would be the appropriate way of understanding that being would not be prescribed by the entity itself. Further, which way of understanding the being of beings in general and as a whole is the correct or appropriate one, if there are several possible ways, would not be 'regulated and prescribed' by those beings and their being. If, for example, extantness merely means perceivability and not the ground of perceivability, then the fact that all the entities within the world can be understood as extant would not imply that entities could not be correctly and appropriately understood in different ontological terms. Thus, the fact that I am capable of being understood as Dasein would not imply that I am not also extant and, as extant, fully amenable to natural scientific—that is, efficiently causal— explanation. Also, whether or not there were any Dasein at all, or only, for example, extant beings, would not be univocally prescribed and regulated by the being of all the beings that are. In a certain sense and to a certain extent, what ontological sorts of being belong to the world would depend upon the manner in which being was intended. And given the fact that the ultimate context of all of Dasein's ways of intending is the structure of purposeful action, which manner would be appropriate at any given time would be an entirely pragmatic concern.

In order to avoid this conclusion, Heidegger needs to distinguish between 'presence' in the sense of presentability and presence as the ground of presentability. If this distinction is preserved, then, for example, the extantness of a thing, as the ground of its perceivability, could prescribe a uniquely appropriate manner of understanding the thing's being. But it is unclear that the early Heidegger has the conceptual resources for making this distinction. Consider the third passage, this one from *Being and Time:* "Of course only as long as Dasein is (that is, only as long as an understanding of being is ontically possible), 'is there' being.

When Dasein does not exist, 'independence' 'is' not either, nor 'is' the 'in-itself'. In such a case this sort of thing can be neither understood nor not understood. In such a case even entities within-the-world can neither be discovered nor lie hidden. In such a case it cannot be said that entities are, nor can it be said that they are not. . . . As we have noted, being (not entities) is dependent upon the understanding of being."[71]

The entire strategy of the metaphysical program of *Being and Time* is transcendental. By giving the necessary conditions for intentionality, one was also to supply the necessary conditions for the intending of the being of beings: that is, the necessary conditions for the understanding of being. These conditions for the understanding of being were then to be used to supply what it means for a being to be. But, as in Kant, this final inference goes through only on the verificationist assumption that what it means to say x is fully specified by the evidence that would fulfill the intention of x. What it is to be is specified by our understanding of what it is to be only if what it is to be is nothing other than the conditions under which we would be warranted in thinking or asserting that some thing is, because our intention that it is would be fulfilled. If there is no such intention, and thus no such conditions (for example, because there does not happen to be any Dasein), then there 'is' no being. This is what the passage says. (In *Letter on Humanism* the late Heidegger tries to avoid this reading of the passage, and the metaphysical pragmatism it implies. We will consider later whether he does so successfully. What is at issue here, however, is determined by more than the reading of this one passage. The whole method of *Being and Time* implies this reading. There is no *Being and Time* without it.) As we saw above, however, the making-present of an entity in perception, for example, directly gives us evidence only for the perceivability of the entity, not for its existence in the sense of the ground for its perceivability. Thus, extantness itself can only mean perceivability. It immediately follows that the only consistent metaphysics to be derived from the program of *Being and Time* is a pragmatic one.

But such a metaphysics is, in the terms of the late Heidegger, subjectivistic and anthropological—and Heidegger, early and late, did not like subjectivism in metaphysics. The early Heidegger saw himself as avoiding the subjectivistic metaphysical trap, but now we see that the metaphysics of *Being and Time* must be pragmatic, against Heidegger's own

71. *B.T.*, p. 255/212.

intentions. It is for this reason that he suppressed the remainder of *Being and Time* and that he himself published no version of *Basic Problems,* permitting its inclusion in the complete works only after he had made clear that it could not be considered the adequate completion of the earlier metaphysical program of *Being and Time.* Heidegger abandoned that program and eventually came to 'attack' metaphysics itself.

The rest of this book contends that the late Heidegger dealt with his unease over the pragmatism implied by the metaphysics of *Being and Time* not by abandoning that metaphysics, as is usually thought, but rather (1) by delimiting the term 'metaphysics' in such a way that a pragmatic position would count as the 'end' or 'completion' of metaphysics instead of as a metaphysical position, (2) by nevertheless accepting the pragmatic position in regard to 'being', and (3) by developing a new sort of nonmetaphysical question concerning being that does not admit of a pragmatic answer. In short, he came to think that pragmatism provides the only viable position concerning the signification of 'being', but he came to believe that there was another issue more important than the metaphysical one. He wanted to change the subject. Instead of asking about the meaning of being in the sense of what it is for a being to be, he came to focus exclusively on the meaning of being in the sense of the horizon in terms of which there can be presenting and, hence, being. This horizon, which Heidegger came to call the truth of being (the analysis of which was merely instrumental to a metaphysical end in *Being and Time*), itself came to be the ultimate matter for thinking. With this transition we have arrived at the late Heidegger.

7 Metaphysics and the Truth of Being

The late Heidegger[1] agrees with the early Heidegger in thinking that philosophy as such is to be identified with metaphysics. As opposed to early Heidegger, however, late Heidegger holds that metaphysics itself, and thus philosophy, is reaching its 'end' or completion. The completion of metaphysics is understood as occurring in a final form of metaphysics, a technological metaphysics whose essence Heidegger characterizes as 'enframing' (*Gestell*). Within the domain of technology (which Heidegger sees as becoming worldwide) a particular understanding of being, being as *Bestand* or 'standing reserve', is dominant. According to this understanding, 'to be' means to be available for use in production or consumption. And, given the domination of this understanding of being, Heidegger holds that (1) philosophy is in the process of dissolving into and being replaced by the positive sciences, and that (2) those sciences themselves must increasingly be interpreted in specifically technological—that is, pragmatic—terms.

As a completion, an end is the gathering into the most extreme possibilities. We think in too limited a fashion as long as we expect only a

1. I use 'late Heidegger' to refer to all the works composed and lecture courses given after approximately 1935, regardless of when they were published. Thus all the essays in *Holzwege* and the work on Nietzsche count as late Heidegger, while "What Is Metaphysics?" does not. I take *Introduction to Metaphysics* to be marginal. For my purposes the chief distinction is that late Heidegger self-consciously understands himself to be 'overcoming' metaphysics, while early Heidegger self-consciously understands himself to be doing metaphysics, regardless of how he believes that what he is doing is different from traditional metaphysics. From this perspective, the essay "The Essence of Truth" still counts as early, though it is crucial for an understanding of the transition as well as extremely helpful in understanding what the late Heidegger has to say.

development of recent philosophies of the previous style. We forget that already in the age of Greek philosophy a decisive characteristic of philosophy appears: the development of sciences within the field which philosophy opened up. The development of the sciences is at the same time their separation from philosophy and the establishment of their independence. This process belongs to the completion of philosophy. Its development is in full swing today in all regions of beings. This development looks like the mere dissolution of philosophy, and is in truth its completion.

It suffices to refer to the independence of psychology, sociology, anthropology as cultural anthropology, to the role of logic as logistics and semantics. Philosophy turns into the empirical science of man, of all of what can become the experiential object of his technology for man, the technology by which he establishes himself in the world by working on it in the manifold modes of making and shaping. All of this happens everywhere on the basis and according to the criterion of the scientific discovery of the individual areas of beings. . . .

The sciences will interpret everything in their structure that is still reminiscent of the origin from philosophy in accordance with the rules of science, that is, technologically. Every science understands the categories upon which it remains dependent for the articulation and delineation of its area of investigation as working hypotheses. Their truth is measured not only by the effect which their application brings about within the progress of research. Scientific truth is equated with the efficiency of these effects.[2]

This sense of the impending end or completion of metaphysical philosophy in the technologically constituted positive sciences is coupled with the claim that another possibility inherent in thinking has been consistently missed by metaphysics in all its forms. Late Heidegger holds that it is possible and has become practically necessary to engage in a thinking concerned with 'the truth of being', or the 'opening' in which being 'occurs', rather than with being, which has been the focus of metaphysics. He refers to this new matter for thinking in a wide variety of ways, but we will tend to use the phrase 'the truth of being' or the Greek word *aletheia*. In turn, the truth of being and with it the variety of ways in which being itself has historically been understood are seen to be 'gifts' of a 'giving' that occurs in and through what Heidegger calls *Ereignis*, or the event of appropriation. Finally, to complete this late Heideggerian liturgy, although most of the time he seems to have a strongly negative attitude

2. E.O.P., pp. 57–58/63–64.

toward the modern, technological world and its dominant pragmatic metaphysics (he sees man's essence in 'danger' through the endless domination of this 'end' of philosophy), he is also unequivocal in holding that only through the domination of technological, pragmatic metaphysics does it first become possible to encounter or to think specifically about *Ereignis* or *aletheia*. He even goes so far as to suggest that enframing, the essence of modern technology, is itself the first form of the thinking that thinks appropriation. "Between the epochal formations of being and the transformation of being into appropriation stands framing. Framing is an in-between stage, so to speak. It offers a double aspect, one might say, a Janus head. It can be understood as a kind of continuation of the will to will, thus as an extreme formation of being. At the same time, however, it is a first form of appropriation itself."[3]

This chapter offers an interpretation of the late Heidegger's thinking concerning the relations among being, the truth of being, and *Ereignis*. To do this is necessarily also to offer an interpretation of the relation between metaphysics—both in general and, in particular, the pragmatic form that is the completion of metaphysics—and Heidegger's attempt at a new thinking concerning the truth of being. As opposed to the interpretation offered by many commentators, and against many appearances to the contrary, my analysis holds that Heidegger's evaluation of modern technological metaphysics is neither wholly negative nor merely ambivalent. Rather, I claim that in one crucial respect—the denial that one can derive general a priori laws that govern all beings from an analysis of what it means to be in general—metaphysical pragmatism and Heidegger's new thinking are identical. In Heidegger's terminology, they both assert that being is not the ground of beings.

For Heidegger, this new thinking differs from philosophical pragmatism, the theoretical expression of enframing, only insofar as pragmatism fails to recognize that the horizon that supplies the condition for the possibility of all understanding and intentionality—which for both Heidegger and pragmatism is a structure of activity—is not itself to be understood as a product of human agency nor to be interpreted and understood pragmatically. In his terminology, pragmatism treats the truth of being as a being that is grounded in the being of man. In short, what is to be criticized in pragmatic metaphysics is not that it makes a mistake in regard to the being of beings but merely that it fails to place

3. S.S., pp. 53/56–57.

the being of beings in its proper context and thus fails to think about something else, the truth of being.

This chapter also asserts that modern technological metaphysics is the 'first form' of the thinking of appropriation insofar as it already implicitly involves a denial that being should be interpreted as the ground of beings, but it does so in a way that fails to allow the truth of being to be explicitly recognized. According to this interpretation, the truth of being can become apparent in and for pragmatism only when pragmatism recognizes (1) that there is no ground, reason, or explanation for the pragmatic way of life that appears in the modern West or, indeed, for any understanding of being, occurring when and as it does, and that in general there is no possible ground or explanation for the fact that there is any understanding of being whatsoever; (2) that formally, the pragmatic, technological understanding of being implies and demands that there are necessary conditions for the possibility of any understanding of being whatsoever, and thus the investigation of those conditions falls outside the region of competence of the pragmatically constituted positive sciences; and (3) that nevertheless, the analysis of these conditions can in no case be used to justify any particular ontology or understanding of being. For late Heidegger, technological thought must come to understand both that there is no ground in being for our ways of understanding being which justifies one way as opposed to others and that nevertheless every understanding of being must stand under certain conditions.

It should be clear to the reader that Heidegger's interpretation of the modern technological understanding of being as *Bestand,* or standing reserve, is precisely the same as the final metaphysical position that we saw Heidegger himself driven to at the end of *Basic Problems.* The early Heidegger found this position unacceptably subjectivistic and for that reason abandoned the project of *Being and Time.* On the interpretation I develop here, the late Heidegger came to believe that there was nothing wrong with the *metaphysics* of that work and that the conditions that *Being and Time* sets out as necessary for the possibility of any understanding of being are indeed necessary. Rather, what is wrong with the early Heidegger from the perspective of the late Heidegger is merely what is wrong with technological metaphysics in general: that is, *Being and Time* gives insufficient attention to the truth of being itself, as opposed to being, and for that reason it fails to recognize explicitly that there is no ground for there being any understanding of being or any particular understanding of being, and that the being or activity of Dasein should not be seen as such a ground or explanation. *Being and Time* is thus confused in regard to its aims. It takes itself to be advancing toward a nonsubjectivist understanding of what it means to be while, in fact, it is advancing toward a pragmatic—that is, subjectivist—understanding of being but a nonsubjectivist, nonpragmatic position concerning the conditions under which being can be understood in any way.

A Note concerning Terminology

In offering this interpretation of the late Heidegger's attitude toward metaphysics, its completion, and what is to succeed it, I do not attempt, as many commentators do, to do justice to the incredible variety and diversity of Heidegger's writings after 1935. Rather, I take him at his word and assume that throughout he was trying to say one simple thing. I thus offer a 'violent' interpretation that gives a unified account of the late Heidegger's attitude toward metaphysics and simply ignores many of the nuances of his various statements of this attitude. Any interpretation of this type must emphasize some texts at the expense of others; this one rests heavily on the expression of Heidegger's views in the 1960s, especially in his essays "The End of Philosophy and the Task of Thinking" and "Time and Being," as well as in the seminar he conducted on the second of these. I believe, however, that the interpretation is faithful to the spirit of a great deal of what Heidegger had to say from 1935 on. At any rate, there are many issues on which it is essential to consult texts from a variety of periods, and I have done so freely throughout.

In addition to the fact that in the essays from the 1960s Heidegger is especially clear concerning the relations among being, the truth of being, and appropriation and, thus, on the relations among metaphysics, the positive sciences, and his 'new' thinking, a second reason for concentrating on this period is that there are substantial and important terminological differences among the works after 1935. This would be less of a problem for interpretation than it is if Heidegger hadn't both made use at different times and in different ways of the same set of ambiguous crucial terms and, in general, stubbornly refused to admit that he had changed his mind, made any crucial mistakes in earlier works, or significantly altered terminology over time. In Heidegger's retrospective writings there is thus a fair amount of cutting and fitting that serves only to confuse the issues involved.[4] For this reason it is more than a mere convenience to use a single consistent terminology with which to discuss and interpret late Heidegger. For the reasons suggested below, I have tended to rely on his 1960s terminology for that purpose.

Much confusion, and many interpretive problems, can be avoided if it is noted that at various times the key word 'being' [*Sein*] is used in at least three separate senses—sometimes even in the same document. First, most properly, and increasingly consistently, 'being' is used to mean what it has traditionally been taken to mean: the 'being of beings', what it is for some entity to be, what is said when it is said that something is. Thomas Sheehan has suggested, felicitously, that it would be helpful and avoid confusion to use the pseudo-English term 'beingness' for *Sein* in this sense.[5] But as Heidegger himself always tends to use *Sein* to render what in English has traditionally been termed 'being' (however else *Sein* is used) and as the terminology from the 1960s finally becomes clear and consistent in using '*Sein*' in this way, I prefer to continue to use 'being' to talk about what it means for an entity to be, as I have done throughout.

Second, the late Heidegger frequently uses *Sein* to say what eventually comes to be said in the terms 'the truth of being', or 'the place of being', or the opening, or *aletheia*. This is especially the case in the phrase 'being itself' or when 'being' is contrasted with 'the being of beings'. I primarily use 'the truth of being'—*never* 'being'—to express this sense. As Heidegger eventually makes clear, 'the truth of being' is a new name—which he hopes is better in important respects—for what in *Being and Time* he calls 'time': "The name 'time' is a preliminary word for what was later called the 'truth of being'."[6] This ambiguity between 'being' as 'beingness', and 'being' as 'the truth of being' is associated with an ambiguity we have already noted in the early Heidegger's use of the phrase 'the meaning of being'. On the one hand, the meaning of being is the unified sense of 'being' which is intended as the intentional correlate of the various categorial intentions directed toward being. It is what *Kant and the Problem of Metaphysics* calls "the significance of 'being' which is pre-

4. E.g., cf. the comments from the seminar (S.S., p. 43/46) concerning the clearly different role assigned to 'being' in *L.H.* from the sense given that word in the "Time and Being" lecture.

5. Thomas Sheehan, *Heidegger: The Man and His Thought* (Chicago: Precedent, 1981), p. ix.

6. S.S., p. 28/30.

comprehended in the question '*Ti to on?*'" In short, 'the meaning of being' in this sense is just what we have called 'being' above, 'beingness'.

In fact, as we have seen, in *Kant and the Problem of Metaphysics* Heidegger specifically calls this question of the significance of 'being' the question 'what is the meaning of being?' In our discussion of the metaphysics of *Being and Time* we tended to use the phrase 'the meaning of being' in this sense, because it is the sense most in keeping with the dominant use of that phrase in *Being and Time* and *Basic Problems*. We did so even though the *late* Heidegger is consistent in claiming that the phrase 'the meaning of being' should be interpreted in the *early* Heidegger in a different way. There is in fact a perfectly legitimate early Heideggerian use of the phrase 'the meaning of being' which goes back to the sense Heidegger gives to 'meaning' in Division 1, Chapter 5, of *Being and Time* and which implies that the meaning of being is the horizon in terms of which there can be any understanding of being in the primary sense. On this reading of the early Heidegger, which becomes normative for the late Heidegger, 'the meaning of being' in *Being and Time* is Temporality, the project horizon for all of Dasein's understanding; and the question of the meaning of being is the question concerning the transcendental conditions for understanding.[7] So understood, the phrase 'the meaning of being' has roughly (but only roughly) the same sense as 'the truth of being'. So the phrase 'the meaning of being' is itself ambiguous between 'being' and 'the truth of being'.

Finally, in the 1940s Heidegger occasionally used '*Sein*' in the sense of what he had already begun to call 'appropriation' (*Ereignis*)—for example, in the *Letter on Humanism*. While leaving open how we are to interpret the extremely difficult word *Ereignis*, we can stipulate that 'being' is never used to mean the same as 'appropriation' in this discussion.

Once we have made these terminological clarifications and distinctions, we can recognize that whole areas of discussion in and concerning the late Heidegger are based on simple terminological confusion. For example, Heidegger sometimes says that metaphysics is the oblivion of being, sometimes that it is the oblivion of the difference between being and beings, and sometimes that it is the oblivion of the truth of being. In the first way of talking it is clear that 'being' is used in the sense of 'the truth of being'. But the so-called ontological difference—the difference

---

7. Cf., e.g., the note at the end of *O.E.T.*, p. 140/201.

between beings and being, which is mentioned in the second formula and looms so large in both early and late Heidegger—also tends to trade on this use of 'being'. Heidegger does believe that traditional metaphysical thinking assimilates being in the primary sense with a being and thus forgets the distinction between being and beings; this is part of what he calls the 'onto-theological' character of metaphysics. He also believes, however, that this trait of metaphysics is rooted in a deeper forgetfulness, the forgetfulness of the difference between being and the truth of being. The unqualified phrase 'the ontological difference' conflates the two distinctions and is thus hopelessly ambiguous, as is the extended phrase 'the oblivion of the ontological difference'. For this reason 'the ontological difference' is entirely avoided here, regardless of the fact that prior to the 1960s Heidegger's use of this phrase is almost ubiquitous.

In what follows, then, I consistently use Heidegger's terminology from the 1960s, regardless of what period we are discussing. 'Being' is always used for 'beingness', what it means to say that some entity 'is'. 'The truth of being' is used as the successor to 'time' and 'the horizon for any understanding of being'; as such it is used in a sense similar to *aletheia*. The term 'ontological difference' is abandoned on the grounds that it is hopelessly equivocal. 'Being' is never used to mean the same as 'appropriation'. The only exception to the use of the late terminology is that I continue to employ the phrase 'the meaning of being' to express the overall signification of the word 'being' rather than to refer to the horizon for all understanding. If I occasionally use this phrase in the second way—which is the way late Heidegger says early Heidegger should be read—I note that I am doing so.

What Is Metaphysics?

It is correct to say that for the late Heidegger the identifying trait of metaphysics is its exclusive emphasis on the being of beings understood as the 'ground' (*Grund* = *arche* = ground, reason, principle; *aitia* = cause) of beings, to the exclusion of concern with the truth of being. The problem with this summary statement is that initially we have very little idea of what it means, because we don't know what it means to say that being is thought of as a ground for beings by metaphysics, and we don't know what is meant by 'the truth of being'. In this section we deal with the first difficulty; in the succeeding section we look at the truth of being directly.

Heidegger sometimes adds helpful additional detail. For example, in "The Onto-Theo-Logical Constitution of Metaphysics," among other places, he claims that "metaphysics is onto-theo-logy" and goes on to explain this term through an analysis of its three components: "Metaphysics thinks of beings as such, that is, in general. Metaphysics thinks of beings as such, as a whole."[8] To think about beings in general, '*to on*', is to think about all beings insofar as they are; it is to ask what it is for any being to be. To think about beings as a whole is to ask about why everything that is, is. It is to ask the question, 'Why are there things rather than nothing?' The metaphysical name for the answer to this question, the being that accounts for the coming to be of everything that is, including itself, is 'God'. In both cases, in asking what it is to be and in asking why it is that things are, metaphysics asks for the ground of beings in the Aristotelian sense of the *archai,* or the principles and causes of the things that are. To think and talk about something in light of its principles and causes is to uncover the 'logic', the *logos,* of those things. So metaphysics is ontology and theology, and this means that metaphysics is the thought that accounts for beings in terms of their ground.

The general metaphysical name for the ground that grounds beings is 'being'. So metaphysics is the science of being as the ground for beings. "Metaphysics thinks of the being of beings both in the ground-giving unity of what is most general, what is indifferently valid everywhere, and also in the unity of the all which accounts for the ground, that is, of the All-highest. The being of beings is thus thought of in advance as the grounding ground. Therefore all metaphysics is at bottom, and from the ground up, what grounds, what gives account of the ground, what is called to account by the ground, and finally what calls the ground to account."[9]

Because being is understood by metaphysics as the ground of beings, metaphysics always drives toward ultimate grounds, the ultimate principles that account for everything else. "Being shows itself in the nature of the ground. Accordingly the matter of thinking, being as the ground, is thought out fully only when the ground is represented as the first ground, *prote arche*".[10] One way of approaching this ultimate ground is

8. *I.D.,* pp. 54/121, 58/125.
9. *I.D.,* p. 58/125.
10. *I.D.,* pp. 59–60/127.

by way of asking about the first efficient or ultimate final cause of all the entities that are taken as a whole, in which case the God of metaphysics can appear. But beings as such and as a whole can be questioned concerning their grounds in other ways, and different determinations of being can appear to metaphysics. "Being is in beings as ground in diverse ways: as *logos*, as *hypokeimenon*, as substance, as subject."[11] In other places this list of the various ways in which being as ground for beings is thought of is expanded and given an almost canonical form, the muster of the historical names for being as ground in metaphysics. Being "shows itself as the *hen*, the unifying unique one, as the *logos*, the gathering that preserves the all, as *idea, ousia, energeia, substantia, actualitas, perceptio, monad*, as objectivity, as the being posited of self-positing in the sense of the will of reason, of love, of the spirit, of power, as the will to will in the eternal recurrence of the same."[12]

It is important to remember that for Heidegger what marks these words for being as metaphysical is that in each of them being is thought of as the ground for what is. The German word *Grund* preserves an essential ambiguity that is present in many of the key words of metaphysics: it refers both to the principles independent of human thinking, that account for things existing and being what they are, and to the principles that are used in our giving an account of those entities. Thus a 'reason' is both an event or cause that motivates or brings about another event and the ground or justification for our believing that some state of affairs obtains. A principle can be either a ground for the being of a thing—for Aristotle the *ousia* (substantiality) or form of a thing is the principle of the thing, that which grounds the fact that it is at all—or a ground for our explanation or account of the thing, as when we argue from first principles. The principle of sufficient reason is both a fundamental axiom of our reasoning concerning things and a statement of what is involved in their being at all. Ultimately, this relation between the two sides of 'principle' goes back to the notion that our beliefs about and apprehensions of things are justified, are grounded, if and only if they correctly uncover and identify the ultimate grounds in and of the things themselves. In the ancient sense, then, to think adequately is to give an account that is fully grounded, and an account is fully grounded only insofar as it shows us the grounds of things themselves. Real knowledge,

11. *I.D.*, p. 60/127.
12. T.B., p. 7/7.

science, always appeals to the essence, the grounds, of the things for which it gives an account.

The emphasis in the biconditional can be read in the opposite direction, however. Something is a principle, a ground, of some thing only if our apprehension and cognition of the thing is fully grounded: that is, fully justified. Heidegger implies that the spirit of modern metaphysics is captured in this shift of emphasis. After Descartes a cognition is grounded if and only if what is cognized is adequate to serve as a principle or ground for the rest of my cognition, and this is the case only if I can be certain of that initial cognition, can know its truth in such a way that doubt concerning it is inconceivable. But since something can be a ground or principle of beings only if its cognition can serve as a ground for our reasoning, only that which is cognized with certainty can be the ground of beings, or the being of beings. After Descartes only the subjectivity of the subject, the self-consciousness of the subject itself, can be known in this way, and all other certainty is mediated by the self-certainty of self-conscious subjectivity. So, in a crucial sense, being is identified with subjectivity. This is the case not only for the out-and-out idealists but also for all those metaphysicians who hold that in one way or another the being of beings is to be understood as the objectivity of the object, or what it is about the object that makes it capable of being intended by a subject. If only subjectivity is known with certainty, and to think is to think something, and only that which is known with certainty can count as the being of a being—as the ground or principle of that which is, in the sense of what it means for a thing to be—then what makes something thinkable must be what it means for that entity to be, its being. And since what it is that makes something thinkable is explainable, understandable, only in terms of the conditions for thinking or self-conscious subjectivity, then what it is for the object to be (the objectivity of the object) is itself grounded in (explained and caused by) the subjectivity of the subject. This subjectivity is thus the deep ground, the *prote arche,* of all beings. The metaphysicians who fall into this group include not only Berkeley and Hegel but Leibniz and Kant, Nietzsche, Husserl, the positivists, and the author of *Being and Time.*

There are several ways in which the history of metaphysics, conceived as that thinking which is concerned with the principles and grounds of beings, can be divided into periods. Heidegger gives us several. For our purposes the most important is the one determined by the division into pre- and post-Cartesian metaphysics. Beginning with the Greeks, the

being of beings—the grounds and principles of an entity insofar as it is—
was thought to lie with the beings themselves. Initially, Heidegger suggests, 'being' is experienced as the self-manifestation of that which is
manifest. That is, for some thing to be, it must be such as to show itself of
itself; it must, as it were, take the initiative and appear. Such appearing,
such making-manifest, was what was initially taken to be what is meant
by 'being'. The ground or principle of any thing, its being, consisted in
such showing. "In the beginning of its history, being opens itself out as
emerging [*physis*] and unconcealment [*aletheia*]."[13] But the emerging can
itself be thought of as having a ground. That something can show itself
rests upon its being there to show itself, upon its being permanently
enduring: "From there [*physis*] it [being] reaches the formulation of
presence and permanence in the sense of enduring [*ousia*]."[14]

Aristotle thinks of that which makes itself present as *energeia*. For
Heidegger, *energeia* must be understood in terms of the difference between the paired oppositions 'moving–not moving' and '*dynamos-ener-
geia*'. In an ordinary change of position the end of a motion signals a mere
cessation of the activity: to reach an end is for the motion toward that end
to cease. But in the motion that results in *energeia* the *ergon*, the work,
"gathers into itself all of the movements of the production" of the entity;
that is, it is at rest in such a way as to appear primarily—to show itself and
emerge—as the completion of those movements. " 'Work' means what is
completely at rest in the rest of the outward appearance—standing, lying
in it—what is completely at rest in presencing in unconcealment."[15] The
actual thing is the enduringly present thing (*ousia*) that shows us the
processes, in various senses, of its coming to rest as it is. In one sense
the work—the resting, enduring *tode ti* that shows up—is the principle,
the being, of the thing. In another sense what the thing shows us—what
it shows itself to be, the various processes of its coming to rest as itself, or
the four causes that identify it as the thing it is—is the proper principle
and ground, the being, of the thing. From these two sides emerge the
notions of existence and essence.

Throughout the history of metaphysics prior to Descartes, the being of
the thing, both its essence and its existence, was seen to be entirely self-
standing, in a crucial sense independent of and lying outside the being's

13. M.H.B., p. 4/403.
14. M.H.B., p. 4/403.
15. M.H.B., p. 5/404.

relation with humanity. For this reason the correspondence view of truth could emerge in the Middle Ages and become entirely natural. But Heidegger thought that with Descartes the reversal noted above occurred. The first mark of this transformation is the rise of certainty as at least the criterion of truth. One must be careful about the character of this subjectivization of being, however. What is at issue is being, not primarily beings: that is, what it means to say that something is or that it is such and such, not *whether* it is or is such and such. Whether some thing exists remains outside the influence and control of the subject, or at least of the subject as self-conscious cognizer, as does what it is if it exists. Prior to Descartes what it is for a thing to be was entirely a matter concerning the thing itself. For it to exist was for it to stand on its own in such a way that, regardless of the state of the rest of the universe, it would be. What a thing is was determined solely as a characterization of the thing's nature itself. Implicitly after Descartes and explicitly after Kant, both what it is for a thing to exist and what the essence of an entity is become relational. As we have seen, for Kant, what it is for a thing to exist is for it to be perceivable or such as to be capable of being perceived. What for the ancients was a consequence of the existence of a thing, an existence distinguished from perceivability as its ground, becomes the existence of the thing itself and, as such, the ground and principle of the thing. As existence is identified with the ability to be intended, the ultimate grounds and principles of the entity must be determined in terms of the conditions under which something can be intended, grounds that express the conditions for intentionality itself. The being of the thing is the objectivity of the thing—and the ground of that objectivity, the principle that supplies its determinacy and our ability to understand and intend it, is the subjectivity of the subject. In Kant's language, the necessary conditions for experience are at the same time the necessary conditions for the objects of experience. Similarly, what a being is is determined with reference to its relation with a subject. That essence is determined in and through the categories, which, with Kant, become explicitly seen as the conditions governing our judgments concerning things.

In one way this reorientation of metaphysics in a subjectivist direction marks an enormous change; in another way it doesn't. Whereas prior to the seventeenth century the understanding of what it is to be a human being was fundamentally shaped by the understanding of what it is to be in general, after Descartes the understanding of being is shaped by the understanding of human being, and behind that by the understanding of what it is to intend. Heidegger lists a whole series of typical characteristics of modernity which he sees as following from this alteration, including the development and dominance of modern science, the rise of social science, the tendency to see the world as a picture to be viewed, and the dominance of formal, instrumental rationality. On the one hand, all of this marks a serious departure from ancient and medieval metaphysics, which always understands what it is for a particular being to be in terms of the being by itself, or in terms of its relation to its ground in God, rather than in and through its relation to humans. On the other hand, the ancient and modern metaphysics are alike insofar as they are both metaphysical: that is, in both cases there is a focus on the ground of the entity, or the principles and causes in and through which the thing is as and what it is. In the ancient metaphysics, how an appearing occurs and that it occurs are grounded in, and explained by, the existence and essence, the *energeia* and *eidos,* of the enduring thing. This same structure is preserved in modern metaphysics, with one difference: 'that *x* is' means explicitly that it can show itself to us, and 'what *x* is' is formally determined by the various conditions for its making itself manifest to us. That there is an appearing is still grounded in the existence of the thing, but 'existence' is now defined in terms of a relation with a subject, and subjectivity is grasped as a deeper metaphysical ground. And, as Heidegger himself often asserts, even the subjectivism of modern metaphysics is presaged in the ancient. After all, the showing and emerging expressed by *physis* itself implicitly involves at least the possibility of a manifesting and emerging for persons and their apprehension. As Heidegger likes to put it, modern metaphysics works out all the possibilities latent in ancient metaphysics, and these possibilities are most clearly explicit in the most contemporary and most 'anthropological' of metaphysics, the pragmatism embodied in modern technology.

Within modern philosophy itself there has been a marked and increasing tendency to emphasize practical models of intentionality at the expense of perceptual models. To some extent, the perceptual metaphysics of Descartes, Hume, and Leibniz have been replaced by the pragmatism of Marx, Nietzsche, and the American pragmatists. In each case, however, the modernity of the understanding of being is preserved. It is only insofar as the being of beings is understood by way of a reference to intentionality that what it means for a thing to be can be understood in terms of serviceability or functionality, just as the metaphysical determination of perceivability is grounded in an analysis of intentionality.

Behind this way of presencing stands the practical subjectivity of the subject as working toward an end and thus accounting for the fact that the things can present their functionality. The self-presence of the agent in its activity is thus taken to involve a deeper sense of presence, which grounds and accounts for the fact that there is such a way of being as functionality or perceivability.

In ancient metaphysics, then, being—the ground and principle of being—is understood as the enduring presence of the entity that accounts for, presences, the manifestations that are presented to us. In modern metaphysics, both classical and pragmatic, being is associated with the self-presence of the subject in and through which objects can become present. In this respect, the late Heidegger's description of metaphysics preserves the early Heidegger's results in regard to the central signification of 'being', always and throughout its history. 'Being' means presence. "Presencing, presence speaks in all metaphysical concepts of being, speaks in all determinations of being. Even the ground as what already lies present, as what underlies, leads, when considered in itself, to lasting, enduring, to time, to the present."[16]

For Heidegger, however, neither the contemporary nor the earlier forms of metaphysics are merely a matter of what professional philosophers say. The various words for being in the history of metaphysics are not merely the idiosyncratic vocabulary of a group of scholars but rather the expression of something deep and pervasive about the way in which being as ground (and this always also means what it is to explain and understand) has been understood by an entire age. That is, the philosophers' words are taken to have successfully articulated a body of practices for coping with things and modes of thinking about things. In this respect the metaphysics of a society is far more than a peripheral academic concern. It is a clue to how, and as what, being is understood in a society as a whole. And this in turn is embodied in every aspect of the way members of a society deal with things, with one another, and with themselves.

Insofar as Heidegger claims that the metaphysics of the modern world must be understood in terms of the essence of the technology of the modern world, therefore, he is making a claim not only about philosophers' understanding of being but also about the understanding of being that dominates the world (in the early Heideggerian sense) in which we

16. S.S., p. 34/36.

live. The contemporary pragmatic way in which being becomes manifest is, for late Heidegger, as the 'standing reserve' (*Bestand*) or calculable material that is there to be used and used up by the technological system of the modern West. "Ever since the beginning of Western thinking with the Greeks, all saying of 'being' and 'is' is held in remembrance of the determination of being as presencing which is binding for thinking. This also holds true of the thinking that directs the most modern technology and industry, though by now only in a certain sense. . . . it is rather being as presencing in the sense of calculable material that claims all the inhabitants of the earth."[17] Such calculable material is to be distinguished from the way being manifested itself to the classical modern philosophers as the objectivity of the object of a theoretical or perceptual cognition by a thinking subject. "Everywhere everything is ordered to stand by, to be immediately at hand, indeed to stand there just so that it may be on call for a further ordering. Whatever is ordered about in this way has its own standing. We call it the standing-reserve [*Bestand*]. . . . It [*'Bestand'*] designates nothing less than the way in which everything presences that is wrought upon by the challenging revealing. Whatever stands by in the sense of standing reserve no longer stands over against as an object."[18] It is more than coincidental that the contrast invoked here, between being as the presence of standing reserve and being as the presence of the object, precisely corresponds to the distinction in *Being and Time* between the handiness of tools and the extantness of perceptual objects.

As with any other determination of 'being', *Bestand* is possible only within a context provided by an original unconcealment that gives man a mode of revealing being. And in the case of the modern world this is the systematic structure of interrelations that go into the ordered whole of technological practice. The 'essence' of technology, or the structure that makes it possible as a way of revealing being, is named by Heidegger 'enframing' (*Gestell*).

The late Heidegger's description of metaphysics and its history preserves a great deal from the metaphysics implied by *Being and Time*. The central signification of 'being' is 'presence', and there are a number of different ways in which 'being' is said, now explicitly stretched out on a historical canvas. Every understanding of being demands for its possibility a horizon in terms of which it and beings can manifest themselves,

17. T.B., pp. 7/6–7.
18. Q.C.T., p. 17/24.

and there is always a correlation between the way in which being is understood and the character of the horizon in which it is understood, as there is between *Bestand* and *Gestell*. But what is the late Heidegger's attitude toward metaphysics as a whole, and toward the metaphysics of the technological world in particular? This last question is especially pressing for two reasons. First, the pragmatic metaphysics of *Bestand* is *our* metaphysics, and this must mean that, on Heidegger's own grounds, in some sense it must be his own in that he lived most of his life in the twentieth century. Second, as we have seen, Heidegger's description of contemporary metaphysics is quite close to the final metaphysical position of *Basic Problems,* and it was the realization that *Being and Time* led to this conclusion that motivated the abandonment of the early program.

The summary answer to these questions has several parts. (1) For the late Heidegger, philosophical metaphysics is—with the technology of the modern world—in the process of being transformed into a kind of pragmatism in which what it means to be is determined by technological practice and its handmaiden, modern theoretical science. For such an understanding, 'to be' just means to be discovered as a standing reserve in a successful practice or to be warranted assertable as 'existing' in a successful theory. "Scientific truth is equated with the efficacy of these effects. The sciences are now taking over as their own task what philosophy in the course of its history tried to present in part, and even there only inadequately, that is, the ontologies of the various regions of beings. . . . The interest of the sciences is directed toward the theory of the necessary structural concepts of the coordinated areas of investigation. 'Theory' means now: supposition of the categories which are allowed only a cybernetical function, but denied any ontological meaning. The operational and model character of representational-calculative thinking becomes dominant. . . . The end of philosophy proves to be the triumph of the manipulable arrangement of a scientific-technological world and of the social order proper to this world."[19]

The reactionary and romantic tone of much of the late Heidegger leaves little doubt that in some sense he thinks of this development as a shame. But (2) what is wrong with all this is not that the metaphysics of the modern world is in error, as if it could be replaced with a new and better metaphysics more in agreement with 'being' itself; rather, what is wrong has to do not with contemporary pragmatic metaphysics but with

19. E.O.P., pp. 58–59/64–65.

metaphysics as such. Metaphysics as such is supposed not to ask a question that needs to be asked, the question concerning the truth of being. "Ontology itself, however, whether transcendental or precritical, is subject to criticism, not because it thinks the being of beings and thereby reduces being to a concept, but because it does not think the truth of being."[20]

It is not even that metaphysics as such asks the wrong or a badly formed question; it is perfectly well ordered. Rather it merely leaves out something important. Heidegger's new 'thinking' aims at rectifying this lack, but (3) the appropriate attitude of this new thinking toward metaphysics is to leave it alone. "The task of our thinking has been to trace being to its own from appropriation—by way of looking through true time without regard to the relation of being to beings. To think being without beings means: to think being without regard to metaphysics. Yet a regard for metaphysics still prevails even in the intention to overcome metaphysics. Therefore, our task is to cease all overcoming, and leave metaphysics to itself."[21]

The rest of this chapter attempts to put some flesh on the bones of this description of the late Heidegger's attitude toward metaphysics and toward the pragmatic metaphysics of the modern world and *Being and Time*. To do this, however, we must understand what Heidegger means by 'the truth of being', by 'appropriation', and by "thinking . . . being to its own from appropriation by way of looking through true time without regard to the relation of being to beings." That is, we must understand Heidegger's attempt to establish a 'new' thinking and to understand how it is supposed to be different from all metaphysics and from the pragmatic metaphysics of the modern world in particular.

The Truth of Being and the Transcendental Conditions of Possibility

The key word in the phrase 'the truth of being' is 'truth'. As we have already seen, from *Being and Time* onward Heidegger consistently interprets 'truth' in light of an etymological reading of *aletheia*, the Greek word usually translated as 'truth'. Etymologically, *aletheia* can be construed as 'unconcealment' or 'unconcealing', so whenever Heidegger

20. *L.H.*, p. 235/357.
21. *T.B.*, p. 24/25.

speaks of the truth of being, he is always talking about the *aletheia,* the unconcealment, of being. That is, he is speaking of the opening in which being becomes manifest and available, in which being itself steps out from concealment, emerges.

Ultimately, in the 1964 lecture "The End of Philosophy and the Task of Thinking," Heidegger abandons the notion that what he means by *aletheia,* unconcealment, can be expressed by the word 'truth'. This does not mean that he ceases to be concerned with the unconcealment of being, however; unconcealment or the opening, he tells us, grants the possibility of being, thinking, and truth in the ordinary sense. And it is precisely this unconcealment, Heidegger claims, that all metaphysics ignores when it focuses on the question of the being of beings. "The opening grants first of all the possibility of the path to presence, and grants the possible presencing of that presence itself. We must think *aletheia,* unconcealment, as the opening which first grants being and thinking and their presencing to and for each other. . . . Insofar as truth is understood in the traditional 'natural' sense as the correspondence of knowledge with beings demonstrated in beings, but also insofar as truth is interpreted as the certainty of the knowledge of being, *aletheia,* unconcealment in the sense of the opening may not be equated with truth. Rather, *aletheia,* unconcealment thought as opening, first grants the possibility of truth. For truth itself, just as being and thinking, can only be what it is in the element of the opening. Evidence, certainty in every degree, every kind of verification of *veritas* already moves with that *veritas* in the realm of the prevalent opening. . . . all metaphysics does not ask about being as being, that is, does not raise the question how there can be presence as such. There is presence only when opening is dominant. Opening is named with *aletheia,* unconcealment, but not thought as such."[22]

These comments have several extremely interesting aspects. Most prominently, it is clear that what Heidegger here calls the 'traditional' notion of truth, understood either as correspondence or as certainty, is understood in terms of the analysis in Husserl's Sixth Logical Investigation of 'being-true' in terms of identification. ('Correspondence' refers here to Hegel's notion that real truth is the self-consciousness of the identity of thought and what is thought about, which is realized in actual beings such as people; it is the objective content of social institutions,

22. E.O.P., pp. 68–70/75–77.

religions, and philosophy. 'Certainty' refers to Husserl's association of truth and the *Evidenz* that grants certainty, especially in regard to the categorial intention directed toward being.) This is an analysis that the early Heidegger accepts. But it is also clear that here the late Heidegger is interested not at all in the question concerning what it is to be true but rather in another question concerning truth: namely, the question concerning the 'possibility' of truth and, with it, of being and thinking. It is not that late Heidegger rejects the Husserlian analysis of what it is to be true, an analysis he formerly accepted; rather, he asks how truth, understood precisely as Husserl understood it, is possible.

Finally, however, this isn't the most interesting aspect of these formulations of the role of *aletheia*. In these passages Heidegger is quite clear both that *aletheia* 'grants' the possibility of being, thinking, and truth in the 'traditional' sense and that metaphysics has never thought about unconcealment. Indeed, late Heidegger consistently maintains that it is a negative criterion of metaphysics that it is the thinking in which the oblivion of the truth of being occurs; that is, the *aletheia* of being is forgotten. But the positive criterion of metaphysics is that it is the thinking that searches for grounds. And what is a question concerning the possibility of x if not a question concerning the grounds for x? Insofar as the question of the possibility of x is treated in a causal manner, what makes x possible are its efficient causes and the general causal setting in which it occurs. In other senses, what makes x possible is the matter x is composed of, or what x is for, or the form of x. That is, in the most natural way of looking at it, the answer to the question of the possibility of x is supplied by the listing of the four causes of x, and to make such a list is a paradigm metaphysical project. Alternatively, when one asks about what supplies the possibility of x where x is something like 'truth' or 'thinking', one could be asking Kant's transcendental question concerning the necessary conditions for the possibility of anything like intentionality or objectivity. But for the late Heidegger this is also a paradigm case of metaphysics. Further, he thinks that this transcendental question, raised in *Being and Time* instead of the question of the truth of being, is what prevented that work from advancing beyond metaphysics. "The experience which attempts to find expression for the first time in *Being and Time* and which in its transcendental manner of questioning must still in a way speak the language of metaphysics has indeed thought the being of beings and brought it to a conceptual formulation, thus also bringing the truth of beings into view, but in all these manifestations of being, the truth of being, its truth as such, has never attained to language, but has remained in oblivion."[23] If Heidegger is not raising a metaphysical question about grounds by raising the question of the truth of being—that is, the question of the possibility of being, then what kind of issue is he raising?

First, we must be completely clear that whatever the sense in which the truth of being is supposed to supply the possibility of being and truth, it does not do so by being the formal cause of being or truth. That Heidegger might be mistakenly interpreted in this way is caused by his own confusions as mirrored in the terminology he used until the 1960s. We have already seen that he uses 'being' for 'the truth of being', and 'the truth of being' or '*aletheia*' for 'truth' during this period, suggesting that 'the truth of being' should be understood as the 'essence' of truth or being, or what it is to be or to be true. But this suggestion is mistaken. Heidegger specifically says that in *Being and Time*, "the name 'time' is a preliminary word for what was later called 'the truth of being'."[24] If the truth of being is at least initially to be identified with the Temporality that is the horizon for the understanding of being in *Basic Problems*, then *aletheia* provides the possibility for truth and being by providing an opening, an open space, in which entities, their being, and the being-identical of intended object and intuited object can occur. And indeed, this is precisely the way Heidegger always speaks of the truth of being.[25] But this open space, this horizon, is not identical with, or what it is to be, or the signification of either truth or being. For Heidegger, early and late, the meaning$_i$ of 'being' is presence, the being-present of that which presents itself, which has traditionally been understood metaphysically in terms of the ground of the presenting. For Heidegger, early and late, the meaning$_i$ of 'truth' is the being-identical of intentional object and its fulfillment in a bodily giving. The horizon in which presence and being-identical can occur is not what it is to be 'presence' or 'being-identical', even if this occurrence is impossible without the open space.

So the truth of being must be understood as providing the possibility for truth, being, and thinking in a way analogous to that in which the horizon of Temporality in *Being and Time* provides the possibility for the understanding of being and truth, and not as if it were the formal ground

23. S.S., p. 29/31.
24. S.S., p. 28/30.
25. See esp. *O.E.T.*, pp. 123–125/183–185.

for being or truth. In *Being and Time* Temporality is the transcendental condition for the possibility of the understanding of being. But, the late Heidegger tells us, *Being and Time* was in error precisely insofar as true time was thought of as the *transcendental* condition of the possibility of being. To this point the only clue we have for interpreting the relation of the truth of being to being, truth, and thinking in the late Heidegger is that the relation is analogous with the relation between Temporality and being in early Heidegger. But we are specifically told that the truth of being in late Heidegger should not be thought of as providing a transcendental condition of possibility, which is precisely the character of the relation in early Heidegger. We are thus left with the problem of seeing how the relation between the truth of being and being is supposed to be similar to the relation between Temporality and being in *Being and Time* yet specifically different from it in not being a relation of providing the transcendental conditions of being. But to deal with this issue we must know exactly what late Heidegger means by 'transcendental', and exactly why he claims that the truth of being does not provide the transcendental condition of the possibility of being, truth, and thinking.

Even though Heidegger came to differ enormously from Husserl and had an incomparably greater knowledge of the history of philosophy, he was Husserl's pupil and in important respects continued to see the history of philosophy through a Husserlian lense. This provides us with a first clue to his understanding of the transcendental. Oddly, for Heidegger, before there was Kant there was Husserl. And for Husserl, 'transcendental' is always transcendental subjectivity, which both provides the ground for the objectivity of objects and, through the method of transcendental reduction to transcendental subjectivity, provides our sole access to the objectivity of objects. To be, for Husserl, is to be an object that presents itself to us as an object through the fulfillment of an intention in and through a dator intuition or series of such intuitions, intuitions that are always in the present tense, as it were. The object's objectivity consists in its ability to 'stand against' us (ob-ject; *Gegenstand*), an objectivity that discloses itself to us in an intuitive representation, a placing-before [*Vor-stellung*].

The problem of the being of the object, then, was the problem of the objectivity of the object. How is it that an object can be an object, something that stands apart from and over against us but nonetheless gives itself to us in intuition? To intend is to intend an object, that which stands against us and is distinguishable from the intuition in which it is given. So the problem of the necessary conditions for the possibility of intentionality—how is it possible to intend?—becomes absorbed in the question of the possibility of the objectivity of objects. Husserl answers by invoking transcendental subjectivity, the subject's reflexive ability to present and represent itself to itself and in doing so to represent the contents of its awareness. The reflexive self-awareness of transcendental subjectivity is accomplished only in and through the ordered structural horizon of internal time consciousness. This time consciousness, as both the primary form of subjectivity and the a priori structure of the organization of all our representations, provides the objectivity of the objects we intend: that is, their ability to stand against and beyond our immediate present-tense intuitions of them. The very transcendence of objects is constituted by transcendental subjectivity.

Late Heidegger's account of Husserl remains faithful to Husserl's own self-description. "The transcendental reduction to absolute subjectivity gives and secures the possibility of grounding the objectivity of all objects (the being of this being) in its valid structure and consistency, that is, in its constitution, in and through subjectivity. Thus transcendental subjectivity proves to be 'the sole absolute being' (*Formal and Transcendental Logic*, 1929, p. 240). At the same time, transcendental reduction as the method of 'universal science' of the constitution of the being of beings has the same mode of being as this absolute being [i.e., reflection], that is, the manner of the matter most native to philosophy."[26]

Given the late Heidegger's interpretation of metaphysics, we can offer the following analysis of the metaphysical character of Husserl's program. For Heidegger's Husserl, objectivity, what it is to be represented as an object, is the being of beings, what it is for them to be. Objectivity is the form, or formal ground, of all beings. Objectivity itself, however, is grounded in transcendental subjectivity, which 'gives and secures the possibility of grounding the objectivity of all objects'. Subjectivity serves as the ground of objectivity in two ways. First, the form of objectivity, what it is to be objective, is just the form of subjectivity, of the reflexive self-consciousness of the subject. The structure of internal time consciousness is both the form of all self-reflexive subjectivity and that in and through which the objectivity of objects and their transcendence is organized. It is for this reason that transcendental subjectivity accounts for and grounds the *transcendence* of objects and is thus "the sole absolute

26. E.O.P., p. 63/70.

being." Second, subjectivity is conceived as the a priori (in a not quite temporal sense) of both objectivity and objects, as providing the not quite causal cause of objectivity and thus of objects. In these senses, then, Husserl's transcendental condition of possibility, transcendental subjectivity, is for Heidegger a metaphysical condition insofar as it provides the ground for the objectivity of objects: it is possible to explain and account for the being of any being by referring to the transcendental subjectivity that serves as its formal and efficient ground. Ultimately, the phenomenological analysis and description of subjectivity are valuable insofar as transcendental subjectivity grounds the way all beings are, and the analysis of subjectivity can thus provide us with laws that govern the being of all beings. It is for this reason that phenomenology, the science that investigates subjectivity, is the method of universal science. Yet subjectivity itself can be seen as dependent upon and grounded on the being of a being, the subject.

So transcendental subjectivity in Husserl is found within a nexus of grounds. It grounds the being of beings, objectivity, and thus can in a deeper sense be seen to be the real locus of the being of beings. At the same time it is itself grounded on the being of the subject. In general, transcendental conditions are metaphysical conditions for Heidegger in that they both provide grounds and are in turn grounded. They are distinctive as metaphysical conditions in that what they provide grounds for is being and not beings, objectivity and not objects. But in doing so, they treat being itself as if it were a being. That is, transcendental conditions explain and ground being, but to explain and ground x is to treat x as some thing that is, so transcendental investigations are metaphysical investigations that treat being as if it were a being, some thing that is.

In the *Critique of Pure Reason* Kant distinguishes between the transcendental and the metaphysical deduction. The Transcendental Deduction begins either with the fact that all experience is temporally organized (in the A edition) or with the fact that all experiences are part of a self-conscious nexus (in the B edition) and argues to conditions that must also obtain if these experiences are to occur. The Metaphysical Deduction starts with a list of the forms of judgment and concludes with a statement of a specific list of categories that apply a priori to every object. That is, Kant distinguishes a *transcendental* argument that determines necessary conditions for experience from a *metaphysical* argument that determines necessary conditions for the objects of experience. Kant does this even though he constructs the transcendental argument for the sake of ultimately drawing metaphysical conclusions concerning the formal and quasi-efficient ground of being, the objectivity of objects, in subjectivity.

Heidegger's reading of Kant consistently refuses to draw the distinction between the two stages in Kant's argument; that is, Heidegger reads Kant in such a way that the transcendental argument as such *includes* the metaphysical conclusion. So, for Heidegger, such transcendental arguments and transcendental conditions are always and as such metaphysical arguments and conditions concerning the determination of the necessary features and grounds of every object insofar as it is an object. We can account for this understanding of Kant and the transcendental if we recall that Heidegger's reading of Kant's notion of the transcendental is dominated by his reading of Husserl's notion of the transcendental.

For Heidegger, early and late, Kant is a metaphysician (for early Heidegger, this is a virtue; for late Heidegger, a vice), a view from which he never wavers. To read Kant as a metaphysician is to read Kant outward from "The Highest Principle of Synthetic Judgment," which Heidegger actually does concretely in *What Is a Thing?* This principle reads: "We then assert that the conditions of the possibility of experience in general are likewise conditions of the possibility of the objects of experience, and that for this reason they have objective validity in a synthetic *a priori* judgment."[27] From this perspective, the point of *The Critique of Pure Reason* is to provide a grounding for the objectivity of objects in reflexive transcendental self-consciousness. The point of the transcendental deduction is the analytic of principles. The possibility mentioned in the phrase "the conditions of the possibility of experience" is interpreted in light of the other phrase, "conditions of the possibility of the objects of experience." Once again, as Heidegger interprets Kant, what distinguishes a condition as transcendental is that it is a condition of possibility of being, not beings. But the sort of conditions involved, the sort of possibility involved, are still identical with metaphysical grounding. Transcendental conditions as such provide the formal ground for the objectivity of objects and the quasi-causal ground for objectivity as such by specifying the grounds for objectivity in subjectivity.

In the second volume of *Nietzsche* Heidegger makes this interpretation of the transcendental explicit. The passage is titled "The Transcendental," its context suggests Kant, and it mentions Kant in its brief concluding paragraph. It is clear, however, that it is meant to apply to the notion of

27. Kant, *C.P.R.*, p. 194, A158, B197.

the transcendental as such. "The transcendental is not the same as the *a priori*, but is rather what determines the object as object *a priori*, objectivity. Objectivity is meant in the sense of transcendence. This word then means that something in the object itself goes beyond that object by preceding it, in representing. Transcendence is grounded in 'reflexion'. Reflexion is transcendental in its true essence, that is, it accomplishes transcendence and thus conditions it in general. The essential and constant re-servation of thinkability, that is, of the representability of something as the condition of all knowledge. I think something."[28]

The late Heidegger always interprets transcendental conditions as conditions for the objectivity of objects. Such conditions always arise in the history of modern metaphysics with its emphasis on subjectivity as the ground for the being of beings. That is, transcendental conditions are seen by late Heidegger as determinations of subjectivity which ground the being of beings in the form of the objectivity of objects. The objectivity of objects itself, understood as the being of beings, always presupposes an optical model of consciousness in which representation intends an object with specific determinations that can present themselves in a theoretical intuition. In the most contemporary sort of metaphysics, however, the pragmatic metaphysics of enframing, the objectivity of the object is replaced as the being of beings by the standing reserve, the serviceability of the functional. In this case it is practical subjectivity that projects the end to be produced in the activity as a goal or value to be obtained; it calculates what is to be done to achieve that goal; and the goal itself is specified in terms of conditions of further use.

But it is possible to see the relation between the availability of the available and its ground in the subjectivity of the practical agent as roughly analogous to the relation between the objectivity of the object and the subjectivity of the subject of theoretical cognition. Within such an interpretation it becomes proper to regard the practical subjectivity of the agent as a transcendental condition: that is, the ground of the being of beings in the modern world. And it is in this sense that the late Heidegger comes to consider the program of *Being and Time* as transcendental and thus as metaphysical. For him, the temporal horizon of Dasein's activity can be seen as the transcendental ground of the being of beings, and this ground is seen in turn as grounded in the being of Dasein. So the whole structure is a metaphysical structure of transcendental grounding.

28. S.H.B., p. 62/466.

But the late Heidegger does not think that the relationship between the truth of being and being is correctly grasped in terms of transcendental grounding; that is, the way the truth of being 'grants' the possibility of being should not be thought of as the way the truth of being provides the transcendental ground for being. He attempts to explicate this difference of relation in several ways. The most general formulation arises from the assertion that the thinking that thinks the truth of being and its relation with being is not metaphysical and does not treat being as if it were a being. It follows that the truth of being is not to be thought of as the ground for being, that being is not to be explained, accounted for, or determined by its relation with the truth of being. From the other side, the late Heidegger attempts to distinguish the relation of the truth of being with being from the relation of transcendental grounding by claiming that the truth of being itself is not grounded in any being but is rather the 'gift' of 'the event of appropriation' (*Ereignis*).[29] What, concretely, would it mean to think of something like a transcendental condition of possibility that did not provide a ground for being and was not grounded in a being?

First, what is it to treat the truth of being, the condition of the possibility of being, as not grounded in any being? In *Being and Time* there is a sense in which there is an ontic condition on the Temporal horizon, which itself is the condition for the possibility of being. There must be a Dasein before there can be the horizon for interpreting being. Both the fact that there is any understanding of being and the particular understanding of being that is prevalent can be explained though a reference to the fact of Dasein's existing and the fact that it exists in the particular determinate manner in which it does. But late Heidegger tells us that the truth of being is a 'gift' of the event of appropriation, and this appropriation should not be seen as a metaphysical ground for either being or the truth of being. Heidegger's formal descriptions of appropriation remain remarkably invariant over his career. Appropriation is the giving (it is always described in verbal rather than nominal terms) that gives both being and time—that is, presence and its horizon—to each

29. The late Heidegger also attempts to distinguish the relation between the truth of being and being from any metaphysical relation of grounding in a number of other ways. Most notably and interestingly he tries to do this by way of a contrast between the belonging-together of being and man in the event of appropriation and the belonging-together intended by the categorial act of identification: See "The Principle of Identity," in *I.D.*, pp. 23–41. As we are primarily concerned with transcendental conditions as metaphysical conditions, however, we will focus exclusively on the very general relations having to do with grounding mentioned above.

other and to Dasein. It is never described as a being. "What lets the two matters belong together, what brings the two into their own and, even more, maintains and holds them in their belonging together—the way the two matters stand, the matter at stake—is appropriation. The matter at stake is not a relation retroactively superimposed on being and time. The matter at stake first appropriates being and time into their own in virtue of their relation, and does so by the appropriating that is concealed in destiny and in the gift of opening out. Accordingly, the it that gives in 'It gives being', 'It gives time', proves to be appropriation."[30] But, of course, appropriation is no being, so it would be a mistake to ask 'what is it?' or to treat it as a being that can be an efficient cause. Rather, it is best to think of appropriation as an ungrounded event, a cataclysm in which being and time occur. For what happens in this event is a 'destining' of being, a determination of the being of beings, and an opening out of time, the organization of a temporal horizon. Needless to say, for Heidegger, both early and late, these always occur together. But what does all of this obscure terminology amount to?

Fortunately, at this point the question is surprisingly easy to answer. What occurs in *Ereignis* is a happening of being: that is, a specific way in which being is understood and thus, in accordance with Heidegger's prevailing verificationism, is. The various periods of metaphysics correspond to the 'destinings' of being. These are 'epochs' of being, not in the sense of mere historical periods (though of course they are at least that) but, for Heidegger, ways of 'holding back' (*epoche*). What is held back in each case is that the being of beings which is revealed is itself a 'gift'; that is, it occurs in an ungrounded event. "A giving which gives only its gift, but in the giving holds itself back and withdraws, such a giving we call sending. According to the meaning of giving which is thought in this way, being—that which it gives—is what is sent. Each of its transformations remains destined in this manner. What is historical in the history of being is determined by what is sent forth in destining, not by an indeterminately thought up occurrence. The history of being means destiny of being in whose sendings both the sending and the it which sends forth hold back with their self-manifestation. To hold back is, in Greek, *epoche*. . . . Epoch does not mean here a span of time in occurrence, but rather the fundamental characteristic of sending, the actual holding-back of itself in favor of the discernibility of the gift, that is, of being with

30. T.B., p. 19/20.

regard to the grounding of beings."[31] This event itself 'consists' in a gift of opening-out: that is, a manner of unconcealment, a determinate mode of 'true time'. In short, appropriation is just the historical occurrence that always involves a change of horizon. All the fancy terminology has only one point: namely, this event is ungrounded. That is, there is no reason for it. There is no reason for it because, treated in its relation to *aletheia*, this appropriating event is no thing and thus can have neither a cause nor a form.

When translated out of his distinctive idiom, the contrast becomes clear between the way in which late Heidegger conceives the origin of both particular ways of understanding being (particular ways of the truth of being or unconcealment) and the fact of unconcealment of being as such and the way in which *Being and Time* and the rest of transcendental metaphysics conceive that origin. For both *Being and Time* and traditional transcendental metaphysical philosophy, what corresponds to the truth of being has its ground in the being and the way of being of human beings. The fact of there being human beings grounds (brings about and explains) the fact of there being a horizon for understanding being at all, and the particular way in which human beings or Dasein are accounts for, brings about, and explains the particular horizon in which being is understood. Because of the way in which he understands transcendental conditions, one thing the late Heidegger takes it to mean to deny that the truth of being is a transcendental condition is to deny that the fact of the being of human beings and their ways of being determine the horizon in which being is understood and given. Rather, a horizon for understanding being is destined to humans, given to them, rather than their producing this horizon.

Concretely, this amounts to the claims that (1) the numerous ways of being (readiness-to-hand, extantness, and so on) tend to succeed one another as dominant determinations of the being of beings (although less dominant modes do, of course, persist in the various epochs) rather than to be 'atemporal' determinations emerging at the whim of Dasein's changing forms of activity; and that (2) neither the fact that there is any understanding of being at all nor the fact that there is the particular one there is at any given time can be explained, accounted for, or grounded in the being of any being, including Dasein. Put in Kantian terms, what is being denied is transcendental psychology, the doctrine that both the fact

31. T.B., pp. 8–9/8–9.

that the conditions for intentionality are met at all and the specific way they are met are 'quasi-caused' by the spontaneous synthetic activity of some transcendental subject and agent of synthesis. But Heidegger seems to accept the Kantian claim that there can be no empirical explanation or ground for the fact and character of the horizon of understanding because all such explanations presuppose some specific form of that horizon. This claim thus amounts to the assertion that there is no explanation, transcendental or empirical, for the occurrence and sheer fact of a temporal horizon, and thus of an understanding of being and intentionality.

As well as being seen as a gift of appropriation rather than as grounded in the being of Dasein, the truth of being is supposed to differ from a transcendental condition in a second respect. Whereas a transcendental condition is seen as the ground for the being of beings, the truth of being is taken *not* to be the ground for the being of beings. In fact, it is asserted that to treat being as having a ground at all is surreptitiously to treat it as if it were itself a being. Further, being itself should not be treated as if it were the ground for beings. In "Time and Being" Heidegger says that "the task of our thinking has been to trace being to its own from appropriation—by way of looking through true time without regard to the relation of being to beings."[32] In the seminar on that essay this passage is interpreted: "Then the phrase 'to think being without beings' was discussed. Along with the expression . . . 'without regard to the relation of being to beings' this phrase is the abbreviated formulation of: 'to think being without regard to grounding being in terms of beings'. 'To think being without beings' thus does not mean that the relation to beings is inessential to being, that we should disregard this relation. Rather, it means that being is not to be thought in the manner of metaphysics, which consists in the fact that the *summum ens* as *causa sui* accomplishes the grounding of all beings as such."[33]

Of course, a transcendental position such as that of Heidegger's Kant or of Husserl does not think of being as if it were some literal being on the order of God that causes everything that is. But insofar as either is a transcendental position, in Heidegger's sense, it does attempt to explain and account for the *form* of every being that is by reference to the transcendental conditions for experience. For Heidegger's Kant and

32. T.B., p. 24/25.
33. S.S., pp. 33/35–36.

Husserl, the being of beings, the objectivity of objects, is determined by the structure of subjectivity; and that structure determines that—and grounds and explains why—every being has the formal structure it has. It is for this reason that they think one can derive metaphysical determinations of all beings that are—for example, that every event has a cause—from an analysis of the conditions of possibility of intentionality. Transcendental philosophy as Heidegger understands it is metaphysics in virtue of the metaphysical form of beings being treated as grounded in the horizonal structure of transcendental subjectivity, which is also the condition of possibility for all intentionality and understanding of being. Given the metaphysical character he takes to be essential to transcendental positions, then, when late Heidegger denies that the truth of being should be seen as a transcendental condition, he is denying that the truth of being can be used to ground a metaphysical account of what the form of all beings must be. That is, he is claiming that even though there could be no being or beings (understood as presencing and things that are, presences) without *aletheia,* the unconcealment accomplished in the truth of being, one cannot reason from the character of the truth of being to the formal structure of the things that are, as transcendental philosophy attempts to do.

From Heidegger's perspective, one can't do so because the truth of being, though necessary for the possibility of being and beings, is the formal ground of neither being nor beings. Being, which admits only of the very general determination 'presence' or 'presencing', is insufficient to determine any necessary rules, laws, or principles that must apply to all entities. The form of such entities is not determined by or grounded in being. In addition, the truth of being cannot explain and does not fix what is determinately meant; by 'being'. Different epochs can have different understandings of being even though they all involve the truth of being. The truth of being isn't the form of being.

To say then, that the truth of being, in late Heidegger, is not the transcendental condition for being, truth, or thinking is just to say (given what Heidegger means by 'transcendental') that the truth of being neither admits of empirical or transcendental explanation or grounding nor can be used to explain, justify, or ground any metaphysical account of the objectivity of objects or of the formal structure of everything that is insofar as it is. If Heidegger is correct in thinking of philosophy as essentially the discipline that attempts to determine a priori (independently of the positive sciences) the necessary formal structure of everything that is and in its transcendental form attempts to do this by way of an analysis of the conditions for intentionality, and if he is right in thinking that the truth of being cannot be used in this way, then philosophy is ended. But all this negative discussion does not quite tell us how we are to discuss positively the truth of being in the late Heidegger. Fortunately, there is no need to engage in a lengthy analysis of this notion, because it turns out that 'the truth of being' really is just a new name for 'true time': *all* that distinguishes them is that the true time of *Being and Time* is thought of as a metaphysical condition, and the truth of being in the late Heidegger is *not* thought of in that way.

We can see this if we look at Heidegger's treatment of time, and its relation to 'opening', in "Time and Being." He begins with an analysis of being in terms of presence and continues with an interpretation of presence and that which is present. That which is present is in general and primarily that which concerns us. (The echoes of *Being and Time* are already beginning.) "What is present concerns us, the present, that is: what, lasting, comes toward us, us human beings."[34] Presence is interpreted in terms of the approaching or reaching toward human beings, the act in which what is present makes itself manifest. "Presence means: the constant abiding that approaches man, reaches him, is extended to him. But what is the source of this extending reach to which the present belongs as presencing, insofar as there is presence?"[35] In one sense this is just the metaphysical question of the ground, but Heidegger, as usual, means to ask a different question. He is asking about the source of presencing or manifesting itself, not the source of the content that is made present or of any particular presentation.

Presencing itself happens in several different modes. For instance, that which is absent, in the sense of that which used to be and is no longer, can presence—that is, be manifest—or be presented *as* absent. There is a presencing of the absence of what has been, and so there is a presencing, a making-manifest, in the mode of having-been-ness. "For one thing, there is much that is no longer present in the way we know presencing in the sense of the present. And yet, even that which is no longer present presences immediately in its absence—in the manner of what has been, and still concerns us. What has been does not just vanish from the previous now as does that which is merely past. Rather, what has been

34. T.B., p. 12/12.
35. T.B., pp. 12–13/13.

presences, but in its own way. In what has been, presencing is extended."[36]

Similarly, there is a presencing in the manner of coming-toward us. The future as coming-toward is thus also a presencing that allows things as expected to be present as expected. "In the future, in what comes toward us, presencing is offered."[37] Unsurprisingly, it is the presencing of the absences of past and future which, through relating one to the other, 'gives and brings about' presence in the sense of the present. "Approaching, being not yet present, at the same time gives and brings about what is no longer present, the past, and conversely what has been offers future to itself. The reciprocal relation of both at the same time gives and brings about the present."[38] The way in which having-been-ness, presence in the sense of the present, and futurity as coming-toward are related to one another and thus 'give' one another (of course, the determinations 'past', 'present', and 'future' are unintelligible except as a set) opens up a 'space', an opening, in which that which is present can present itself. And it is only as a 'unifying unity' that the three dimensions of time can themselves approach us and bring about a kind of presencing toward us. For the time-space, the open region in which beings can appear, itself approaches us and makes itself manifest; it itself presences in the unity of past, present, and future. That is, there is a manifesting that is time itself and is the unity of past, present, and future. This is true time: "True time is the nearness of presencing out of present, past, and future—the nearness that unifies time's threefold opening extending."[39]

All of this could have come out of the final pages of *Basic Problems;* in fact, for all intents and purposes, it does come out of the early Heidegger. When the late Heidegger attempts to describe *aletheia* or the truth of being directly through an account of true time, the description is fundamentally indistinguishable from the description the early Heidegger gives of Temporality as the horizon for all understanding of being. Nevertheless, as we have seen, the late Heidegger thinks there is a substantial difference between the truth of being and the ultimate horizon for the understanding of being in *Being and Time.* The difference is that the truth of being is not supposed to be a metaphysical determina-

36. T.B., p. 13/13.
37. T.B., p. 13/13.
38. T.B., p. 13/14.
39. T.B., p. 16/17.

tion, while the horizon for the understanding of being *is* a metaphysical determination.

If we combine this recognition (that late Heidegger thought the horizon for the understanding of being in early Heidegger, Temporality, was a metaphysical determination) with our analysis of the way in which the late Heidegger tried to distinguish his own project from metaphysics, we can see that the difference amounts to a difference in the relations in which these respective structures are taken to stand. In the program of *Being and Time*, Temporality (*Temporalität*) is taken to be identical with the meaning of the being of Dasein (*Zeitlichkeit*); thus, Temporality is grounded, both formally and efficiently, in the being of a being, Dasein. In late Heidegger, the truth of being is the gift of appropriation, but it has no ground or explanation in any being.

Similarly, the early Heidegger thinks that Temporality can be used to ground (explain and justify) a certain metaphysics in regard to beings, a determinate way of thinking of the being of beings. In traditional fashion, he thinks he can use a transcendental argument concerning the conditions for understanding to arrive at and ground an understanding of the being of each being. Even though early Heidegger differs from Kant in holding that beings can be in a variety of ways, he does believe that each being itself determines the appropriate manner for approaching it, the appropriate manner for understanding its being: "The mode of uncovering and the mode of uncoveredness of the extant obviously must be determined by the entity to be uncovered by them and by its way of being."[40] And, he holds, we can practice the discipline of ontology if we first do fundamental ontology, the ontology of the being that is capable of intending. In contrast, the late Heidegger holds that an understanding of the truth of being, of the horizonal structure in which the presencing of what is present can occur, cannot be used to justify or ground any determinate metaphysics. In fact, he believes, we will be released into appropriation and the truth of being only when we stop trying to think of being, and alongside being the truth of being, as if they were the ground for beings.

So the truth of being differs from Temporality only in its relations with being and beings. Temporality is seen as grounded in a specific being, Dasein, and as in turn grounding a particular, determinate understanding of the being of beings. The truth of being, on the other hand, has no

40. *B.P.*, p. 70/99.

ground in any being and cannot be used as a step in a two-stage transcendental argument capable of grounding determinate metaphysical determinations of beings. But this characterization of the difference between early and late Heidegger leaves us with an unresolved issue. What, exactly, is the relation between Heidegger's 'new thinking' (which is concerned with the truth of being and appropriation) and the kind of metaphysics that he takes to be dominant in the modern world, the technological metaphysics of enframing and the standing reserve? What alterations are necessary in this technological metaphysics to transform it into the new thinking?

It should be clear that they are very close to one another. The metaphysical outcome of the program of *Being and Time* was not what Heidegger had hoped it would be; he came to recognize that the fundamental ontology of *Being and Time* could be used only to ground a subjectivistic metaphysics—a metaphysics that defines the being of each being only in relation to Dasein's mode of uncovering, ultimately goes back to practical activity as the basic way of Dasein's being, and thus leads to a pragmatism in regard to the being of beings. What it means for a being to be depends upon the way in which it can be practically approached, an issue that is decidable not a priori by philosophy but only by actual practice, technological and scientific. This position, needless to say, is just the theoretical formulation of the metaphysics of the essence of technology. And the key element in this position, Temporality as the horizon for all understanding of being, is the same as the key element in late Heidegger's thinking, the truth of being. In the final section of this chapter we turn to the question of the relation between the pragmatic metaphysics of the modern world, which is the metaphysics implied by *Being and Time,* and the thinking of the truth of being and appropriation.

"A First Form of Appropriation Itself"

Certain aspects of the late Heidegger's attitude toward the technological character of the modern world are clear and constant over time. Technology isn't understood primarily as a way in which human beings happen to make and use tools. Rather, modern technology is interpreted by way of its 'essence', with 'essence'—understood as it is in the essay "On the Essence of Truth"—as what allows for the possibility of technology in the ordinary sense. In this case, the essence of technology—what makes modern technological practice possible—is a certain way in which being is revealed and unconcealed, the definite mode of the truth of being that Heidegger calls *Gestell,* 'enframing'. This manner in which being is given 'releases' or unconceals being as 'standing reserve'. As we have seen, being as standing reserve is supposed to differ from all the ways being is unconcealed in all earlier epochs in its extreme subjectivism. Concretely, this means that the being of any entity is understood to vary as a function of the way in which it can be successfully approached and coped with. Whether it is possible to approach and cope successfully with an entity or group of entities in any particular way is an issue that can be determined only through the attempt to do so; therefore, the determinate being of any entity can be determined only through technical practice and positive scientific inquiry. It is for this reason that philosophy as metaphysics ends itself in the sciences: if metaphysics decides that to be is to be available for use, that whether a being is available for use and the way in which it is available to be used can be determined only by the pragmatic success or failure of the actions that presuppose it or of the scientific theory in which it is intended and asserted to exist, then metaphysics as a discipline that treats the being of entities has transformed itself into practice and science.

For late Heidegger, the essence of technology, enframing, in unconcealing being in the extreme subjectivist manner of standing reserve, places human beings in an extremely 'homeless', 'rootless', and 'traditionless' position. "Everything is functioning. That is precisely what is awesome, that everything functions, that the functioning propels everything more and more toward further functioning, and that technicity increasingly dislodges man and uproots him from the earth."[41] This rootlessness amounts to the way in which technicity dissolves all traditional and substantial determinations for being human—by measuring the value of all factical human determinations in light of their pragmatic efficacy and by giving humans the seeming power, through technical mastery of the natural and social environment, to recreate their own facticity and 'nature' from the ground up. It is this technical revolt against human rootedness in place and social tradition, not the end of philosophy, that the late Heidegger perceives as the primary danger of enframing. "As far as my own orientation goes, in any case, I know that, according to our human experience and history, everything essential and of great magnitude has arisen only out of the fact that man had a home and was rooted in a tradition."[42] In particular, he is concerned that the

41. O.G.C., p. 56/206.
42. O.G.C., p. 57/209.

rootlessness of enframing will destroy the human essence, which he now conceives as the ability to respond to the epochal transformations of being and, ultimately, to *Ereignis,* the event of appropriation. We will see below why he should think so.

In all this we can see the strong strain in Heidegger of the romantic rejection of modernity and formal, instrumental rationality that characterizes much of German thought in the nineteenth and twentieth centuries. We can also see how the Nazi ideology, with its emphasis on the land and the folk and its own kind of romanticism, could have exercised an initial attraction for him in the 1930s. Further, given the fact that for late Heidegger the event of appropriation and the inauguration of a new relationship with being are never grounded in humanity or in human agency, we can understand the passivity in the face of technological and political issues that is characteristic of his last years. This attitude is in the starkest contrast with the attitude prevalent in the technological world itself, which takes all things to be within the power of human control. For late Heidegger, "only a God can save us," and we do need saving. Thus in speaking of Western political and cultural attempts to deal with and control the technological relation to being, he characterizes them as "half-way measures," because, he says, "I do not see in them any actual confrontation with the world of technicity, inasmuch as behind them all, according to my view, stands the conception that technicity in its essence is something that man holds within his own hands. In my opinion, this is not possible."[43]

And now we have come full circle: the technological notion that man and the being of human beings is the origin and ground of all unconcealment of being, and that the way of being and revealing is within man's power, is precisely what marks the technological world as metaphysical for late Heidegger and hence different from his own new thinking. It is from this standpoint that from the 1930s onward he consistently criticizes pragmatism as the philosophical expression of technicity, calling it incapable of really apprehending the true character of modern technology as a way in which being is unconcealed. "They [Americans] are still caught up in a thought that, under the guise of pragmatism, facilitates the technical operation and manipulation [of things], but at the same time blocks the way to reflection upon the genuine nature of modern technicity."[44]

43. O.G.C., pp. 55–56/206.
44. O.G.C., p. 61/214.

It is at just this point, however, that Heidegger's response to the essence of technology and to pragmatism as its philosophical expression becomes more complicated. Almost all his remarks on the metaphysical character of enframing focus upon the way in which what is properly seen as the truth of being—and hence as not grounded in any being—is experienced in the modern world as grounded in and at the disposal of humanity. But according to the ideal conception of metaphysics that the late Heidegger develops, there is in general a second relation of grounding that is typical of metaphysics. In metaphysics, being is conceived as the ground of beings. In certain types of metaphysics, being in the guise of God serves as the ground and explanation of all beings by counting as their efficient or final cause. But even when this specific characterization is lacking, metaphysics is supposed to retain its 'theological' character insofar as being is conceived as the ground of beings by counting as their formal cause. Every metaphysical research program involves first determining the a priori structure of what it is to be and then using this knowledge to derive general laws that cover all beings. Traditional transcendental philosophy, for example, counts as metaphysical insofar as the reflexive character of the self-conscious subject (the subjectivity of the subject) is conceived as specifying the form of the concept of an object in general (the objectivity of the object) and therefore can ground a priori the principles that hold true of all beings. It is precisely in this sense, however, that pragmatism—whether in the shape of technological practice, or in the shape of American pragmatism, or in the shape of the implications of Heidegger's own thought in *Being and Time*—is no longer metaphysical. For pragmatism, the investigation of the conditions under which it is possible to intend entities, is either an empirical, pragmatic investigation like all others or, as it is in *Being and Time,* an investigation whose results imply that there are no definite a priori determinations of the being of beings beyond the entirely abstract determination of 'presence'. All that such investigations tell us is that those things are which show up in successful practical dealings with the world, either directly or indirectly through our theories, and that they are as the character of those dealings show them to be. And, at least for the pragmatism of *Being and Time,* the necessary conditions for experience are not at the same time the necessary conditions for the objects of experience.

So it is not true to say that for late Heidegger the essence of technology is merely the metaphysical positing furthest removed from appreciation of the truth of being and appropriation. Rather, "the essence of technology is in a lofty sense ambiguous. Such ambiguity points to the mystery of all revealing, i.e., of truth."[45] It is ambiguous for Heidegger in that it is a mode of the truth of being which at the same time is the most extreme form of subjectivistic metaphysics, in that it takes the activity of man to be the ground of all being (including its own manifestation as a way in which being is revealed) and an advance away from metaphysics, in that it denies a grounding role to being vis-à-vis beings. It is "Janus faced." We are told that "this destining, enframing, is the extreme danger, not only for man's coming to presence, but for all revealing as such," insofar as "the coming to presence of technology threatens revealing, threatens it with the possibility that all revealing will be consumed in ordering and that everything will present itself only in the unconcealedness of standing reserve."[46] That is, the tendency to interpret all things pragmatically as human products or as determined in their being for human using makes it possible that it will become impossible to respond to any new giving or granting of being, any *Ereignis* or transformation of the way being is experienced, as anything other than a new instance of standing reserve. Enframing is, oddly enough for a non–a priori move, a totalizing mode of unconcealment. At the same time, we are told that "we look into the danger and see the growth of the saving power,"[47] and that enframing "is a first form of appropriation itself"[48] insofar as it already announces the end of philosophy and metaphysics and thus makes possible a new relation to being in which being is experienced in relation to the truth of being and appropriation rather than in relation to beings as their ground.

Enframing itself, pragmatism, doesn't experience being in this other relation, however. According to late Heidegger, to do this it would need to experience that enframing itself—our contemporary manner of un-concealing being—is not grounded in human activity but is rather, as a manner in which being is unconcealed, an ungrounded 'gift' of appropri-ation. All that is necessary is that we experience technology by way of its 'essence' as a "destining of a revealing," an ungrounded gift. We do this when we ask how the pragmatic world itself can come to pass. "When . . . we ask how the instrumental comes to presence as a kind of causality, then we experience this coming to presence as the destining of a reveal-ing."[49] How are we to translate this opaque claim out of the late Heideg-ger's idiom?

45. Q.C.T., p. 33/41.
46. Q.C.T., pp. 31/40, 33/42.
47. Q.C.T., p. 33/41.
48. S.S., p. 53/57.
49. Q.C.T., p. 32/40.

The point Heidegger is emphasizing here is the narrow line that separates the last form of metaphysics, enframing, from his new thinking. This line is just the metaphysical notion that the Daseinish activity that provides a context for the possibility of any encounter with being or beings is itself a product of human activity and can itself be accounted for—explained, grounded—pragmatically in the same way as the things that show up within that context. In Heidegger's terminology, this would amount to treating the truth of being as if it were a being. But for late Heidegger, that context itself is neither grounded on nor grounds beings, although it does make being possible. The truth of being is thus an unexplained occurrence (it is no thing) that makes all relation with being and beings possible but does not provide the form of all beings. Pragmatism knows that nothing provides the form of all beings; it is anti-essentialist to the core. But it does not recognize that (1) all intentionality and activity nevertheless stand under necessary conditions for their possibility; that (2) these conditions cannot be treated pragmatically—that is, as standing reserves that vary their determination depending upon how they are approached and used; and that (3) the fact that these conditions are met cannot be explained either empirically or transcendentally. Pragmatism *is* Heidegger's new thinking without the truth of being.

With this result we have come to the end of our interpretation of the late Heidegger on being, the truth of being, and metaphysics. We are left, however, with two pressing problems. First, so much of our interpretation has been couched in Heidegger's own opaque and confusing terms that it is difficult to see how to evaluate his claims, both because they are difficult to translate into a neutral, non-self-authenticating idiom and because we are not sure what criteria to use in the evaluation. This last consideration leads to the second problem. If one doesn't share the late Heidegger's rather idiosyncratic vision and intuition—if, indeed, one finds his reactionary, romantic, antimodernism repugnant rather than attractive, as I do—then is there any reason to take his thought at all seriously? Is there anything like an argument structure to be considered and evaluated?

In the last chapter I hazard both a non-Heideggerian statement of the late Heidegger's thought concerning the truth of being and a reconstruction of his argument structure, both of which can be considered and evaluated by a non-Heideggerian-speaking audience.

8 The Argument Structure of Late Heidegger

The central concept in the late Heidegger is the 'truth of being'. On the one hand, the truth of being is supposed to be necessary for the possibility of truth in the sense of semantic content (or the possibility of truth and falsity), thinking, any understanding of being, and through the latter any understanding of the things that are. It is supposed to be so in such a way, however, that it does not determine or ground either the being of beings or beings themselves; if it did ground these, then it would be, for Heidegger, a metaphysical concept—and he denies that it is one. On the other hand, the notion of the 'truth of being' is supposed to be unique in the history of thinking in that it is not taken to refer to any entity or the determination of any entity, or admit of any ground or explanation. Rather, the truth of being is taken to be a gift of 'appropriation', the ungrounded 'event' that 'lets' being and time, presence and the open space of the horizon of presence, 'belong together'.

On the basis of the interpretation presented in the last chapter, we can isolate five claims that are central to the late Heidegger. Together they serve not only to characterize his thought but also to flesh out his use of the phrase 'the truth of being'. (I) The truth of being is necessary for beings and their being, and a necessary condition for intentionality (thinking) and truth. Nevertheless, (II) the truth of being does not ground beings or their being and cannot be used as an explanation or reason for beings or their being. (III) The truth of being is not identical with Dasein, the being of Dasein, or what it means to be Dasein. (IV) The truth of being is not grounded in Dasein in any way. In fact, (V) the truth of being is not grounded at all but is an ungrounded gift of *Ereignis*.

259

The first two claims serve to specify the relations among the truth of being, being, and beings themselves. The last three assert in different degrees of generality the claim that the truth of being is entirely ungrounded. Clearly, if (V) is true, (III) and (IV) must be true, but the truth of (V) is not necessary for the truth of (III) and (IV).

The extreme difficulty involved in understanding and evaluating the late Heidegger's thought arises from the fact that the 'truth of being' and, behind it, 'appropriation' are not supposed to be beings, determinations of beings, or identified with the being of beings. If, as Heidegger holds, 'being' is to be understood in terms of presence, then the supposed horizonality of the truth of being becomes crucial. The truth of being can never present itself, can never be made manifest in an intuition or show itself as presentable. Although the late Heidegger frequently emphasizes the need to 'experience' the truth of being, the implicit logic of his thought indicates that no experience can be an intuition or representation of the truth of being. Similarly, if truth is understood in terms of the fulfillment of an intention in a direct having, then it is difficult to see how any claims about the truth of being could be either true or false.

Heidegger's reiterated insistence that the truth of being loves to hide or necessarily involves a self-concealment (*lethe*) at the very moment that it is unconcealment (*aletheia*) comes back to this circumstance. Nevertheless, insofar as late Heidegger attempts to articulate the truth of being and does in fact make certain attempts to articulate a series of relations among the truth of being, appropriation, being, and beings, there must be some sense in which what he says admits of evaluation, if only to the extent of being judged either intelligible or unintelligible. In fact, we will assume in this chapter, as we assumed in the last, that 'the truth of being' is a 'theoretical' notion in that Heidegger arrives at it through an argument that what is and is observed could not be the case unless the truth of being 'were given' in some sense. What distinguishes it from ordinary theoretical notions is that the truth of being is not supposed to be a being—that is, a presence or a ground of presencing—whereas ordinary theoretical notions are taken to refer to entities or the determinations of entities. If this approach is accepted, then to assert that Heidegger's claims are true is just to say that the arguments he presents in favor of the truth of being are cogent ones, even though those arguments themselves imply that there could never be a presentation or manifestation of the truth of being.

Heidegger's Transcendental Pragmatism

In this section we examine the connection between claim (I), that the truth of being is necessary for the possibility of truth and the understanding of being, and claim (II), that the truth of being nevertheless does not ground beings or their being. Understood in terms of (I), the late Heidegger's position is transcendental in the sense that it rests on a transcendental argument, which argues from the fact of an understanding of being and semantic content to a set of conditions that make those facts possible. His argument in favor of this thesis is, of course, just *Being and Time,* as we analyzed it in Part I of this book. Heidegger's transcendentalism differs from other such positions, however, in asserting that these conditions cannot be used to ground a metaphysical position. That is, understood in terms of claim (II), his position is pragmatic in that it is in a deep sense anti-essentialist.[1] Not only does the late Heidegger hold that what kind of thing any particular entity is, and hence how it must be understood in order to be understood correctly, is not fixed solely by the entity itself; his position also implies that what it means for a thing to be, the ontological sort of the entity, is not determined solely by the entity itself. Further, this position implies that what ontological sorts there arc varies in relation to the way being is revealed. The position is pragmatic in that the being of beings is seen to vary in terms of the ways in which the world can be successfully dealt with and coped with. It is because he thinks the entire metaphysical tradition has been tending toward this pragmatic position—which he feels is reached in principle in Nietzsche—that Heidegger thinks metaphysical philosophy is 'completed' in this kind of pragmatism.

Late Heidegger's pragmatism is unique in two respects, however, both of which arise from the transcendental character of his thought. First—as opposed to most pragmatists—he is pragmatic, in regard to being, for transcendental reasons. That is, it is the transcendental results in *Being and Time* concerning necessary conditions for intentionality which are used as premises in the argument that leads to pragmatism concerning the things that are. As we will see, because of the specific character of those conditions for intentionality, they not only cannot be used in the

1. Cf. Richard Rorty, *The Consequences of Pragmatism* (Minneapolis: University of Minnesota Press, 1982), esp. the essay "Pragmatism, Relativism, Irrationalism," pp. 160–175, for the anti-essentialism of pragmatism.

way that has been traditional in transcendental arguments, to ground a metaphysical position, but can be used to show that no a priori metaphysics can be justified and that pragmatism is the only plausible metaphysical stance.

Second, because the pragmatism is based on necessary conditions for intentionality, Heidegger's position is different from most pragmatism in being restricted. It is restricted in that Heidegger is emphatically not pragmatic in regard to the truth of being itself. Even if the traditional metaphysical and epistemological concerns of philosophy seem to be naturalized in late Heidegger, the structure of the truth of being is not naturalized: there can be no pragmatically determined research into the truth of being and no positive science of the truth of being. Even though the truth of being is not supposed to be a being and thus cannot properly be said to have an essence, Heidegger describes it in the anti-anti-essentialist terms used in *Being and Time* to discuss Temporality. It is this anomalous position of the truth of being that accounts for his at best ambivalent attitude toward modern pragmatism. But the transcendental character of the truth of being, as the necessary condition for any understanding or understanding of being, is also used in the argument in favor of metaphysical pragmatism.

In effect, then, late Heidegger pulls apart two aspects of transcendental arguments that have traditionally gone together. In Kant and Husserl, for example, the conclusions of a first part of the argument, which concern the necessary conditions of possibility for intentionality or knowledge, are used as premises in a second argument that concludes with assertions concerning the necessary conditions for the possibility of the objects of intentionality or knowledge. The necessary conditions for experience are seen to be the necessary conditions for the objects of experience, and those conditions prescribe the concept of an object in general: that is, the objectivity of objects or the being of beings. Heidegger reserves the term 'transcendental' for full-blown metaphysical arguments of this type, and one of his reasons for denying that after *Being and Time* he used transcendental arguments is that he accepts and uses only the first stage in the traditional transcendental structure. Precisely because of the particular conditions he uncovers in *Being and Time*, Heidegger is led to the conclusion that the second stage cannot be carried out. Instead, these transcendental conditions are used as premises in an argument designed to show that no a priori metaphysics is plausible. Unsurprisingly, the outline of this argument is contained in *Basic Problems,* although in a hidden and confused form, because Heidegger *thought* he was arguing to a very different conclusion.

As we have already seen, the metaphysics of *Basic Problems* appears to end in an *aporia*. Early Heidegger wants to maintain that the subjectivism and implicit idealism inherent in the modern metaphysical tradition is mistaken. He argues that it is wrong to think of Dasein as a 'worldless' subject, a pure cognizer to whom objects appear within the realm of its own self-consciousness, which is placed as an observer vis-à-vis objects presented to a faculty of representation. If Dasein is understood in this way, then we must be confronted with Descartes's epistemological problem: namely, how can one ever know the relation between that which is presented to self-consciousness and that which is in itself? Given the parameters in which this question is set, the only possible response is Kant's. The distinction between appearance and reality is internal to the realm of experience because the being of the object, the very objectivity of the object or what it is to be an object that can be represented as transcending any particular experience, is itself determined by the conditions under which self-consciousness can occur. In making self-consciousness possible, Kant sees the synthetic activity of understanding and imagination as also fixing and determining the being of the object experienced.

From the early Heidegger's perspective, Hegel and the nineteenth century—while expanding the subject of this activity and this experience to the ideal community of knowers, discarding the traditional metaphysical remnant of the thing in itself, and replacing it with the movement of spirit in the object itself—make no essential change in the modern position. But (also from the early Heidegger's perspective) this entire subjectivist picture is based on a bankrupt understanding of what it is to be Dasein. The bulk of the published portion of *Being and Time* is, as we have already argued, an extended argument designed to show that no self-consciousness is possible unless Dasein is being in the world, an agent actively working on and with things to achieve self-defined ends. Heidegger argues that if this ontology of Dasein is correct, then Descartes's initial epistemological problem can never legitimately arise. Dasein is always 'out there' with and among things in its activity. Dasein is just the revelation, the unconcealment, of things in and through its temporally organized activity. And if this basic alteration in the way in which we understand the being of Dasein is accepted, then, Heidegger argues, our fundamental way of understanding metaphysical issues must also change. As Dasein is being-there, the there in which beings are revealed, and it is impossible for beings to be revealed unless their being is understood, Dasein must also be the unveiling or revealing of the being of beings. Insofar as Dasein understands beings as they are, it must also have a prior—an a priori—understanding of their being, or of what it is to be that which Dasein understands. And as Dasein is no longer seen as an isolated worldless subject, the contrast between a subjective sphere and a sphere of being disappears, and with it the temptation to understand the being that Dasein understands as some sort of projection of that understanding itself.

As early Heidegger likes to put it, the horizon of Dasein's understanding, the structure of temporal action, is more objective than any object in that it opens up the possibility of understanding the being that beings themselves have and display. Dasein's activity is an open space in which things can display themselves and their being, rather than a productive agent that forges that being. Temporality is the transcendence itself in which Dasein transcends beings toward their being and thereby comes to understand what it is for beings as such to be. It is because he has this image that early Heidegger can claim that the being of individual beings itself 'regulates' the appropriate way in which that being can be understood.

It is the deep problem in this argument, however, that leads to an *aporia*. As we have seen, in order to argue in favor of the position that the being of Dasein is to be understood in terms of temporality and purposive activity rather than as self-conscious subjectivity, Heidegger must base his argument on phenomenological grounds. And phenomenology is essentially verificationist. The meaning of any intentional act, including linguistic acts and purposeful acts, is specified in terms of the conditions under which the act would be satisfied, or fulfilled. In the course of the argument of *Being and Time* Heidegger discovers that intentional acts can specify and determine a content to be fulfilled only insofar as those acts themselves are part of an ongoing course of purposeful, temporally organized, activity. This is the heart of the argument of *Being and Time:* there can be no self-conscious subjectivity, no intentionality, without the being in the world of Dasein. It follows that because evidentiary or fulfilling acts are intentional (that is, evidence, in order to be evidence, must be grasped with a determinate sense as fulfilling some other intention), nothing, no 'experience' or 'intuition', can count as evidence—as fulfillment of some intention having a sense—unless it is placed within a context provided by an ongoing series of acts. This is the discovery that all understanding, all cognition, involves interpretation, or the placement of that which is intuitively presented within a context or horizon of interpretation in which there can be evidence for or against a claim.

Now, for both Husserl and the Heidegger of this period, the being of any being, or what it is for that entity to be, is itself the object of a categorial act that accompanies the intention directed toward the entity. If this is the case, then the being of any being must be specified only within a context of interpretation, a structure of activity in which the act directed toward the being of a being occurs. What it means for any being to be, but not whether that being is, is dependent on the interpretation of that being—the character of the horizon in which it is understood— insofar as the meaning of the act directed toward the being of that entity is determined as the conditions under which that act would be fulfilled; and those conditions are fixed only in and through the context of an ongoing activity. If Heidegger admitted only one structure of activity, then this conclusion would be compatible with a univocal sense of 'being'. But given the priority he accords to practical action, such a position would leave semantic, linguistic, and mental content unexplained. So Heidegger opts for the claim that a variety of senses of 'being' correspond to differently structured horizons of activity, 'extantness', 'handiness', and so on. As all such horizons are similar in being Dasein's horizon of activity, however, there is an analogical unity to the meaning$_i$ of 'being'. No matter how articulated, 'being' always signifies 'presence': the manifesting of a being to Dasein in and through the presentation of itself in evidence.

It is at this point that we can see the *aporia* emerging. 'Being' itself, remember, is the object of a categorial intention, and the meaning of this intention is determined by the conditions under which it would be fulfilled, under which a being would in fact be. We are never confirmed in thinking that some being is, simply because we have an intuition of it; presence is not identical with being presented. Rather, the evidence for the being of an entity consists in a coherent system or series of manifestations: x is if and only if it is present to present itself, and it is so present only if it is there to be presented, if it is presentable. But (1) what it is to be presentable, what must occur if our intention that x is is to be fulfilled—whether that x must be presentable in confirming perception or as usable in a practical way, or must act as Dasein acts—is specified, fixed, and determined by the interpretive horizon in which Dasein approaches *x*. (2) As with Kant's modal categories, presentability is a determination that makes essential reference to Dasein—there is no possibility of presentability without the one for whom and through whom there can be presence. In order to avoid this consequence the early Heidegger plays with the metaphysical idea that 'being' should be identified with the ground of presence. But eventually he comes to hold—correctly, on his own terms—that the evidence for being, and hence the meaning of 'being', reaches only as far as presentability, not the ground of presentability. (3) As the being of an entity, what it means for the entity to be, is fixed within the horizon in which the being is interpreted, and as 'being' itself always means something like 'presentability for mode of presencing *y*', there is no a priori reason why any *x* can't present itself in different modes: for example, why *x* can't both be an extant entity and Dasein. Determinations of being cannot be correctly seen to be mutually exclusive on a priori grounds. Since for me to be Dasein just means that my behavior is successfully interpretable for some purposes as itself purposeful, and for me to be extant is just for me to be successfully interpretable according to the scientific laws of physics, biology, and the like, there is nothing metaphysical that precludes the possibility that I am both. Which ontological kinds I belong to, if any, is just a pragmatic and scientific question, even if it is an objective question. The being of a being cannot be seen as 'determining and regulating' a unique appropriate way to understand that being and its being, even though whether any being is in any determinate mode does depend on that being itself to the extent that not every entity can be successfully interpreted in every way. (4) As the ontological sorts that have being vary with the temporal structure of interpretation, and these interpretive structures are themselves 'for the sake of' Dasein and thus evaluable pragmatically, which *sorts* of entities have being itself becomes an empirical and pragmatic issue. There is no way in which this can be decided philosophically or a priori.

The *aporia* of the early Heidegger's metaphysics can now be stated simply. Conclusions (1), (2), (3), and (4) taken together contradict the claim that 'being' is not to be understood subjectivistically: that is, that how the being of an entity is to be understood is specified uniquely by the being of the entity itself, that the being of an entity is independent of Dasein to the extent that it is to be identified with the ground of presence or the explanation for the fact of presentability, and that the being of any *x* is completely independent of the way in which it is approached.

It is the argument of Part II of this book that Heidegger, confronted with this *aporia,* divided the issue between being and the truth of being, keeping the conclusions of the second horn of the dilemma with regard to being and asserting the antisubjectivist conclusions in regard to the truth of being. Being is seen as interpretable pragmatically and hence as a possible object of scientific investigation, but the truth of being is not. Both the 'nature' and the 'determinate structure' of the truth of being are independent of the way in which they are cognized by Dasein; regardless of how it is interpreted, the truth of being is always a horizonal structure of true time that withholds itself and grants the possibility of presencing; regardless of how the truth of being in an epoch is interpreted, it grants the determinate understanding of being that it does.

If it is the case that Heidegger handles the *aporia* in his early metaphysics in the way I have suggested, then the argument that takes us from assertion (I), that there are necessary conditions for the understanding of being, to assertion (II), the pragmatic conclusions in regard to metaphysics—(1) that the being of any being can be discovered only through a pragmatically understood positive science, (2) that the being of a being can be correctly understood in a variety of ways, and (3) that there is a multitude of ways of correctly understanding 'being'—is just the argument (discussed in Chapter 6) given in *Being and Time* and *Basic Problems:* There is no additional argument on this topic in the late Heidegger. At most there are a series of *aperçu* concerning the drift of the disciplines in the contemporary world, the plight of philosophy both internally and in relation to the other disciplines, the bankruptcy of metaphysical appeals to the ground of beings, and the technological character of the modern world. All this aids greatly in our understanding of the nature and consequences of modern pragmatism but neither adds to nor detracts from our reasons for accepting something like the truth of this position, even though it does add to our reasons for believing that pragmatism is currently dominant.

Quite clearly, then, late Heidegger is no longer interested in the classic metaphysical questions concerning being. Rather, he is interested in the truth of being, the opening in which being, in any of its modes, can be unconcealed and understood. As we have seen, however, all that distinguishes the description and articulation of the truth of being in late Heidegger from the comparable description of Temporality and Dasein's being in the world in early Heidegger are the claims that the truth of being ought not to be seen as grounded in the being of any being or in being itself, and that the truth of being does not ground being or beings.

This second claim is incorporated in (II), which we have just discussed. The first claim seems to involve the assertion that it is wrong to see the truth of being as any determination of any being, including Dasein, insofar as any determination of any being admits of ground and explanation.

The Truth of Being, Dasein, and Grounds

At this point we have passed over to an examination of assertions (III), (IV), and (V), and in this section we inquire into the sense of these claims and Heidegger's possible grounds for holding them.

We can begin to get a handle on the way in which late Heidegger treats issues concerning the relations among the truth of being, Dasein, and any hypothetical grounds for the truth of being if we place his discussion in the context of other twentieth-century discussions of the relationship between 'man' and the transcendental conditions for knowledge and intentionality. Michel Foucault, in Chapter 9 of *The Order of Things*, "Man and his Doubles," considers a variety of such discussions and provides an account of their intellectual history. He tells us that contrary to appearances, "before the end of the eighteenth century, man did not exist. . . . He is a quite recent creature, which the demiurge of knowledge fabricated with its own hands less than two hundred years ago."[2] Obviously, 'man' here can't mean 'member of the human species'. For Foucault, 'man' is a strange creature who has the character of being a naturally and historically determined object that can be known as such— as any other being is known—by the positive, empirical sciences and at the same time provides the conditions for the possibility of all experience and knowledge and hence is transcendental to all positive knowledge, providing its a priori necessary form and structure. "Man . . . is a strange empirico-transcendental doublet, since he is a being such that knowledge will be attained in him of what renders all knowledge possible."[3]

For Foucault, the tensions and possibilities of modern thought arise out of this position of 'man'. Everything that man says or does has a double aspect. It is the act of a real, positive being, grounded in and caused by the natural and historical factors that operate upon that being. As Richard Rorty puts it, it is possible "'in principle', to predict every

2. Michel Foucault, *The Order of Things* (New York: Vintage Books, 1973), p. 308.
3. Ibid., p. 318.

movement of a person's body (including those of his larynx and his writing hand) by reference to the microstructures within his body."[4] Beyond this sort of physicalism, which applies only to human behavior described in extant terms, we all know how each of our acts admits multiple social scientific explanations from psychology, sociology, and history. At the same time, the very existence of positive knowledge presupposes that what man says and does belongs to a different order from that of nature and history; it belongs to the order of semantic content and the logical space of reasons, in which what is said and done is determined as true or false, warranted or unwarranted, successful or unsuccessful. Insofar as knowledge does exist, it must occur within a logical space of reasons, evidence, and experience in which what one does, says, and believes is understood not as a natural event that exists or does not exist depending upon the causes that operate on it but as assertions to be evaluated for truth. Understood in this way, it seems that 'man' can't be comprehended simply as a being like any other but rather supplies the space of reasons in which anything like beings and explanations can appear.[5] The tension in modern thought arises out of the apparent necessity of both these ways of understanding man and the apparent impossibility of combining them in a single coherent description—either the positive, scientific description or the transcendental account is dominant—but if Foucault is right, every modern attempt to grapple with man involves both sides.

The first representation of 'man' understood in this way—the original Adam, so to speak—appears, of course, in Immanuel Kant. In the "Paralogism" chapter of *The Critique of Pure Reason,* Kant distinguishes between "the mere apperception 'I think', by which the transcendental concepts are made possible"[6] and the I that I know as object "when I am

---

4. Richard Rorty, *Philosophy and the Mirror of Nature* (Princeton, N.J.: Princeton University Press, 1979), p. 354.

5. Foucault discusses Heidegger in a thinly veiled fashion in "The Retreat and Return of the Origin," a section of the chapter cited above. He sees Heidegger as a thoroughly typical modern thinker who contrasts the ordered sequence of temporal moments in which natural and historical events can occur with the 'opening' in which ordinary time itself can 'happen', and which has no proper place in the ordinary temporal series because all temporal moments presuppose that it has 'already' occurred. As a determination of man, however, it cannot have temporally preceded most of those moments. For Foucault's Heidegger, this transcendental 'origin' is such as to recede, withdraw, hide itself from us, even though it is the light in which all presence occurs and we advance toward it in advancing toward the future. See *The Order of Things,* p. 328.

6. Kant, *C.P.R.,* p. 329, A343, B401.

conscious of the intuition of myself as determined with respect to the functions of thought."[7] On the one hand, this second 'I', the I as object, "is not the consciousness of the determining self, but only that of the determinable self, that is, of my inner intuition (insofar as its manifold can be combined in accordance with the universal conditions of the unity of apperception in thought)."[8] The 'I think' of apperception, on the other hand, is and can be no object whatsoever; it is pure self-reflexive subjectivity, the form of representation rather than any representation or thing represented. "Through this I or he or it (the thing) which thinks, nothing further is represented than a transcendental subject of the thoughts $= x$. It is known only through the thoughts which are its predicates, and of it, apart from them, we cannot have any concept whatsoever, but can only revolve in a perpetual circle, since any judgment upon it has always already made use of its representation. And the reason why this inconvenience is inseparably bound up with it, is that consciousness in itself is not a representation distinguishing a particular object, but a form of representation in general, that is, of representation in so far as it is to be entitled knowledge."[9]

The difficulty with this account of the relation between the empirical and the transcendental is the same one that Foucault notes. In some sense the substance that is known and the subject that is not known, because it is no substance but merely the self-reflexive form of subjectivity and intentionality itself, are taken by Kant to be one and the same being. The entire context of the discussion is the methodological solipsism that Kant inherits from the seventeenth and eighteenth centuries. It is involved with what Hegel called Kant's 'subjective idealism': the transcendental form of knowledge and representation is identified with the self-conscious subjectivity of individual persons. The connection is made through the suggestion that both the form of knowledge and representation and the self-consciousness of the individual are the *result* of the synthetic activity of the subject. My empirical self-consciousness, my awareness of myself in and through my awareness of my having particular thoughts—what Kant calls my determinable self—is taken as the appearance of my determining self: that is, my self as spontaneous agent of the synthetic activity that grounds the form of all knowledge and

7. Ibid., p. 368, B406.
8. Ibid., B407.
9. Ibid., pp. 331–332, A346, B404.

representation. Just as the natural object is taken to be the way in which a thing in itself must appear to a being with the cognitive faculties we have, and is not some second thing, the empirical ego is the way in which a being that engages in spontaneous synthetic activity must appear to itself, given the character of that activity, but is also not any second thing. Yet for just that reason I can have no knowledge of myself as thing in itself but only as substance, even though I must think of myself as a spontaneous agent insofar as I am self-conscious and take myself as acting on rational grounds. I am, for myself, a "empirico-transcendental doublet."

From the standpoint of the late Heidegger, it is clear what is happening here. The form of representation, which Kant calls the transcendental unity of apperception and thereby identifies with the individual subject, is being treated as *a* being, which therefore stands in need of a ground in *a* being, even though we have and can have no experience of this being but only of ourselves as an object and of our experiences and evaluations of the objects that we do experience as having certain formal relations among themselves insofar as they can be intended in intentions having semantic content. It is as if Kant is saying that the form of representation must have a cause (even though the concept 'cause' can have no application in this case); that that cause must be a being (even though we can have no experience of that being and thus cannot apply the concept 'existence' to it); and that that being must be identical with the being I am aware of and which I know as myself (even though that object is caused in its behavior and the ground of the form of representation can not be).

As we have seen, the early Heidegger inherits much of this problematic from Kant (and Husserl). The major modification he makes is the shift in priority from pure (that is, cognitive) self-consciousness to practical action as the primary locus of intentionality and semantic content. He thinks this modification allows for a description of the being of Dasein in such a way that the desideratum of the Kantian discussion is met: that is, the being of the being that is man can also be seen to be identical with the form of semantic content and thus as the horizon for every understanding of being and beings. *Zeitlichkeit,* the meaning of the being of Dasein, is also the same as *Temporalität,* the meaning of being in general in the sense of the form and horizon of all intentionality; and both are taken to be identical with the temporal structure of Dasein's activity itself. Thus, even though it is impossible, as Kant thought, to talk about subjectivity in terms of the ontological determinations of substance, this does not mean for the early Heidegger that no ontological determination of the form of intentionality is possible; we can give an account of temporality as the being of Dasein using the *existentialia* appropriate to the description of Daseinish activity. "He [Kant] has not shown that the 'I act' itself cannot be interpreted in the way in which it gives itself, in this self-manifesting ontological constitution. Perhaps it is precisely time which is the *a priori* of the ego—time, to be sure, in a more original sense than Kant was able to conceive it. He assigned it to sensibility and consequently from the beginning, conforming with tradition, he had in view natural time alone. It does *not* follow from the inadequacy of the categories of nature that every ontological interpretation whatever of the ego is impossible. That follows only on the presupposition that the same type of knowledge which is valid for nature is taken as the sole possible basis for knowledge of the ego. From the impropriety of applying the categories to the pure ego there follows the necessity to inquire beforehand into the possibility of a suitable ontological interpretation of the subject, one that is free from the entire tradition."[10]

From the standpoint of the late Heidegger, to raise the question of Temporality in the context of an "ontological interpretation of the subject" is already to fail to free oneself from the entire tradition. We can understand why he thinks this, as well as see how he would propose to deal with 'man', the "empirico-transcendental doublet," if we look once again at the traditional two-stage structure of transcendental arguments: first, one asks for the necessary conditions for intentionality, or language, or experience; second, one uses the results of the first investigation to ground an account of the being of beings. We have seen that because of the results of early Heidegger in regard to the first stage of the argument, late Heidegger divorces the first job from the second—properly metaphysical—stage of determining the necessary features of all beings.

At this point our focus shifts to the first stage. We have already noted that both Kant and the early Heidegger identify the formal conditions for representation or intentionality or practical activity with the being of man, with what it is to be human or a subject or an agent, and that these conditions are fulfilled is explained by recourse to the being of a being that has that kind of being. There are thus two assumptions built into the first stage of traditional transcendental arguments. The formal conditions for intentionality are identified with what it is for the one who is inten-

10. *B.P.*, pp. 145–146/206–207.

tional to be, and the fact that those conditions are fulfilled in any particular case is explained by the fact that a being with that type of being exists. In Kant, for example, the form of representation necessary for awareness of objects, which is a certain way in which representations are related and accordingly is itself never an object, is taken to be what it is for an individual subject to be self-conscious; and that representations have that form is taken to be the result of the synthetic activity of a being that has the being of a subject.[11] Similarly, in early Heidegger the meaning of Dasein's being, *Zeitlichkeit,* is taken to be identical with the horizon for any understanding of being, *Temporalität.* Further, that the conditions for intentional action are fulfilled is taken to be grounded on the existence of a specific being with Dasein's kind of being.

Late Heidegger denies both these implicit assumptions. And after we have seen what he thinks the impact is on ontology of the conditions for intentionality and purposive action, we can understand why he moves in this radical direction. According to the pragmatism inherent in the late Heidegger, Dasein's being, what it is for a Dasein to be, is to be identified with the interpretability of a being as acting purposively. A being is interpretable as acting purposively and thus as being a Dasein only if a series of conditions is fulfilled, conditions specified by what it is to act purposively and thus to be intentional. According to the metaphysical transcendental tradition, that those conditions are fulfilled is taken to be grounded on a metaphysical fact about that being, that that being exists as intentional. Just as in the case of scientific metaphysical realism, a second level of explanation is added: one explains a particular act by alluding to the fact that the actions of this agent, which can be and are encountered, can be successfully interpreted as falling into a purposeful pattern; then one explains that it can be so interpreted because the deep metaphysical being of the thing grounds or explains the interpretability of the agent as acting in that way. But the evidence in favor of the being's interpretability as an agent is identical with the evidence in favor of the being's being an agent; there is no other. Given verificationism, there is no being of the Dasein over and above the interpretability of the actions as purposive, and the being of the being that is Dasein isn't the metaphysical cause or ground or explanation of the fact that its actions are interpretable as purposive.

11. The obvious problem here—that Kant accounts for the fact of transcendental apperception through the activity of a subject which, as a self-conscious subject, is identical with that apperception—has been frequently noted.

In short, just as for the pragmatism implicit in the late Heidegger the distinction between the perceivability of the extant thing and the metaphysical ground for that perceivability—the extantness of a being—collapses (as is evidenced in the decline of metaphysics and its replacement by empirical science and practice), so the distinction between the interpretability of a being as Dasein and the metaphysical ground for that interpretability also collapses, (as is evidenced in the rise of social science and the decline of philosophical anthropology). "Philosophy," as Heidegger says, "turns into the empirical science of man, of all of what can become the experiential object of his technology for man."[12]

This leaves us with late Heidegger's second modification of the traditional understanding of the first stage of transcendental arguments. In the tradition, as in Kant and early Heidegger, the being of a being that is intentional is identified with the conditions for intentionality. The subjectivity of the subject is taken to be specified by the conditions for intentionality. It is obvious that here those conditions are taken to be the essence or formal cause of the being that is intentional. But late Heidegger denies that the truth of being, which we have identified with the conditions for intentionality, is to be seen as a being or as the being of a being, including the being of Dasein. Once again the seeds of the late Heidegger can be found in the early. For the early Heidegger, no Dasein can be Dasein outside a community of Dasein, and the character and the nature of the ends and practices of the particular Dasein are intelligible determinants of a Dasein or, indeed, actions of a Dasein at all only insofar as they both take place within a context provided by the actions and ends of other Dasein and are recognized as actions of a Dasein by the others. To be Dasein is to engage in standardized action that is recognized as action and is evaluable as appropriate or inappropriate, and no Dasein is capable of any of this by itself.

So the conditions for intentionality, or for the behavior of the individual being that is interpretable as a purposive Dasein, include a social condition: the being who is to be interpreted as Dasein must be interpretable as an appropriate member of a community of Dasein. And that it is so interpretable is a condition that necessarily not only depends upon the way its actions can be successfully interpreted but also upon the character of the activity of the others. Further, the fulfillment of some of these social conditions—for example, that there is a correct and incorrect way

12. E.O.P., pp. 57/63–64.

to assert semantic contents—is entirely independent of the existence or behavior of any individual Dasein. These conditions can thus never be fulfilled by an individual Dasein by itself. That is, to say that an individual *x* is a Dasein presupposes the truth of a variety of claims, and only some of these claims concern *x* or are determinations of *x,* even relational ones. Similarly, to say that *x* has some particular intentional determination presupposes an entire structure that is wholly independent of that Dasein. For example, that what I do now is write a sentence presupposes a whole set of truths concerning English grammar and semantics, as well as other conventions, that are entirely independent of my existence or actions. I could cease to be or stop talking English tomorrow, and English would still be English. The conditions for a being's being intentional are thus not all determinations of the being; hence, these conditions cannot be straightaway identified with the essence of that being.

These social conditions for intentionality can be fulfilled in a variety of different ways; that is, the practices and ends within a community can vary without affecting the fact that they are successfully interpretable as practices and ends. In particular, they can vary to the extent that what the members of such communities must be interpreted as interpreting 'being' to signify, if they are to be interpreted successfully, can vary across communities and history. And given the role such social practices play in conditioning the possibility of Dasein, the purposive behavior of any given Dasein that is a member of such a community must be interpreted as in accord with that understanding of being.

It would also seem to be the case that one could not explain or ground either the fact that the conditions for intentionality are fulfilled or that the way in which they are fulfilled has changed by alluding to the intentional—Daseinish—activity of Dasein. Whatever any Dasein does is what it is as a Daseinish activity only in terms of a set of social conditions and constraints that are independent of these acts themselves. Given a set of practices and ends, I can choose and control who I am by choosing and controlling which ends to adopt, but even my acts of choice and control are the acts they are and acts at all only insofar as that set of practices and ends is always already in place. That an act of Dasein is an act of Dasein presupposes a historical and social context that is not the product of that act or of the agent of that act, so neither that act nor that agent can be properly seen as the cause of that context or its determinate character.

This emphasis on the social and historical positioning of the individual Dasein partially accounts for the shift in late Heidegger's model for the multiplicity of the understandings of being. For early Heidegger, extant-ness, handiness, and so on, are alternative ways of being that can be and are invoked in the same period by members of any community. In late Heidegger, the various metaphysical names for being are historical grant-ings of being that are dominant in different communities at different periods. As such, they are totalizing determinations that dominate all the interactions with beings of the members of a community and are beyond the control of any member, or even all members acting together. Every act of every Dasein counts as the act it is only insofar as the dominant social practices have the shape they do. So every act—even one that attempts to alter and control the shape of those practices—once again implicitly affirms that the practices are as they are. Putting these two models together, the ontological determinations appear as variations within a dominant way in which being is given in an epoch, variations that have analogues in each epoch. In a similar vein, language is seen in early Heidegger in terms of the activity of asserting on the part of individual Dasein for the purpose of communication; in late Heidegger it comes to be understood more explicitly as involving a 'saying' to Dasein on the part of language itself, to which the individual must respond. Language 'calls' Dasein, instead of Dasein's using language. Language embodies the way in which being is already granted to a historical community; it is the house of being in which humans dwell.

So the being of Dasein, existence in Heidegger's sense, cannot prop-erly be seen as the ground of the truth of being in the sense of its being the quasi-efficient cause of the truth of being. Dasein's existence does not ground or account for the fact that the conditions for intentionality are met. Nor can Dasein be correctly seen as the ground for the truth of being in the sense of being the efficient cause of a particular way in which the conditions are fulfilled, correlated with a particular understanding of being. Nor is it possible to identify Dasein and the truth of being through seeing the truth of being as the formal cause or essence of Dasein. In fact, as late Heidegger maintains, the being of Dasein is neither identical with the truth of being nor the ground for the truth of being, nor can Dasein itself or even all Dasein together be correctly understandable as the ground for the truth of being or any particular understanding of being.

In light of this conclusion, we can now see how the late Heidegger ought to handle Foucault's problem of 'man' as the "empirico-transcen-dental doublet." Dasein is a being; as such its actions admit potentially of multiple explanations. Among these are presumably those explanations that treat Dasein as Dasein: that is, as intentional beings that act pur- posively within a community of agents who follow practices and have ends not of their own making and are not under their intentional control. Presumably, this behavior also admits of physicalistic descriptions and explanations. In either case, what Dasein does has a ground and is explainable. To treat Dasein as Dasein is not to deny that what it does is explicable and understandable; it is to explain and understand what it does in a particular way. Nevertheless, that there is any Dasein at all, whether the one being interpreted or the interpreter, stands under a variety of necessary conditions; some have to do with the character of the individual interpreted as Dasein, and others do not. There are necessary conditions for the possible interpretability of anything as intentional action, language, belief, and knowledge. The fulfillment of these condi- tions allows us to understand what the particular Dasein does as having semantic content and as thus capable of being right or wrong, correct or incorrect, appropriate or inappropriate. But the fact that such conditions must be fulfilled if the being interpreted is to be successfully interpreted as Dasein in no way implies that that being can't be interpreted in other ways or that the actions of that Dasein are inexplicable or ungrounded. Such implications would go through only if we were to accept as hidden premises the metaphysical claims that the being of Dasein grounds the interpretability of a being as a Dasein and thus precludes other types of interpretation of that being, and that Dasein is to be identified with the conditions for intentionality. But it is these claims that the late Heideg- ger's anti-metaphysical stance gives us reasons to reject.

Heidegger wants to go even further. He maintains that the truth of being has no ground at all, admits of no explanation, and is an un- grounded gift of 'appropriation'. This claim, in its most general form, seems to have two sides. Neither the fact that there is any truth of being at all—that is, that the conditions for intentionality are met at all—nor the fact of any change in the way those conditions are fulfilled, any change in the truth of being, can properly be seen as having any ground or explana- tion whatsoever. This is the cash value of assertion (V), that it is always inappropriate to look for the ground of the truth of being and that it is thus inappropriate to treat the truth of being as a being. What argument could be presented for these claims?

When we attempt to answer this question directly, it seems that Hei- degger's claims here contradict his own genuine, if reluctant, pragma- tism. How is it possible to know a priori that the truth of being as such or any changes in the truth of being cannot be treated as a being, which in that case could be explained and grounded? Although purposive human action to change the way in which being is understood, to change the structure of the social practices in which any Dasein must exist as intentional, must fail of its object, it is nevertheless the case that those practices do in fact change and that the understanding of being does alter. The late Heidegger wants to maintain that these changes are discontinuities that admit of no explanation. In this respect he is a precursor of Foucault, who emphasizes the breaks and discontinuities in the history of the episteme.

One might speculate that the argument in favor of this position is based on a recognition that all historical and social scientific explanation presupposes something like an intentional idiom and thus must ascribe some particular understanding of being to the agent whose action is to be explained. Thus, all explanations explain the acts of individual Dasein through reference to a particular set of practices and horizon of understanding, but they are incapable of explaining the fact that this understanding of being or set of objective social determinants of action are dominant at that time. So, it might be claimed, a change in the dominant understanding of being must appear as a break or ungrounded event, admitting of no social explanation. This might be the case, but the a priori argument presented is certainly not valid. It rests, at best, on the contestable claim that every social scientific explanation must make use of the intentional idiom. And if pragmatism is the correct approach to such issues, then whether this assertion is true can only be decided empirically.

Similarly, the late Heidegger wants to claim that the fact that the conditions for intentionality are fulfilled at all is an ungrounded event of appropriation. This amounts to the assertion that not only is Dasein or its being not the ground of the fulfillment of the conditions for intentionality but that there is no possible adequate ground or explanation for the interpretability of beings as Dasein: that is, for the circumstance that the conditions for such interpretation are fulfilled. Given the extraordinary character of those conditions, including the social ones, this might very well turn out to be the case. If the truth of being could successfully be seen as a being, however, such explanation would be at the same 'metaphysical level' as that which is to be explained and thus would not run counter to the anti-metaphysical character of pragmatism. That is, what would be attempted would be the explanation of one verifiable circumstance—that there are Dasein and thus that the conditions for intentionality are in fact fulfilled—by reference to another verifiable circumstance rather than to the 'existence' or 'being' of the metaphysical ground of the first circumstance. So, if the truth of being could be seen as a being, then there would seem to be no a priori argument with the conclusion that the truth of being is ungrounded, and whether or not it is would then be a scientific/pragmatic issue. But our only reason thus far for denying that the truth of being is a being is based on the assertion that it is ungrounded and hence cannot be a being, as all beings admit of explanation and have grounds. So the claims that the truth of being is no being and that the truth of being has no ground would seem to fall into a tight little circle, and we are left with no reason to think that either claim ought not to be evaluated in the usual way, pragmatically. The next section, however, suggests another possible argument in favor of the claim that the truth of being cannot successfully be considered to be a being, an argument based on general systematic grounds of consistency and independent of the assertion that the truth of being lacks a ground. If such an argument were successful, then we would have reason to hold that the truth of being has no ground.

We are now in position to summarize the results of the last two sections. What is distinctive about the late Heidegger can be expressed in the five propositions set forth at the beginning of this chapter. My translations of these claims out of Heidegger's idiom are as follows. (Ia) There are necessary conditions that must be fulfilled if there is to be any semantic content, and thus any intentionality, possibility for truth or falsity, or understanding of what it means for something to be. Nevertheless, (IIa) the necessary conditions for intentionality in no way determine what it means for any being to be. Any number of understandings of being are possible, given the conditions for the possibility of semantic content. (IIIa) The necessary conditions for intentionality include social conditions such that it is an error to conceive the conditions for intentionality as constituting the essence of Dasein. (IVa) The fact that the conditions for intentionality are fulfilled is not explicable by the being of Dasein or even the existence of a Daseinish community, because the existence of Dasein and of such a community is just the fulfillment of the individual and social conditions for intentionality. (Va) The fact of the fulfillment of the conditions for intentionality, as well as the predominance of a particular way in which those conditions are fulfilled and the way in which being is understood at any time, admit of no possible explanation.

(Ia) is the premise of the argument strategy of the late Heidegger; it is taken as demonstrated in *Being and Time,* and the argument for it is presented in the first part of this book. (IIa) follows from (Ia), given the specific character of the conditions for intentionality; it is the implicit conclusion of *Basic Problems,* and the argument for it is developed in that work and presented in an abbreviated form in the first section of this chapter. (IIIa), the non-identity of the meaning of Dasein's being and the conditions for intentionality, follows from the social aspect of those conditions. (IVa) is a consequence of the pragmatism inherent in (IIa). (Va) has not been demonstrated and, lacking additional argument, is at best an empirical claim, although Heidegger takes it to be fundamental to the truth of being.

What is unique in the late Heidegger is that he is pragmatic in regard to metaphysics while remaining transcendental in regard to the conditions for intentionality. His metaphysical pragmatism is in fact a consequence of his transcendental semantics. I have previously argued that for reasons of consistency, pragmatism can follow only from such a semantics and that all pragmatism either must be based on a transcendental semantics or is self-contradictory.[13]

Relativism, Pragmatism, and Being

To what extent is the doctrine we have ascribed to Heidegger a plausible and consistent one? There are two central features of Heidegger's thought as we have interpreted it. First, an argument that has the form of the first stage in a classic transcendental argument is used to show the priority of practical social activity over other types of intentionality. Second, this result is used in an argument designed to establish a pragmatic anti-realism in regard to traditional metaphysical issues while maintaining an anti-pragmatic stance regarding the conditions for intentionality.

With the possible exception of the emphasis on temporality, the principal doctrines of the early Heidegger concerning the primarily practical character of intentionality are hardly unique in the twentieth century. A whole series of philosophers, including John Dewey, the late Wittgen-

13. See Mark Okrent, "Hermeneutics, Transcendental Philosophy, and Social Science," *Inquiry* 27 (1984), 23–49; "Relativism, Context, and Truth," *Monist* 67 (July 1984), 341–358; and "The Metaphilosophical Consequences of Pragmatism," in *The Institution of Philosophy: A Discipline in Crisis?,* ed. Avner Cohen and Marcelo Dascal (Totowa, N.J.: Rowman & Littlefield, 1988).

stein, and the contemporary American neo-pragmatists—who arise out of a strictly analytic context—have made very similar points. If there is anything distinctive about the early Heideggerian claims, it is the structure of the argument that can be extracted from the discussion, not the conclusions asserted.

Aside from the large-scale claims concerning the truth of being and appropriation as nongrounded nonbeings, the interesting aspect of the late Heidegger is the way in which he uses early conclusions regarding intentionality to motivate an anti-realist, non-idealist, anti-metaphysical attitude toward questions regarding being and the being of particular entities, while remaining anti-pragmatic regarding the truth of being or the conditions for intentionality and any understanding of 'being'. It is as if epistemology and metaphysics are being 'naturalized' in a manner not very distant from the one Quine suggests, while semantics continues to be treated transcendentally.

If we ignore the question of the cogency of the arguments we have ascribed to Heidegger, we can raise two issues concerning the coherence and self-consistency of these doctrines. As is the case with any criticism of metaphysical realism, including all the varieties of pragmatism, it is possible to accuse this position of relativism. And since we are already supposed to know that relativism is an internally inconsistent view, if it can be shown that Heidegger's views imply relativism, we will have reason to accuse him of self-contradiction. But it seems possible to criticize the Heidegger we have reconstructed from the other side, so to speak. If one is pragmatic and anti-realist in regard to ontology, what is to prevent one from being pragmatic all the way down? Isn't it inconsistent to preserve an area of thought from pragmatic constraints if as a general rule all ontological questions are to be decided pragmatically? And even if some questions are not to be decided pragmatically, why choose semantics, of all things—as opposed to logic, for example—as the area of such issues?

As it turns out, we can treat both these areas of concern more or less simultaneously. Heidegger's position is not viciously relativistic or inconsistent precisely insofar as it denies that a pragmatic conception of truth applies in any simple way to questions in transcendental semantics: that is, denies that the truth of pragmatism itself as a position concerning semantics and intentionality is a contingent matter to be decided by a pragmatically conceived positive science. We can see this if we look at the traditional concerns surrounding relativism.

It has often been asserted that if one denies the classical metaphysical doctrine that the being of an entity determines a unique way in which that entity can be correctly comprehended, and thus apparently denies the correspondence view of truth, then one must be committed to a form of relativism. And as we have known since Plato's *Theateatus*, relativism is a self-defeating doctrine. Therefore, the argument runs, every form of anti-metaphysical realism, including pragmatism, must be self-refuting.[14] Most recently this argument has been used in informal discussions about Rorty, Nelson Goodman, and Hilary Putnam. Since we have interpreted Heidegger to be quite similar to these American neopragmatists in certain respects, it seems that the same considerations can be raised about him.

Before we can evaluate this line of argument, we must have a clearer idea of what is meant by the term 'relativism'. Most generally, 'relativism' is used to characterize any doctrine asserting that something, whatever it may be, has a certain determination only in relation to, or relative to, something else, whatever *it* may be. For example, a 'relativism' concerning 'to the left of' would be the eminently sensible position that for *A* to be 'to the left of' is for it to be to the left of some *B;* that is, 'being to the left of' is a relative determination or a two-place predicate. In practice, the use of the term 'relativism' has been restricted in two ways: in general, to characterizations of doctrines concerning philosophically interesting terms, including 'meaning', 'knowledge', and 'truth'; in particular, to doctrines claiming that one or more of these philosophically interesting terms are not merely relative terms (which they all are in a variety of more or less trivial ways) but predicates with one more place than is usually thought.

The word 'relativism' has historically been used most prominently to characterize views concerning 'truth', especially those that seem to deny the correspondence view of truth. That view itself is 'relativistic' in a straightforward and innocuous manner. According to the correspondence view, 'truth' is a property of sentences or, if you prefer, propositions. A proposition is true if and only if a certain relation, 'correspondence', obtains between what the propositional content of the sentence asserts and the way the world, or some portion of it, is. If sentences are

14. The easiest way to block this consequence is to adopt a position, such as Kant's, in which there is only one possible horizon for understanding and intelligibility. In that case, even though 'truth' can in some respects be seen as relative to something like a set of categories, there is no danger of self-contradiction because only one such set is possible.

seen to bear the properties 'true' and 'false', then—because sentences have semantic content only relative to a language—'truth' is seen as a three-place predicate involving a sentence, a state of affairs, and a language. This kind of three-place doctrine concerning truth is not usually seen as relativistic, however, because the relation between sentence and language merely fixes the determinate meaning of the sentence to be evaluated for truth. Once that meaning is fixed, this relation is in no way seen to affect that evaluation itself. For the sake of simplicity we will stick to propositions as the subject of 'truth' (without implying any position on the familiar conflicts concerning sentences and propositions).

The most familiar forms of relativism are those regarding 'truth'. Such doctrines claim that what it is for an assertion to be true must be analyzed in terms of a predicate of one more place than is ordinary. In the simplest forms, the truth of a proposition is taken to involve the relation of a proposition, the 'world', and the beliefs of the one asserting or believing the proposition; thus, one and the same proposition can be both true and false depending upon who asserts it. In more complex forms, truth is taken to be a predicate involving a relation with intersubjective determinants such as 'language', 'vocabulary', 'world-view', 'episteme', 'conceptual scheme', 'theory', 'form of life', 'set of practices', or whatever. What these various doctrines share is a commitment to the view that the truth of a proposition varies as a function of one or more of these determinants in such a way that the same proposition can be both true and false— independent of changes in the state of affairs the proposition mentions— depending on the social, practical, linguistic, or epistemic commitments and/or affiliations of the asserter or interpreter of the proposition.

The classical problem with most forms of relativism concerning truth was pointed out by Plato in the *Theateatus*. The relativistic claim is itself an assertion or proposition; thus, its truth must depend on the very same features that relativism claims are relevant in setting the truth value of every proposition. That is, since the proposition that asserts relativism is itself a proposition, if it is true, it is self-referring. But, then, the truth of any assertion of relativism itself is relative to whatever additional factor that assertion asserts is relevant to truth in general. Now, using Plato's simplest case (against Protagorean relativism), consider A who believes in relativism. She also believes that B does not believe in relativism. According to A, then, relativism must not be true for B—but A holds that relativism is universally true: this is what she takes the word 'true' to mean. So, according to A, relativism must be true for B. Thus, one proposition—that relativism is true for B—asserted by the same person, A, in a single belief state, is, given relativism, both true and false. This is a blatant self-contradiction; therefore, relativism concerning truth in terms of belief must be false. One must remember that the relativist concerned with 'truth' does not set out to be contradictory, any more than the relativist concerned with 'to the left of' does. Both merely read the propositions they are interested in, 'x is true' and 'x is to the left of', as elliptical, even though the latter has ordinary linguistic practice on his side and the former does not. It would seem that similar arguments could be constructed regarding the more complex modern types of relativism.[15]

At first sight, Heidegger's views on truth do not appear to fit neatly into the structure we have used to discuss relativism, but this is an illusion. As we have seen, any discussion of Heidegger on truth is complicated by his confusion, throughout the better part of his career, between 'truth' and a certain kind of necessary condition for the possibility of truth: first the meaning of the being of Dasein and then the truth of being. If we take this complication for what Heidegger eventually correctly recognized it to have been all along, a confusion, Heidegger's views on truth can best be understood—as I have argued—through a comparison with Husserl's views on truth. In general, both see truth as the being-identical of the object and meaning of an empty intention with the object and meaning of an intuitive presenting or giving. Nothing in this by itself appears to involve relativism, and in Husserl it doesn't. For Heidegger, however, both the fact and the determinate meaning of an unfulfilled intention and both the fact and the meaning of every presentation or giving are dependent upon and in that sense relative to the intentional context or horizon in which the intention or its fulfillment occurs. What is given, in a strict sense, is given only for and in terms of a determinate intentional horizon that forms the 'fore-having' of an interpretation. To change that horizon is to change both the empty intention and the evidence. If this is so, it seems that the truth of a given proposition—that is, whether there is a capacity for the being-identical of that proposition's empty intention and fulfillment in evidence (laying aside the further Husserlian/Heideggerian complication that the intention of beings, as well as propositions, are seen to be capable of truth and

15. For a more complete discussion of the varieties of relativism, see Okrent, "Relativism, Context, and Truth."

falsity)—varies as a function of the interpretive horizon in terms of which the evidence is collected. And this is a standard relativistic position that can be treated in the manner suggested above. But we will see that the situation in regard to most varieties of pragmatism, including Heidegger's, is less simple than this summary would suggest.

As Rorty, among others, has quite correctly pointed out, there is nothing in pragmatic views, including Heidegger's, that implies relativism in any vicious sense in regard to what might be called 'first order' or 'ontic' propositions: that is, propositions concerning beings. For a pragmatism such as Heidegger's, it is not only the evidence that varies as a function of the intentional horizon but also the empty intention. In practice, this amounts to the intentional horizon of any set of assertions or 'language' in a certain sense determining the domain of objects referred to and constituting the members of that domain as objects. Because of this, two assertions that appear similar—and in fact might be homophonic—but function within different realms of discourse or 'vocabularies' can differ in truth value, but they can do so only insofar as they in fact refer to different entities and have different meanings. Within a given intentional horizon, whether or not an assertion is true is wholly objective; it is determined solely by the way the world shows itself to be within that horizon. And this is what is correct for Heidegger about the correspondence view of truth. Rorty makes the same point in regard to his own brand of pragmatism: "Given a language and a view of what the world is like, one can, to be sure, pair off bits of language with bits of what one takes the world to be in such a way that the sentences one believes true have internal structures isomorphic to relations between things in the world. When we rap out routine undeliberated reports like 'This is water', 'That's red', 'That's ugly', 'That's immoral', our short categorical sentences can easily be thought of as pictures or as symbols which fit together to make a map. Such reports do indeed pair little bits of language with little bits of the world."[16]

Thus, pragmatism in general and Heidegger's brand of pragmatism in particular need not involve any insuperable relativistic problems concerning propositions about beings within the world. To say that an ordinary assertion about things within the world is true is always to say that what that assertion says about the entities within the world matches up pretty well with the way the entities within the world show themselves to be or

16. Rorty, "Pragmatism, Relativism, Irrationalism," p. 162.

would show themselves to be under ideal conditions, given the same intentional horizon in which the original proposition has semantic content. At this level the 'relativism' of the position emerges only in the fact that an assertion cannot have any semantic content or the content it does in fact have, nor can the entities within the world show themselves at all, let alone in the way they do, apart from a particular set of determinate social linguistic and actual practices. Since there is no meaning of that assertion apart from that set of practices, it is proper to say that truth is a relation among an asserting, the entities within the world, and an intentional horizon. But the evidence relevant to establishing the truth or falsity of the proposition can be encountered only within the same horizon in which the proposition can be meaningfully asserted; evidence that can be encountered within another horizon does not bear on the issue; and a similar or homophonic proposition made within another intentional horizon and having a different truth value just does not have the same semantic content, doesn't say the same thing, and is not the same proposition.

If a problem of relativism arises for pragmatism, it must arise at a different level. It seems possible to raise the question of which 'language', which 'vocabulary', which intentional horizon is the right or correct one. In fact, this is the very question that metaphysics in Heidegger's sense was designed to raise and answer. To find a ground for beings in their being is to give an explanation of why it is that we must approach beings in some particular way. But according to both American neopragmatism and Heidegger as we have interpreted him, there is no determinate answer to this question, because being cannot be seen as grounding and justifying a particular intentional horizon. Rather, the being of entities is seen as varying as a partial function of those horizons themselves ('partial' because not every horizon is equally successful pragmatically). It seems that for pragmatism, the truth of answers to questions like 'What ontological sorts are there?' and 'What ontological sort does x belong to?' varies as a function of the intentional horizon in which the issue is raised or x is approached. And it would seem that this sort of claim could be attacked as viciously relativistic.

There are really two kinds of cases here. The first kind of 'ontological' assertion makes claims concerning, in Heideggerian terminology, being as such: claims concerning what it means for something to be. Thus Aristotle's analysis of 'being' in terms of substance being, Kant's discussion of the categories necessary to the concept of an object in general, and even Quine's claim that 'existence' is univocal and is to be associated with the existential quantifier all count as being about 'being' in this sense. It seems that issues concerning the ontological sorts that populate the world can be decided by reference to such claims. Thus, if it is the case that to be, in the basic sense, means to be substance in Aristotle's sense, then neither artifacts nor Dasein are—because neither is supposed to be any variety of substance. But there appears to be a second class of propositions that concern the being of particular beings, propositions such as 'This x is a Dasein', or 'If this x is to be understood, it must be interpreted as a Dasein', or 'This x is extant', or 'If this x is to be understood, it must be interpreted as extant'. Such claims often arise in discussions of appropriate methodology, especially in fields—similar to contemporary social science—where there is considerable confusion concerning the basic concepts. We will deal with the first class of claims first.

Ontological assertions have usually been interpreted as claims regarding the ground that explains and accounts for the fact that the world, or the entities within it, can be appropriately understood in a certain way. Entities are understandable as substances because they are substances. But pragmatism, whether in Heidegger's form or any other, is a kind of verificationism. And it seems clear that there can be no evidence concerning the metaphysical ground of the interpretability of the beings within the world in any definite way. Rather, such claims are properly understood, according to pragmatism, as hypothetical assertions concerning the ability to succeed of a particular understanding of being: that is, of a particular type of social linguistic and actual practice. That is, 'For any x to be means y' should, according to pragmatism, be interpreted as 'If one approaches the world with social and linguistic practices A, which have end B, and for which for any x to be means y, then one will be successful in achieving B'. But it seems possible for different types of practices to be capable of being successful for different ends or, perhaps, equally capable of realizing the same ends. Whether any particular practice—that is, any particular understanding of being—is successful for achieving that for the sake of which it is, of course, is an empirico-pragmatic issue. It therefore seems possible for different and apparently competing ontological claims both to be true.

For example, given the understanding of being that is embodied in the set of practices involved in modern physics, it seems true to say that there are no beings that act according to final causality and hence no beings that are Dasein. According to the understanding of being that is embodied in our ordinary language and practice, there clearly are beings that act for the sake of ends. These two claims seem to be in straightforward contradiction. Given our pragmatic interpretation of ontological discourse, however, they need not be seen as contradictory. The first assertion says, for the pragmatist, that for some purposes the linguistic and social practices of modern physics, which involve an understanding of being according to which there are no Dasein, are successful. The second says that for some purposes the linguistic and social practices of ordinary life, which involve an understanding of being in terms of which there are Dasein, turn out to be successful. Clearly, these claims need not conflict.

Notice, there is a disanalogy between the way pragmatism treats assertions concerning beings and the way it treats assertions concerning being. Homophonic assertions about beings which admit of different truth values are treated as having different semantic content in virtue of being assertions made within and in terms of different sets of social and linguistic practices. Apparently contradictory assertions about being are treated, through a translation into pragmatic terms, as different assertions within the same set of discursive practices. They are treated as being about the potential success of different types of practices, but the claims that those practices are or are not capable of success are themselves both made within the same set of practices. As long as such claims remain couched in an ontological idiom, they must appear contradictory; and pragmatism, countenancing the possibility that two such ontological claims might be true, must appear as a vicious type of relativism. But when such claims are understood pragmatically, they cease to count as contradictory at all.[17]

Propositions concerning the being of particular beings, on the other hand, appear to be hybrids. One who says that '*A* is as a Dasein' is implicitly saying that there is an *x*, described in such a way as to count as *A*, that can be successfully coped with as a Dasein. To say '*A* is extant' is implicitly to say that there is an *x*, described in such a way as to count as *A*, which can be successfully coped with, for some purposes, as extant. This kind of translation makes such assertions seem ontological asser-

---

17. In one sense this pragmatic translation of ontological claims is merely a generalization of the way Kant treats the modal categories. E.g., 'existence' is interpreted in terms of a relation of the being with our faculties: i.e., the perceptibility of the object. Such an interpretation need make no reference to any ground of the perceivability of the being, although neither Kant nor the early Heidegger quite succeeded in convincing himself of that.

tions, and our discussions of the implications of some of Heidegger's analyses have treated them in that way. But such a reading depends upon the prior identification of an 'A' that can be treated in these two ways and is specified in both claims. And this presupposes that the two sets of practices mentioned in the translations themselves share at least the feature of being able to identify the same A. If this condition is not met, then 'A' refers differently in the two claims, and the claims are best seen as ordinary ontic assertions that cannot come into conflict because they are claims in different vocabularies with different fulfillment conditions.

According to pragmatism, then, there is no problem of relativism for ontological claims, because they should be treated as claims about the possible success of social practices for coping with the world, not as assertions regarding being or the ground of interpretability. According to pragmatism, there is no problem of relativism for ontic claims, because meaning varies as a function of intentional horizon. This leaves us with two questions, however. First, if ontological assertions are claims made within a single set of practices regarding pragmatic issues, within which set of practices and in which vocabulary are these claims stated? Second and more important, what is the status of the claim that ontological propositions are 'best' treated, or properly treated, as pragmatic claims concerning the potential success of types of practice and that ontic propositions are 'best' treated, or properly treated, as types of acts within a system of social practice? That is, for pragmatism, what is the status of the propositions that assert the truth of pragmatism itself? We will deal with the crucial second problem first.

There is a limited number of alternatives. If one assumes that pragmatism is true, then either the propositions that assert the claims of pragmatism are themselves contingent propositions whose truth must be demonstrated in the same way as that of any other proposition—by being verified in and by some pragmatically understood positive science—or they have some other status. In either case, the propositions that assert pragmatism and those that appear to deny it (by affirming the claims of some variety of metaphysical realism) can be claims made either within the same intentional horizon or within different ones. If made within the same horizon, the assertions of pragmatism and realism can either concern the same issues or (as with the pragmatic analysis of assertions concerning being) in a hidden fashion concern separate issues.

We begin by considering what seems the more plausible position and the one adopted by most pragmatists: that pragmatism is itself a contingent position which, if true, must be demonstrated in the ordinary pragmatic way. There are then three possible options. First, pragmatism and metaphysics could share an intentional horizon and in fact conflict by being concerned with the same issue: for example, the conditions under which there could be semantic content, truth, and so on. But insofar as pragmatism tends to share roughly the same values and goals as the metaphysical tradition, the values and goals common in the history of the West, a strong case can be made for the *pragmatic* success of the metaphysical way of speaking, while it is anything but clear that the pragmatic way of speaking will be at all successful in accomplishing those ends. In this case, on pragmatic grounds, the pragmatist should assert that pragmatism is false.[18]

The second option is to regard pragmatism and metaphysics as claims made within different horizonal frameworks and thus incapable of coming into direct conflict. Two different ways of talking about the issues pragmatism discusses—roughly, as we have developed them, the character and possibility of intentionality, language, knowledge, the understanding of being, and so on, and the status of claims concerning being, each of which is capable of a certain utility in achieving its respective ends—would then seem possible. We do in fact have two ways of talking about these issues, the pragmatic one and the traditional metaphysical one, and these could be treated as different sets of discursive and practical practices. And it is at least plausible to claim that metaphysical realism, given its role in the rise of the West, has been and continues to be quite successful at achieving its ends. Nevertheless, the pragmatist—Rorty, Heidegger, or whoever—wants to claim that the pragmatist's way of treating these issues and understanding claims concerning being is the correct one. If we assume that the question of the truth of pragmatism is itself a pragmatic question, and that it is possible to have at least two competing intentional horizons for dealing with it, the pragmatist is put into the following position. From her own standpoint and using her own vocabulary, the pragmatist must assert that the pragmatic understanding of language—in particular, ontological language—is true and correct and that the metaphysician ought to adopt it: that is, that it is true in respect to the metaphysician. If she fails to do at least this much, then pragmatism, in that it makes only claims concerning how such issues should be treated, makes no difference to the way in which people think

18. Cf. Okrent, "The Metaphilosophical Consequences of Pragmatism."

and act or the way in which being is understood—that is, it makes no difference at all. In that case, pragmatism on its own grounds can have no point and is incapable of pragmatic warrant. On the other hand, insofar as the metaphysician has pragmatic warrant for talking, believing, and acting as he does, the pragmatist on her own grounds must assert that the metaphysician's way of treating these issues is correct and true. This is a contradiction analogous to the one Plato uncovered respecting Protagorean relativism. If A is the pragmatist and B is the metaphysician, the contradiction is that for A, B's claims are both true and false in B's terms.

The third possibility is to assume that the propositions stating pragmatism and those asserting metaphysical realism are assertions within the same intentional horizon but concern different issues. But as the issue involved in pragmatism is precisely how one should treat such conflicts, and the metaphysical realist denies that this pragmatic analysis is at all correct, assuming the truth of pragmatism here generates exactly the same contradiction as does the previous case. If the truth of pragmatism is a pragmatic issue treated along these lines, then, for the pragmatist, the metaphysical way of talking must be both successful and unsuccessful.

In all three cases the problems arise from the fact that it is seen to be a contingent issue whether or not pragmatism itself is true, an issue which is seen to turn, for the pragmatist herself, on whether or not pragmatism and metaphysical realism are successful on their own terms. If this is what the truth of these positions turn on, then it is possible for the pragmatist, insofar as she commits to the truth of pragmatism, to find herself having to admit that on her (the pragmatist's) own grounds, the metaphysical realist is both right and wrong. And, given the extraordinary success in the West of the metaphysical way of talking, this is likely to be precisely what she will be committed to.

It follows that if the question of the truth of pragmatism is treated as a contingent pragmatic question to be decided empirically by the positive disciplines, then pragmatism is a self-refuting position on the grounds that it is viciously relativistic. That is, if the truth of pragmatism as a position is treated by the pragmatist as an issue to be decided pragmatically, then—regardless of whether that assertion is treated as about beings or about being, within the same horizon or different ones—the position is viciously relativistic. The other alternative for the pragmatist is to treat the assertion of pragmatism itself as not understandable as having a truth value that is evaluable pragmatically. And this, we have been arguing, is precisely the position the late Heidegger adopted. In this case, however, it seems that pragmatism is self-refuting for lack of internal consistency. According to our analysis in Part I, every assertion, in order to have semantic content, must be asserted within the context of a set of Daseinish practices and would thus seem ultimately to stand in need of practical confirmation if it is to be true. So, insofar as it is held that assertions of the truth of pragmatism itself are evaluable not pragmatically but in some other way, it looks as if pragmatism contradicts its own basic doctrine. This is 'the criticism from the other side' mentioned at the beginning of this section.

I would suggest that this problem can be seen as motivating Heidegger's own desperate recourse to the view that assertions concerning the truth of being are not really assertions at all. Fortunately, this move is not really necessary. The view of language and assertion that we ascribed to the early Heidegger directly concerns the conditions under which an asserting can count as an asserting, can count as having semantic content. The primary conditions under which this can occur have to do with the operation of asserting within a certain social structure of intentional action, and they arise out of considerations having to do with the conditions for intentionality in general. It is only from these conditions that claims regarding the priority of a pragmatic notion of evidence or a pragmatic conception of truth are derived. Now, consider the claim that 'every assertion, insofar as it is meaningful, must stand under certain conditions of possibility having to do with its placement within a social context of purposeful action'. That claim itself seems to be an assertion, and I see no reason not to treat it as one. As such, if it is to be meaningful, it stands under the very conditions that it specifies. And, quite clearly, if it is true, it does so: it is an English sentence asserted in the context of philosophical discussion, a discussion that is theoretical but stands under the same sort of social constraints as any other. What is it for this assertion to be true? What evidence could count in favor of its being true?

We have suggested that Heidegger implicitly claims that the truth of this assertion must be demonstrated in a transcendental argument and that the truth of claims of this type do not have the same sort of pragmatic status as do claims concerning either beings or being. As the conclusion of a transcendental argument, even if a somewhat truncated (non-metaphysical) one, this claim is taken to be universal and necessary. Every assertion within every language, it is claimed, must meet these conditions if it is to have semantic content and thus in fact be an assertion. But in terms of which set of practices and in which language is *this* claim true? As a universal claim this assertion in order to be true, must hold true in every language in which a judgment is possible concerning what counts as language and assertion. And, given that every language must be capable of distinguishing the meaningful from the meaningless, it must hold in every language. Indeed, as we have seen, this must be the case if we are to avoid a vicious form of relativism.

But this is just the claim that nothing can count correctly as an assertion, as having semantic content, or as being capable of being true or false unless these conditions are met, and that this is the case regardless of which language or set of practices are operative in deciding the issue of whether some thing or event counts as an assertion in a language. That is, the transcendental claim amounts to the assertion that in terms of any intentional linguistic horizon y, it must be possible to distinguish the meaningful from the meaningless, the semantically evaluable from that which can not be so evaluated; and that insofar as so distinguishing is possible, that which is seen as being semantically evaluable must be recognizable from within y as also meeting a set of specified conditions.

The argument in favor of this claim is just the one we extracted from *Being and Time* and outlined in the first part of this book. This argument ultimately rests on the circumstance that nothing can count as or be recognized as a language or intentional horizon (y) unless entities interpreted as operating in terms of y are interpretable as making the distinction in question concerning what *they* determine as semantically evaluable; and the only possible evidence that could count in favor of *this* is that what they do is implicitly understandable as responding differentially according to precisely these specified conditions. The structure of this argument is remarkably similar to the sort of argument Quine and Davidson advance in favor of the principle of charity, and both arguments concern the same topic, the conditions under which something can count as a language.[19] But this kind of argument—which, if cogent,

19. E.g., in one of Quine and Davidson's arguments in favor of the principle of charity, the base step involves noting that at least part of what it is to recognize that what another group is doing is using a language is to assign linguistic meaning and semantic content to its members' various performances. But this can be done only if we can discover that there are conditions under which various 'assertions' are allowed or assented to by the members of the group. The argument proceeds in two steps. First, given holistic considerations concerning the way in which linguistic connections among various assertions can effect assertability, one can in general assign such conditions only for a whole structure of assertions at once. So, in general, we have reason to believe that a particular performance has a particular semantic content only insofar as we have reason to believe that it is part of a

yields a universal and necessary conclusion—in no way contradicts the conditions for meaningful discourse which the proposition in question states.

So, to avoid contradiction, claims concerning the necessary conditions for assertion must be self-referring; that is, they must meet the very conditions they set. Heidegger's early claims regarding intentionality and Dasein do so. Because of their universal and necessary character, in order to be true these claims would need to be verifiable both in and for every language, but they must be so in such a manner as not to contradict the very strictures on assertion and evidence which they state. If the argument Heidegger gives in *Being and Time* is cogent, then this restriction is also met. The claim that there are necessary conditions for intentionality and language, claims concerning 'the truth of being', are meaningful only within and for particular social and linguistic contexts. But the claim that these are the conditions for language and intentionality as such is true only insofar as this assertion is in principle verifiable within *every* social and linguistic context. And this is precisely what the argument we have developed from *Being and Time* is designed to show.

Having seen that this is the structure of Heidegger's overall strategy, we can also, perhaps, understand why the late Heidegger became committed to the proposition (V) that the truth of being is entirely ungrounded and inexplicable. An argument can be constructed on the premises that (1) x can be grounded and/or explained if and only if x is a

---

system of performances which themselves have semantic content. Second, for us to recognize a correlation between assent and conditions for assent, it is necessary that we be capable of recognizing the regularity of conditions governing the linguistic usage of the others. We are entitled to assert that the sentence 'Gavagai' has the specific meaning expressed by our sentence 'It is raining' only if in general the aliens genuinely assent to 'Gavagai' only when it really is raining. That is, we are entitled to assign the semantic content of 'It is raining' to 'Gavagai' only if most of the aliens' uses of 'Gavagai' are true (that is, only if we would consider most of those uses true). Combining this with holism, we reach the conclusion that in order for us to have reason to think that what an alien group is doing is using a language, most of what they say must be true (by our lights). And, given verificationism, if we assume that others are speaking a language, we must also assume that most of what they say is true. This is the principle of charity. The family resemblance between this argument and the argument structure we elicited from *Being and Time* should be obvious.

The version of this argument given here is a generalization of specific formulations that appear throughout the writings of Quine and Davidson. See, in particular, Quine, *Word and Object*, chap. 2, and Davidson, "Radical Interpretation," "Belief and the Basis of Meaning," and "Thought and Talk," all in *Inquiries into Truth and Interpretation*, pp. 125–170.

being, and (2) x is a being if and only if assertions concerning x have the status of assertions concerning beings, or of what we have called 'ontic' assertions. There is ample textual evidence that the late Heidegger held positions that commit him to both (1) and (2). But claims concerning the truth of being have a different structure and evidential status from those concerning beings. It follows from this plus (1) and (2) that the truth of being is no being and that it is thus completely ungrounded and inexplicable. The weak link in this argument seems to be the manner in which the word 'being' is used in (1) and (2), for it is not clear that the sense in which all and only 'beings' (or things that are) can be explained is the same sense of 'being' in which all and only beings can be referred to in 'ontic' assertions.

The argument of *Being and Time* turns on the considerations that nothing can be recognizable as a language unless its speakers are interpretable as distinguishing the meaningful from the meaningless, and that this interpretability occurs when and only when those speakers can be understood as responding differentially according to the conditions in question. It does not follow, however, that every speaker in every language is equally capable of stating and discussing these conditions. And this raises one final question. Several pages ago we claimed that apparently contradictory statements concerning being must be treated as statements within the same intentional horizon, but we postponed discussion of exactly which horizon this could be. Similarly, if assertions asserting the truth and falsity of pragmatism are treated in the way we have suggested here—as claims concerning features that are necessary for the possibility of semantic content, truth, and so on—then they must also be treated as claims within a single intentional horizon that admits of determinate, unequivocal, truth values. The obvious candidate for the vocabulary or discourse in which claims in regard to the conditions for intentionality and language could be formulated, and in which the discussion with metaphysical realism could take place, is philosophy. But for Heidegger, 'philosophy' is essentially metaphysical. That is, philosophy is the attempt to find a metaphysical ground that underlies the interpretability of the world in a particular way; thus, it can't be the discourse in which claims in regard to conditions for the understanding of being are used to show that there can be no such ground. In this respect, however, Heidegger is misreading both philosophy and its history. Not all philosophy has been metaphysical in Heidegger's sense of looking for a ground for beings and being. Even leaving aside such twentieth-century figures as

Dewey, the late Wittgenstein, Heidegger himself, and problematic cases such as Nietzsche (whom Heidegger sees as the last metaphysician), one can still point to such anti-metaphysicians as those opponents of Plato, the Sophists, and those opponents of the Stoics, the Pyrrhonian Skeptics. If we continue to call such people 'philosophers'—and I see no alternative to ordinary usage in doing so—then we can tentatively suggest a reading of the word 'philosophy' and its history alternative to the one Heidegger affirms.

Philosophy includes all those enterprises that take a stand on what it is 'to be true', or what it is to know or to be a language or to intend, and on what, if anything, is necessary to any of these—regardless of whether that stand accepts the metaphysical assumptions or not. In short, philosophy is the field of discourse in which the necessary conditions for and character of discourse and intentionality themselves—together with semantic content, meaning, truth, and knowledge—are called into question. It is the discipline that is concerned to discover necessary features and concomitants of systems that are capable of generating semantic content. As such, it may be designated as 'transcendental semantics'. So understood, pragmatism and Heidegger's own contributions fit rather well into 'philosophy'. Instead of being seen as a rejection of philosophy and its procedures, as Heidegger tends to see it, his work should be seen as a position that uses philosophical procedures and modes of argument to make philosophical points that attack the dominant tradition within philosophy, the tradition characterized by the necessity for metaphysics.

It is not that Heidegger is wrong in seeing philosophy as having predominantly involved the search for the metaphysical grounds for being and beings, and the understanding of being; he is right about this. Rather, that it has been so has rested upon a dominant answer to a prior question: namely, 'What conditions must be met if there is to be any semantic content, intentionality, or presence?' The traditional Platonic answer to this question has asserted that these are possible only if there is a ground of beings that accounts for the presentability of beings. But this dominant view has been denied before in the history of philosophy, and if our interpretation is correct, Heidegger is also denying this position. If philosophy is understood as the attempt to answer the prior question of transcendental semantics, the question of 'the truth of being', then Heidegger remains a philosopher. If he is a philosopher, then he shares a space of discourse with his opponents, the metaphysicians. And if this is the case, then Heidegger's claims concerning the conditions for intentionality, language, being, the understanding of being, and the truth of being can and should be evaluated as philosophical claims and judged in the same context and according to the same criteria of evidence as those of his opponents.

In this book I have presented Heidegger in this way, as a philosopher, so that it could become possible to evaluate his assertions, his arguments, and his discourse.

Index

Library of Congress Cataloging-in-Publication Data

Okrent, Mark, 1947–
    Heidegger's Pragmatism: Understanding, Being, and
the Critique of Metaphysics/Mark Okrent.
      p. cm.
    Includes index.
    ISBN 0–8014–2094–6 (alk. paper)
    1. Heidegger, Martin, 1889–1976—Contributions in theory of
pragmatism. 2. Pragmatism. I. Title.
B3279.H49036 1988
193—dc19   87–26014